EVERYTHING IS GOD

EVERYTHING IS
GOD

THE RADICAL PATH OF
NONDUAL JUDAISM

Jay Michaelson

Trumpeter
Boston & London
2009

Trumpeter Books
An imprint of Shambhala Publications, Inc.
Horticultural Hall
300 Massachusetts Avenue
Boston, Massachusetts 02115
www.shambhala.com

9 8 7 6 5 4 3 2 1

First Edition
Printed in the United States of America
Distributed in the United States by Random House, Inc.,
and in Canada by Random House of Canada Ltd
♾ This edition is printed on acid-free paper that meets the
American National Standards Institute z39.48 Standard.
♻ This book was printed on 30% postconsumer recycled paper.
For more information please visit www.shambhala.com.

Library of Congress Cataloging-in-Publication Data
Michaelson, Jay, 1971–
Everything is God: the radical path of nondual Judaism/
Jay Michaelson.—1st ed.
p. cm.
Includes bibliographical references and index.
ISBN 978-1-59030-671-0 (pbk.: alk. paper)
1. Judaism—Doctrines. 2. Dualism (Religion) 3. Pantheism.
4. Panentheism. I. Title.
BM602.M53 2009
296.3—dc22
2009010427

עס איז מער ניטאָ ווי ער אַליין און ווידער קערן אַלץ איז גאָט

Es is mehr nito vie Ehr alein un vider kehren altz is Gott.
There is nothing but God alone and, once again, all is God.
    —R. YITZHAK ISAAC OF HOMEL

The world is holy! The soul is holy! The skin is holy! The nose is holy! . . .
Everything is holy! everybody's holy! everywhere is holy!
    —ALLEN GINSBERG

CONTENTS

EVERYTHING IS GOD

INTRODUCTION

You surround everything and fill everything.
You are the reality of everything and are in everything.
There is nothing beyond You and nothing above You,
Nothing outside of You and nothing inside of You.
—R. Samuel Kalonymous, *Song of Unity*

ONENESS

What is Jewish Enlightenment? Well before the term entered common usage, and centuries before it became associated with rationalist philosophy, Jewish mystics pondered the prophet Daniel's prediction that "the enlightened (*maskilim*) will shine like the radiance (*zohar*) of the sky."[1] The Zohar, the masterpiece of Kabbalah which takes its name from that verse, explains that the enlightened are those who ponder the deepest "secret of wisdom."[2] What is that secret? The answer varies from text to text, tradition to tradition, but in the Zohar and elsewhere, the deepest secret is that, despite appearances, all things, and all of us, are like ripples on a single pond, motes of a single sunbeam, the letters of a single word. The true reality of our existence is *Ein Sof*, infinite, and thus the sense of separate self that we all have—the notion that "you" and "I" are individuals with souls separate from the rest of the universe—is not ultimately true. The self is a phenomenon, an illusion, a mirage.

This view is called "nonduality" ("not-two"), and it is found at the summit of nearly every mystical tradition in the world. Nonduality does not mean we do not exist—but it does mean we don't exist as we think we do. According to the nondual view, the phenomena, boundaries, and formations which constitute our world are fleeting, and empty of separate existence. For a moment, they appear, as patterns of gravity and momentum and force, like letters of the alphabet, momentarily arrayed into words—

and then a moment later they are gone. In relative terms, things are exactly as they seem. But ultimately, everything is one—or, in theistic language, everything is God.

To be sure, this is a God very different from the ordinary one—a "God beyond God," as it were, neither a paternalistic judge nor a partisan warrior, but Ein Sof, Being and Nothingness, without end or limit, and thus filling every molecule of this page and every synapse in the brain. God is who is reading these words and writing them, who is thinking and what is thought. (Indeed, this book could well be titled *Ein Sof Judaism.*) This is the world without an observer, with no inside and no outside, in which That (what seems to be without) and You (what seems to be within) are the same. And with this radically different conception of God come very different expressions of Judaism: elite, often hidden traditions quite unlike the mass religion of rituals, myths, and dogmas.

Moreover, because nonduality so flies in the face of everything we see—which is dualistic, divided into subject and object, self and other, and a thousand other antinomies—mere belief is insufficient, and a different kind of knowing is required, a more intimate intercourse with the truth. As a philosophical view, nonduality is but an interesting and debatable proposition. Internalized as a psychological reality, however, it can be transformative; it is the very content of enlightenment.

For example, it's rather banal to be told, in Ram Dass's analogy, that "you're not a wave—you're water." But to inscribe such a view upon the heart, and to understand that the phenomena of body and mind are not mine, not me, and not self, is to simultaneously erase and enlarge the personality, and to transmute the present into the Presence of God. It can also be quite disorienting; if there are no distinctions in the absolute (e.g., forbidden and permitted, self and other, light and darkness, body and mind), then the religion of the relative, with its rules and prohibitions, suddenly becomes incoherent. This is true for all mystical traditions: mysticism blurs the boundaries which religion seeks to enforce. Thus nondual Judaism, like other such traditions, has been, for almost a millennium, carefully guarded and hidden.

Yet Judaism does differ in one important respect from other nondual paths. Whereas most traditions regard the knowledge of nonduality as the ultimate wisdom—the last stop on the road, so to speak; the final teaching—in the Jewish mystical tradition, nonduality is the beginning rather than the end of wisdom. Jewish mystics begin with the shocking, and proceed to the ordinary. Thus Kabbalah begins, rather than ends, with the Ein Sof, and devotes most of its attention to the finite, to the *sefirot* and their qualities, to the world and its demands. And the Jewish contemplative spends less time establishing nonduality than asking how best to live in its light. If the experience you are having right now is a dream of Infinite Mind, what becomes of God, Torah, and Israel? How can Ein Sof be known in the mind, heart, and body of the lover of wisdom? These are the primary questions, respectively, of parts 1 and 2 of this book.

Of course, some would say that to read a book on nonduality is like trying to wake up from inside of a dream. And yet, awakening does happen.

TWO QUESTIONS

To speak of nondual Judaism is to explore two complementary subjects: *nondual* Judaism, and nondual *Judaism*.

On the one hand, we may approach nonduality from within a Jewish perspective, and ask questions about how it is expressed. Where did it appear in Jewish history, and why? How does it relate to the fundamental topics of God, Torah, and Israel? How does it function in the religious life, whether conceived traditionally or nontraditionally? There is no claim here that all Judaisms are nondualistic at heart. There are nondual Jews, dualist Jews, and many more Jews who have never thought of the issue at all. So what might be the benefits, or costs, of being a *nondual* sort of Jew?

On the other hand, we may pose questions from the nondual perspective, and ask what relevance Judaism has, if all is really one. That is, we might ask not "why be a *nondual* Jew" but "why be a nondual *Jew*"? For some, the question is beyond the bounds of normative conversation. For many of us, however, it begs to be asked. If nonduality, in whatever expression, enables one to be fully awakened from the dream of separation and to live a loving, compassionate, wise life, then why involve oneself with Jewish language, text, and tradition—so much of which is dualistic, distracting, and occasionally disrespectful of other paths? If everything is God, why be Jewish?

In my own life, both nonduality and Judaism have been deeply transformative, and correspond roughly to absolute and relative, universal and particular, head and heart. As we will see, there is little separating the nondualistic philosophies of Judaism from those of Hinduism, Buddhism, and other traditions—not nothing, but little. Nonduality, if true, is necessarily a universal truth, and all schools and teachers are but skillful means of apprehending it. However, as we will also see, nonduality does not erase the world in a hazy cloud of oneness. All is zero (*ayin*), and all is one—but one manifests as two. The general takes the form of the particular; the One wears the drag of the many. And so, as the world is reborn, our particularities matter anew, and with my background and accidents of birth, the Jewish way continues to resonate in my heart.

At times along the nondual path, I have surrendered all that is particular: not just all that is Jewish, but also many important particularities of gender, sexuality, class, and ethnicity. Yet when I "return to the marketplace," to paraphrase the Zen ox-herding parable, all these forms return. Jewish forms are neither superior nor necessary. But they are superior and necessary *for me* because they are the vocabulary of my heart, and the technology of my body.

The "benefit" of nonduality is ending the tyranny of the egoic illusion and awakening to the truth. The "benefit" of Judaism is responding to that truth with acts of love and devotion; integrating it into a culture, community, and ethical tradition; and naming it as God. The world of *yetzirah*, the domain of the heart, needs its forms, its faces, its God. As Rabbi Arthur Green, one of today's leading progressive nondual teachers, has written, "the step from 'wonder' to 'God' is not an act of inference, but an act of naming."[3] Judaism provides, for some of us, the grammar and vocabulary of that utterance.

Nondual Judaism is at once quite old and quite new. As an esoteric doctrine, it has been around since at least the twelfth century. It animates much of the Kabbalah and was a central tenet of Hasidism. But more Jews are nondualists today than at all other times in history put together. In Israel, nonduality is in the mainstream of contemporary spirituality; pickup trucks drive by with bumper stickers that say "Ein Od Milvado" (There is nothing but God), and the phrase is shouted at shrines and in forests. In America, nonduality is a central feature of neo-Hasidism, Jewish Renewal, and other new forms of Kabbalah and Jewish mystical revival. And the concept of nonduality clearly echoes the notion, popular in the 1960s, that "all is one."

Of course, exploring nondual *Judaism* necessarily involves the concept known in English as "God." As we will explore in detail, particularly in chapter 3, this concept can be extraordinarily misleading. To begin with, there have been many God-concepts in the last twenty-six hundred years of Jewish tradition. Sometimes, God is an anthropomorphic warrior, or gardener, or mother, or father, with preferences and emotions. Other times, God is a cosmological creator, perfect and unchanging; and at others, God is a provider, an abandoner, a schoolmarm, or a scold. Sometimes Jews say we experience God in judgment; other times we experience God in love. But really, what we have been doing, all these centuries, is embellishing different experiences with the name of God.

The nondual understanding of God as Ein Sof, Infinite, at once negates and reaffirms all of these images. On the one hand, Ein Sof refuses all category, including that of "God." If you have an idea of God, that's not It. And yet, because God is Nothing, God is the true reality of Everything, and refractable in an endless number of prisms. The nondual God is at once entirely transcendent ("surrounding all the worlds," in the language of the Zohar; the "upper unity" in the Tanya, the nineteenth-century Hasidic text which we will explore in some detail.) and entirely immanent ("filling all the worlds"; the Tanya's "lower unity"). It is the only mask there is.

I like to think of it this way. First, if you have some belief in God, drop it. Let the atheists, or your own doubt, totally, utterly win: there is no one minding the store, just matter and energy combining and separating. There is nothing in this moment that cannot be explained by science and reason.

But then, take science seriously, and remember that there is no self either: consciousness is an illusion of the brain, after all. Believe the postmodernists, the Buddhists, the Darwinists, the cognitive materialists, and the Hasidim when they say that this sense of ego, while essential for our survival, causes us to mistake a pattern of phenomena for something that's actually there. Really, there is no soul, just a buzz of neurons. So: no God, no self. And then . . . what?

What's left, after the self is subtracted, is what nondualists mean by

"God." Other names are fine as well. Empty phenomena, rolling on; the Divine Play; Indra's Net; the Dharma; causes and conditions; the substance of Nature, and its laws; the *Shechinah* and the Holy One; as you like it. YHVH, the primary Jewish name for God, basically means "Is."

And now everything reappears. The self manifests as it does, with all its talents and neuroses. The breeze still blows, of course. And God, too, half-projected, half-imagined, but still nonetheless with an aroma of Presence, appears as well. But the "God" that reappears here is a God of more masks than before. In the Kabbalistic schema, the term "God" is only one of the ten *sefirot*, or emanations of the One to the many. Like our personalities, "God" is a mask, a way of speaking about the world: of naming it. As Daniel Matt says, "'God' is a name we give to the oneness of it all."[4] All of it—not just chocolate and summer days, but cancer and prisons too; "all is One" may sound like a bromide, but in fact it is a challenge.

In reluctantly choosing to use the word "God"—and given how much the word is misused, and for what reasons, my reluctance is considerable—I take a slightly different view from Professor Matt. For me, Ein Sof is the oneness of it all, but "God" is the name I use when "It" becomes "You," when knowledge becomes love. God is the companion, the Presence ever-present, the half-projected face of the universe, the ghost within the machine. I recognize that this act of naming has attendant benefits and costs. It reflects my truthful experience, but it also raises the stakes; it shelves me together with fundamentalists, fideists, and fools; and it leads to any number of dangerous mistakes: mistaking the finger pointing at the moon for the moon itself, mistaking the means for the ends, and mistaking one's own path for the only path.

If secularists object to the use of the word "God," many religionists may object to my definition of it. For centuries, nondual Jewish theologians have been accused of pantheism ("where atheism and religion shake hands," according to one popular notion), because this "God" is stripped of personality. This objection, though, misses two points. First, as we have just seen, nonduality does not erase Divine personalities but sees them as what they are: masks. Indeed, as we will see in chapter 3, the more masks, the better. Second, nonduality insists on transcendence, the view that "God is the world's place, but the world is not God's

INTRODUCTION

place."[5] (Of course, if God is "more than" the world, we might ask what this "more than" actually is. If it is anything we can define, then it is part of the universe. If not, it is, from our perspective, nothing.) That God is Is, but also the Naught surrounding it, is what is meant by the Ein Sof, the God beyond God: both the transcendent other, and the transparent immanence of the real.

Still, the traditionalists are right that the nondual return of "God" is different from the naive version. Now "God" is almost a way of speaking, and one mask among many. Indeed, we may experience this "God" in any number of ways: as bridegroom, or bride, or nature, or love. Because all these images are masks, all are available to us, though ultimately, as the psalmist says, only silence is praise.[6]

As before, there is no pretension here that this is what all Jews (or others) mean when they talk of God. But it is what is meant when I address this moment as You, rather than as It. This and nothing more. Only You; only This; only I; only Love.

NEITHER ONE NOR TWO

Nonduality is the oneness before the number one.
—RABBI DAVID AARON[7]

So nonduality means that all is one?

Yes, and no. Perhaps the most mysterious, misunderstood, yet also the most revolutionary aspect of nonduality is that it stands not just for "all is one" but, rather, that it stands for "all is one," "all is two," and, for good measure, "all is zero" as well.

Let us envision it this way. By the age of two, all functional human beings have figured out the difference between inside and outside, between self and world. It is the first essential stage in human development—and most of us spend the great majority of our lives there. Our lives are comprised of dualities, binaries, and boundaries.

A second stage is possible: unitive consciousness which returns to the predifferentiation of infancy. At first, it only occurs at certain peak moments—lovemaking, abject terror, encounters with the numinous. But gradually, it is possible to extend the light of the Ein Sof into everything, in the words of the Lubavitcher Rebbe, to be in unitary consciousness more and more of the time. As Rabbi David Cooper has written:

> As nothing can be separated from it [Ein Sof], everything is interconnected in a Oneness, a unity, that cannot be divided. Things that in relative reality appear to be polar opposites—light and dark, hot and cold, male and female, determinism and free will, heaven and earth, good and evil, and so forth—are in absolute terms inevitably contained in the Oneness of Boundlessness.[8]

This sense of oneness is what many people call "enlightenment." It is the state of no-mind, in which one knows oneself to be Nothing, and being Nothing, one with everything. Rarely do any of us inhabit its space for more than a fraction of our lives—and yet it is a reservoir of wisdom and compassion, comfort and joy. In my experience, it is worth the effort to reach it.

Yet even this is but an intermediate phase. That "all is one" is exactly half of the picture. After all, if everything is really one, does that not also include the experience of two? The third stage, then, is to "transcend and include" (Ken Wilber's phrase) both the dual and the nondual, to return to the experience of duality while maintaining the consciousness of unity. This is what David Loy calls the "nonduality of duality and nonduality."[9] It is what the Zen masters mean when they say "in the beginning, mountains are mountains. During zazen, mountains are not mountains. Afterward, mountains are once again mountains." That is to say: in the initial dualistic consciousness, mountains are experienced as mountains. In unitive consciousness, the mountains disappear as separate entities and are only motes on the sunbeam of consciousness. In nondual consciousness, the mountains are both: both everything and nothing, both existent and nonexistent.

Rabbi Aharon of Staroselye, a great but little-known nondual Jewish sage whose work we will explore in detail in this book, calls this seeing from "our point of view" and "God's point of view." Both points of view are of the same reality—they are just different points of view. Ours sees objects, people, and things. God's sees only Godself. The object is to see both as two sides of the same coin. *Neti-neti*, the Vedantists say: not-this, not-that. Neither twoness nor oneness, neither *yesh* nor *ayin*, but both, and thus neither. It's not quite paradox—it's enlightenment.

The Kabbalistic math of this reality is that 2 = 1 = 0. Fortunately, I don't have to be good at math anymore.

I'd like to return to a symbol I suggested in the introduction to my first book, that of the two triangles of the Jewish star. The downward-pointing triangle represents the "first stage," the world of ordinary experience, in which there is self and other, figure and ground. This is the view of *aretz*, of earth, of all of us, with our histories and loves and heartbreaks and joy. The upward-pointing triangle represents the "second stage" of unitary consciousness, in which there is no self, no other, no figure, and only the one Ground of Being. This is the view of *shamayim*, of heaven, of ultimate reality, the way things actually are. The star together is the "third stage" of nonduality: of both-and and neither-nor. It is the Ein Sof that is both Many and One, hidden God and manifest *Shechinah*, and in being both, is Naught, or *ayin*.[10] Here it is on one enormous chart (Hebrew terms are defined in the glossary):

2	1	2 = 1 = 0
dualistic	unitive	nondual
immanent	transcendent	both
aretz	*shamayim*	both
yesh	*ayin*	both
corporeal	incorporeal	both
living in *yesh*	*bittul ha-yesh*	both
self	no-self	Self
relative	absolute	both
form	emptiness	emptiness is form
everything	nothing	both
manifestation	essence	both
expression	realization	both
ordinary mind	no-mind	"ordinary mind"
mochin d'katnut	*mochin d'gadlut*	*ratzo v'shov*[11]
tzimtzum	*shefa v'atzilut*	*ratzo v'shov*
hitlabshut (envelopment)	*hitpashtut* (expansion)	*ratzo v'shov*
yeridah (descent)	*aliyah* (ascent)[12]	*ratzo v'shov*
plurality	unity	union of unity and plurality

memaleh (filling)	*sovev* (surrounding)	both
materialization	annihilation	both
our point of view	God's point of view	both
confusion	enlightenment	confusion is enlightenment
samsara	nirvana	nirvana is samsara
apparent	real	both
many	one	both and neither; 0, 1, and 2
the "real"	the "ideal"	both
good and bad	no good and bad	both
good and evil	all is God/perfect	both
self and other	all is one/no other	I/Thou (Buber, Levinas)
God or no God	God-beyond-God	both
I'm here, God's there	all is God	both
prayer, myth, ritual	contemplation	both
sacred and profane	all holy	both
ethics	no ethics	nondual ethics
problems	perfection	both
tikkun olam	all is perfect	all is perfect, but you make it better
pursuit of justice	acceptance	both
yang; action	*yin;* nonaction	both
farq (separation)	*jam' al-jam'* (union)	*al-farqath-thani* (God's return to separation)
passion	dispassion	compassion
movement	stillness	both
seeking	nonseeking	seeking without seeking
path	no path	path
hope	without hope	hoping without clinging
particular	universal	both
conditioned	unconditioned	both
damaged	undamaged	integrated
human	being	human being
eros	thanatos	both
diversity	union	both
mountains	no mountains	mountains

existence	consciousness	both
in the world	apart from world	return to world
kadosh baruch hu	*shechinah*	union
sefirot	*ayin*	Ein Sof
presence	absence	absence in presence (Derrida)
thesis	antithesis	synthesis
earth	heaven	heaven on earth (Hasidism)
polytheism/monotheism	monism	all three

The list could go on, but the point, I hope, is clear. Nonduality is not only oneness. It is oneness-in-twoness, the extraordinary in the ordinary. Is it a mere coincidence that so many of the symbols of the world's religions are based upon this coincidence of opposites? The cross of heaven and earth, the six-pointed star, the yin and the yang. To what does their joining gesture? This is why so many nondual sages say that the only thing keeping you from enlightenment is searching for it. If only you'd stop trying to see yourself through your own eyes! You, with your neuroses and shadows and wounds—*tat tvam asi*, "you are that." This moment of your experience is God masquerading as you.

As a lived phenomenon, the experience of the chart is one of *ratzo v'shov*, running and returning. This experience is not one of an Aristotelian golden mean, or some vacuous sense of "balance," but rather of transcending binarisms to include both sides of them. Sometimes we experience life as the ego tells us we must: as a separate self, with boundaries to be defended and needs to be met. Other times, we see this ego as being like a computer program, running according to causes and conditions, just like the trillion miraculous programs executing all around us at every moment. Or consider nonduality from the perspective of earth-based spirituality: sometimes, we feel at one with all, part of the great cosmic dance, the cycle of birth and death—and other times, we revel in our own uniqueness, our individuality, our humanity and sex and joys. Along such a path, we do not seek a midway point, somewhat godly and somewhat human, but rather a vibrant oscillation between the poles of everything and nothing, separation and union.

Of course, most of us spend the overwhelming majority of our lives at "stage one," experiencing ourselves as selves sandwiched between our ears—and we suffer as a result. So, for most of us, just getting to "stage two," in which the ego melts away for a blessed moment or two, remains the primary work. Besides, stage two is wonderful: spend time in the presence of enlightened masters, and see for yourself the palpable stillness of no-mind, the great compassion that emerges naturally from wisdom. Know that you can become such a person yourself. Please, do not rush to integrate too quickly.

Gradually, though, the mind states of spirituality, even the most lofty, will become less and less urgent, as God becomes more and more transparent. Slowly, not only may you see infinity in a flower, you may not even need to. The flower, having become infinite, may now be but a bloom—and wholly Divine in being so. Both-and, neither-nor, all of it, the emptiness and the form, yielding and wrestling. Duality and nonduality are the ultimate nonduality. As the nondual sage Nisargadatta said, "Love says 'I am everything.' Wisdom says 'I am nothing.' Between the two, my life flows."[13]

THREE ASPECTS

As we have already mentioned, the kind of "knowing" that constitutes the liberation of nonduality is, of necessity, richer than solely intellectual cognition. For that reason, this book is divided into two major parts, the first devoted primarily to theory, the latter to practice. Part 1 begins with ten ways of understanding the concept of nonduality and then explores a variety of sources that are used in Jewish and other traditions to express it. Later, part 1 approaches nonduality from the three aspects of mind, heart, and body, here mapped (somewhat idiosyncratically) onto the traditional Jewish doctrines of God (creation: theology and mysticism), Torah (revelation: Jewish myth and practice), and Israel (redemption: history, peoplehood, messianism).

These three aspects recur in part 2, only now from the perspective of practice (how nonduality may be lived and experienced) rather than theory (what nonduality is). Here, I draw on the schema of Rabbi Aharon of Staroselye, the leading disciple of the founder of Chabad Hasidism and perhaps the most systematic expositor of nondual Judaism. R. Aharon's two major books are, like the two parts of this book, divided into theory (*Shaarei HaYichud v'HaEmunah*, "The Gate of Unity and Faith") and practice (*Shaarei HaAvodah*, "The Gate of Practice"), the second of which articulates three core practices corresponding to mind, heart, and body: contemplative meditation, ecstatic prayer, and performance of the *mitzvot*. (They also correspond more or less to Hinduism's *jnana, bhakti,* and *karma* yogas, which perfect wisdom, devotion, and action.) For R. Aharon, these three aspects of practice had both personal-mystical and cosmological value. For the individual mystic, they comprise three aspects of knowledge. Contemplation reveals the truth of things; ecstasy provides the emotional, unitive experience of that truth; and ritual and ethical action cause that truth to manifest in all aspects of life. On a theological or cosmological level, these three faces of nondual practice unite the mind with God, enable God to unite with Godself, and extend the light of the Ein Sof into all of existence, leaving nothing out.

Here, I expand R. Aharon's categories somewhat, addressing both traditional Jewish contemplative meditation and other forms of nondual meditative practice, asking not just how prayer works but also how the more general Jewish heart-practice of *tshuvah* (discussed in chapter 7) and consciousness of our imperfection works with a perspective that all is perfect, and exploring several Jewish practices from an embodied, nondual perspective. In addition, I devote a separate chapter to the question of ethics and the problem of evil, which, as we will see, can be particularly tricky for nondualists. A concluding chapter restates the major themes of the book in the context of knowing, not knowing, and knowing anew—the great *ratzo v'shov* of the nondual path.

Doubtless, some of these aspects of nonduality will be of more appeal to some readers than others. By temperament, some may prefer the emotional, experiential, and practical to the intellectual, rational, and theoretical, while others will prefer the reverse. I have tried to accommodate both of these and more. I assume no belief or faith whatsoever. I take nothing for granted, and question everything. I am especially sobered to remember that, in geological time, we humans are but an instant away from tree-dwelling monkeys; it's best to hold all ideas lightly, not to presume too much of our capacities. Yet I do take seriously the possibility of authentic religious consciousness, and I do not seek to reduce it wholly to something else. And I do not dumb it down. In our day, there are many who seek to relegate religion to the reactionaries—and many reactionaries who are glad to comply. But if we aspire to the heights of a Baal Shem Tov, a Ramakrishna, a Buber, or an Abraham Joshua Heschel—and there is no reason why we should not do so—then we must reject such efforts to divorce heart from head, spirit from matter. Obviously, such separations fly in the face of the absolute. Yet even in the sphere of the relative, they demean our humanity, and by extension the unfolding intimacy of the One who has chosen to dance within us. Having yearned for such a courtship, and its eventual consummation, She has donned the garb of multiplicity. Let us find the joy He, and We, deserve.

At first, most of us imagine that we are essentially selves, and some of us believe that there is a God as well. Nonduality invites us to suppose nothing, believe nothing: that there is no God, but also that there is no self. When there is merely no God, we remain as we were. But when there is also no self, then what is left is the Ein Sof, the God beyond "God." Simply what is; simply this; and not-this as well, "surrounding" as well as "filling" all that can be predicated.

And from that fullness, which is also utter emptiness, God reappears, and the self reappears as well—only now as masks, perspectives, ways of seeing, modes of speech. Some masks are more real than others; some are merely imaginary. But that becomes a subject for a different conversation. In silence, all disappears. From silence, all is born.

Part One

SHAMAYIM: THEORY

1

PERSPECTIVES: TEN PATHS TO EVERYWHERE

God is not far from you.
—Deuteronomy 30:11

[God] does not exist, [God] is existence itself.
—Christopher Isherwood and Swami Prabhavananda[1]

What is nonduality?

The nondual perspective is one which holds that our immediate, superficial perceptions of separation—of duality—are not ultimately correct, and that in its deepest reality, all of being is one. The boundaries we see all around us, between you and the outside world, between tables and chairs, are not ultimately real—though they may be partially true, or true in some relative way. Literally, nonduality came into the English language as a translation of the Sanskrit word *advaita*, which refers to the nondual tradition of Vedanta, a philosophical movement of Hinduism. In Jewish vocabulary, nonduality is expressed as Ein Sof, the Infinite, the ultimate reality of Being according to the Kabbalistic tradition.

There are many ways to approach nonduality, and many ways it can be described.[2] Some are logical, others experiential. Some are religious, others secular. Some are theoretical, others experiential. Nearly all, however, insist that language is inadequate to describe nonduality. This is not because of a desire to be mysterious, but because language denotes; it describes; it marks and distinguishes one thing from other things; and it is part of the social community that created it. Yet if language is inherently dualistic, and inherently social, it is inherently incapable of describing that which is not an object to which one might refer, and which is not other than oneself.

By way of analogy, imagine describing the color "red" to a blind person. We might think of associations in our experience—heat, for instance—but these only suggest something of the tone of red; they cannot describe what redness is. Nor does the scientific account of wavelengths and frequencies, which says nothing about how redness is experienced in perception. Likewise, when speaking of the ineffable, language can only hint, gesture, and point, for any time I use a word, I define (demarcate, differentiate) its referent, and if nondual Being is everything and nothing, then such definition is self-contradictory.

Thus it is tempting, in writing a book such as this, to simply "gesture at the moon": to provide poems and cryptic utterances which hint at a truth that is beyond communication. Occasionally, I will do just that; there is something in language which, when uttered from a place of stillness, resonates with silence anew. But this chapter tries a different way: it offers ten different perspectives on the non-perspectival, ten ways of looking at looking. Reflecting the structure of this book, the first five ways of looking are conceptual, the second five experiential. Doubtless, as the introduction noted, some readers will prefer rigorous logic, in contrast to the apparent vagueness of spirituality, while others will find the heady material too abstract, and prefer invitations to intuition and the wisdom of the heart. That is fine.

One pedagogical note. Traditional Jewish sources usually depict nonduality from the top down—that is, beginning with an infinite God and moving to the consequences—rather than from the bottom up, deriving insights from experience and then working our way "up" from there. Here, I've reversed the priority. For most people today, to start with God is to start from an unproven, uncertain, and highly debatable premise. Moreover, as the introduction noted, the word "God" carries with it all sorts of associations that have nothing to do with the nondual view: a character who acts in history, for example, or has some special relationship to prayer or ethics or ritual.

"It does not exist, it is existence itself," say Swami Prabhavananda and Christopher Isherwood of the Atman, commenting on Patanjali's yoga aphorisms. The Atman here is the true Self, which is one with Brahman, the Ein Sof, all that is. Thus my rephrasing in this chapter's epigraph, "God does not exist—God is existence itself."

At first, this may seem a privation. But if the boundaries of self and other allow this truth to penetrate, then the seeming loss of the Friend is replaced by an intimacy greater than that which can be dreamed. This is not a question of dogma or cosmology, whether there is or is not an agent named the deity. It is a matter of ascribing the holy name to the immanent and transcendent, of addressing the true as God. To say "You" to the world is to transform the speaker, for now the You is the consciousness of I as well. There is, in a sense, no one else here. But then again, you aren't either; only God, Godding. This is not solitude, but blessed dissolution, a dissolving which, the instant it is complete, re-creates all that we see and know, the self and its trials, justice and community—all reborn the instant separateness dies. Consider the surrender an act of grace.

NON-SELF, VERSION 1: THE SELF IS A PHENOMENON

Who are you?

Beyond your name, your familial role; beyond your profession and avocation—who are you? When pressed to reply, most of us offer something to do with a self, a personality—perhaps even a "soul," something distinctively individual, psychological or spiritual. Our answers are usually vague, but firm; we exist, after all, even if we can't quite pinpoint what that means. Both the amorphism and the solidity are natural; identity formation is part of the maturation process, and draws on external factors, such as personal, professional, and familial roles; physical traits such as gender, age, and body type; and internal characteristics, such as personality, thoughts, habits, preferences, and feelings.

Yet for all that, it's quite hard to define what this "self" actually is. Look closely at the personality (or mind, or heart, or soul), and you discover that it is more a label than a reality—a phenomenon of perception, not a thing in itself. As a simple experiment, raise your right hand right now. Go ahead: just pause for a moment, raise your right hand, and then put it down. Now, whether you did or didn't raise your hand, reflect on what actually happened. Did the thing you call "you" really raise your right hand? In fact, what likely happened were a series of mental processes, all of which were conditioned by factors outside of "you." Maybe there arose a sense of curiosity, or playfulness, or even obedience, which was probably learned when you were a small child, or which maybe has something to do with genetic predispositions. Or, if you didn't raise your hand, maybe some feeling of laziness, obstinacy, or contrariness arose—just as much learned from experience, from other people, from a thousand outside sources. Of course, the bundle of all of those feelings, plus myriads more, is conventionally referred to as "you." But the bundle never actually does anything—it's a label, nothing more. What actually acts, thinks, feels, dreams are one or more mental factors, usually in combination, none of which is actually "you." They are the conditions which are necessary for the action to take place—not "you." Who moved? The conditions moved.

This is a very simple example. But no matter how often you repeat the experiment, you will never find the "you" doing anything; it will always be some combination of mental and physical factors. We conventionally say that "I am happy" or "I am sad"—but is there really an "I" behind the happiness or sadness? Or is there only the experience of joy or sorrow itself? And yet, no one would claim that joy or sorrow is "me," right? Suppose someone does something to make you angry. Are "you" really angry? Or is it more accurate to say that anger arose in the mind, because the conditions for anger were present, without any input from "you" at all? Indeed, perhaps "anger is present" is more accurate than "I'm angry," even if the difference doesn't seem like much at first.

This is how both Buddhist *vipassana* meditation and Hasidic *bittul ha-yesh* lead to liberation: not by some positive doctrine, but by a process of elimination. Keep looking, and the self is never there. In fact, all of your hopes, fears, dreams, loves, hates, tastes, predilections—each instance of who you are—is wholly caused and constituted by non-you elements. Now, we may get very used to these movements of the mind and come to understand them as ourselves. But that doesn't make it so. Take a look for a few minutes (or hours, or weeks). As a reaction, idea, or emotion arises in the mind, try to notice it (obviously, a context of concentrated meditation makes this far easier) and query whether it's "you" or something that is "not-you." In my own spiritual practice, I've done this for many months at a time while on silent meditation retreats, and, at least in my experience, it's "not-me" every time.

Now, of course, we all experience the *phenomenon* of the self—but this is just the way things seem from a certain perspective. The well-known Theravadan Buddhist teacher Joseph Goldstein compares the notion of the self to that of the Big Dipper. Really, there's no Big Dipper, right? We all know this; there are just stars, light years apart from each other in reality, which viewed from a certain perspective look like the Big Dipper. Change the perspective, and the Big Dipper disappears. Now, does that mean there's no Big Dipper? Well, it depends; from a certain perspective, of course there is, but not in any objective sense. Not really. Likewise, this self, which the ego fights so hard to aggrandize and protect, is just a label of how things look from a certain angle. A vital one, but just a label. And likewise with every phenomenon we experience.

What is there, really? Well, we'd have to ask the scientists, who presumably would tell us something about protons and electrons, or molecular bonds, or perhaps biology or chemistry. In traditional cultures, though, the constitutive elements of creation are known as the "four elements." Rabbi Shmuel Schneersohn, the fourth Lubavitcher Rebbe, explained in a 1869 discourse titled *Mi Chamocha* (literally, "Who is like You?") that

> When you carefully examine the nature of all physical beings, when you contemplate them well, you will find that material things are not actually material. For example, the substance of wood is actually made up of the four elements: fire, water, air, and earth, and yet, while it has all four elements, its existence is not any one of them. Rather, its being is the power that combines the four elements. So, the essence of its being is the Word that causes it to be (*davar hamehaveh oto*) and sustains it: the [Divine] Utterance . . . [W]hen you separate the elements, nothing remains. Thus there is no material thing without Godliness.[3]

There is never any "there" there, to paraphrase Gertrude Stein; only various elements combining in different ways. Indeed, usually we don't even experience the phenomena we think we experience. For example, if you are sitting in a chair, is the "chair" holding you up right now? Or is it really the various molecular properties of wood, metal, or plastic? Is the "chair" white, black, or another color, or is it the chemical properties of the pigmentation? And do you ever perceive the "chair," or rather, different elements of it, like its size, color, and texture? Perhaps this seems obvious, yet we all suffer by wanting this thing and not that one, and by failing to realize that all things, both pleasant and unpleasant, are simply evanescent aspects of Being, arising and passing away like sparks from a fire.

More than chairs or constellations, though, it is the notion of the individual soul that causes us to suffer. The human ego is the product of billions of years of evolution; without it, our ancestors wouldn't have run away from predators, fed themselves, or reproduced. We are hardwired to identify with the processes of our brains, to see ourselves not merely as bodies (which, we all know, will one day return to the Earth) but as truly distinct individuals, as personalities. Yet, our neuroscientists tell us, consciousness is not some immaterial, immortal phenomenon; it's a trick of the brain.[4] Our mental computers are executing programs at astonishing speed, but they are only programs, which the computers learned from somewhere else. The ego is a phenomenon— part of the world, not an observer or controller of it. Mind states are just patterns that arise and pass. None of it is I, me, or mine.

But try telling me that when I am in pain. The Jay program needs protection, love, aggrandizement, recognition; he needs to get what he wants, on shallow and deep levels. And most of the time, I identify with that program; I *am* Jay, so I need these things, and get angry, sad, hurt, upset when I don't get them.

Once in a while, though, usually in the stillness of meditation, I see that "Jay" is a phenomenon that arises. Nothing is under Jay's control; in fact, "Jay" is part of what's not under control. Feelings arise—joy, loneliness, inspiration, anger—and "Jay" has nothing to do with it. In fact, the sense of "Jay" only arises when there's something there to provoke it. This is the gateway toward releasing the *yetzer hara*, namely, the perspective that the self is what matters most in the universe.

For some, seeing through the illusion of the self is experienced as diminishment. Yet for the Hasidim, it is a gateway to *bittul ha-yesh*, nullification of the sense of self, and thus the highest of aspirations. For moving from nonself to nonduality is really quite simple: if there's no self, what is there?

NON-SELF, VERSION 2: SELF-INQUIRY

If *bittul ha-yesh* and insight meditation gradually divest us of the delusion of self, self-inquiry—asking, over and over again, "who am I?"—attempts to immediately locate the Nothing, Self, or God within. Initially, as we saw above, most of us identify with our names, or senses of self-identity. I'm Jay, of course. But very quickly, this simple response becomes insufficient. As we have seen, "Jay" is a label, not an answer. It refers to me, but does not answer who or what I am. And then, as I refine my answer, I find not subjects but only objects of consciousness: the personality, memes, predilections, habits, and impulses of the self which arise in every moment. "Jay" is something which arises when the circumstances are right, and passes at other times. So that's not "me," right?

Keep looking, keep asking, and nothing is found—or perhaps Nothing. What the Vedantists call the Self (Atman), the Buddhists call nonself, and the Hasidim call the *ayin* are three perspectives of the same phenomenon: the egoless, timeless emptiness, the nothingness one finds when one looks for oneself. It is an answer to the riddle of self-inquiry, which finds nobody home, but somebody seeming to notice. The Vedanta sage Ramana Maharshi (1879–1950) urged his disciples: "Always and at all times seek for the source of the ego, the apparent actor, and on the attainment of that goal . . . the ego will drop away of its own accord, and nothing will be left but the all-blissful Self."[5] Likewise in Hasidic traditions, in which *bittul ha-yesh*, annihilation of the self, takes place both ecstatically, in the furnace of prayer, and contemplatively, by means of introspection. (We will explore methods for self-inquiry in chapter 6.)

From the seeming paradox of self-inquiry is born a radical reorientation. Normally, we identify with the body, or the space between our ears, or some phenomenon of consciousness or soul or personality that arises, habit after habit, over time. Each of us thinks he or she is this individual who moves around through the world and bumps into others along the way. Eventually, however, we identify not as the body in the world but as the world itself, the space of consciousness in which all of life appears to unfold. Consider the shocking, unsettling, counterintuitive novelty of this idea: that all of reality really is in your head—only it isn't your head. Once, responding to a questioner who asked, "But the ant still stings, correct?" Ramana answered, "Whom does the ant sting? It is the body. You are not the body. So long as you identify yourself with the body, you see the ants, plants, etc. If you remain as the Self, there are no others apart from the Self."[6]

This shift in awareness, born of self-inquiry, leads to the notion of the Self as Kosmos, as primordial awareness, as the timeless utterance of "I AM." Here's Ken Wilber, in an unpublished form called "From You to Infinity in 3 Pages" (to get the full effect, substitute your name for mine):

> What you have been seeking is literally and exactly That which is reading this page right now. That Self cannot be found because it was never lost: you have always known *you* were *you*. That I AMness is a constant condition of all that arises, is the space in which it all arises, has nothing outside of it and thus is complete Peace, and radiates its own beauty in all directions. Jay arises in the space of that I AMness, Jay arises in this vast spaciousness, this pure openness. Jay is an object, just like a tree or a cloud that arises in the space of the Self that *you* are. I am not talking to Jay right now, I am talking to *you*. That which is aware of Jay is this ever-present Self. This Self is aware of Jay arising right now. This Self is God. God is reading this page. Jay is not reading this page, God is reading this page. The Self is aware of Jay and aware of this page. *You* are not Jay. *You* are what is aware of Jay. What is aware of Jay is an I AMness that itself cannot be seen but only felt, felt as an absolute certainty, unshakeable is-ness, I AM that I AM eternally, timelessly, unendingly. There is only this I AMness in all directions. Everything arises spontaneously in the space of this great perfection that is the Self, which is reading this page right now.[7]

NON-SELF, VERSION 3: INTERSUBJECTIVITY AND POSTMODERNITY

If the preceding perspectives on non-self seem too empirical, or even naive, consider the insights of the last fifty years of postmodern philosophy, which have relentlessly insisted that what we call the "self," that is, the modern subject, is actually a social construction, an assemblage of memes, narratives, and values entirely made up of historically conditioned factors. My supposed need for security, home, and hearth is a late capitalist, bourgeois affectation conditioned by nineteenth- and twentieth-century advertising and cultural production. My tastes, preferences, styles, and self-identifications all are cultural constructions—even notions of feminine and masculine, sophisticated and down-to-earth, sane and insane.

Consciousness is really made up of memes, units of information that replicate themselves, a bit like genetic information does.[8] In fact, every notion that you have, about politics, justice, identity, music, love, whatever, is a meme, constituted outside of "you" and replicated in sophisticated ways. To think that they are "you" is what the epistemologist Wilfrid Sellars called "the myth of the given." It's what happened when Descartes moved from the arising of thought (*cogito*) to the existence of the full-on modern subject (*sum*). A postmodernist would reply: yes, the thought arose—but that doesn't mean there was a "you" thinking it. There was just a set of memes thinking the thought, interpreting it, and constructing a self on the basis of it.

Neuroscientifically, writes Daniel Dennett, "human consciousness is itself a huge complex of memes,"[9] a vast assemblage of learned behaviors, which, like software, operate the hardware of the brain.[10] Enlightenment, in turn, is what the philosopher Susan Blackmore calls "waking up from the meme dream."[11] As Blackmore puts it, "we are just co-adapted meme-complexes. We, our precious, mythical 'selves,' are just groups of selfish memes that have come together by and for themselves."[12] The false self is a meme complex.

"Memes" may be a novel coinage, but what the word stands for is familiar on an anecdotal level. To take a Jewish example, the mainstream Jewish community is today very interested in "identity formation." Notice that term: identity is something that is formed. Go on a trip to Israel, and you'll have more of a "Jewish identity." Don't go, and you won't. In fact, all identity is formed; none of it is really "you." Identities are collections of memes, rhetorical moves and cultural practices, learned from outside and then assimilated into the mind. One who aggregates these memes under the rubric of an "identity," says Ken Wilber, is simply "the mouthpiece of . . . a structure he doesn't even know is there."[13] Some of these structures are good, others not so good. But it's a mistake to confuse memes for a self. One who does so, Wilber continues, "is not speaking, he is being spoken."[14]

If you like, you can even name your memes: the controller, the child, the traditionalist, whatever. For example, the Zen roshi Genpo Merzel uses voice dialogue to enable his students to see that, really, we are always performing one or another of these roles, like actors in a play.[15] Seeing these voices and memes face to face can be of great therapeutic value, as shunned voices are known and recognized, and points directly to non-self. For Genpo, the self is like a corporation: it's a set of agreements, a point of reference, and nothing more. All these voices are just the employees—only, unlike actual employees, most of them have no idea what the mission of the corporation actually is.

I remember sitting at Penn Station in New York one morning, and the obviousness of non-self simply appeared, in the midst of the crowd. All around me, I watched as thousands of people were replicating memes unconsciously, mistaking memes for self. Habits learned, dispositions, instincts. And suffering the predicament: natural desires to make more, do more, be more. If it weren't for these desires, we'd be extinct; in this sense, happiness is "unnatural." But it is possible too for consciousness to awaken, see what is happening, and look around, and then happiness becomes the most natural thing in the world. Life a profusion, flowing in a trillion faces, ants to adam, eagles to eve. And no separateness, no arrogance: Jay is also a feature of the ocean, and this voice too, though perhaps more aware of conditions. But that morning in Penn Station, early morning, tired and waiting for my train, there was an I behind the I, full of compassion and joy.

THEOLOGY

Another "way in" to nonduality is to begin from the premise of theism and work "downward" from there. For many, this suggests beginning from the conclusion. However, like philosophers before them, most Kabbalists begin from the premise that there is a One, that which does not change, and deduce that because the One is infinite, it is all there really is. In the example used by the sixteenth-century Kabbalist Moses Cordovero (discussed in the next chapter), if we suppose that a physical object is just that object and not God, we have supposed limit in the limitless, which is a contradiction. If the object has its own separate existence, then the Ein Sof exists everywhere but suddenly stops at the border of the object; it is thus not Ein Sof. Therefore, the object must be filled with God. Whatever its form, its substance is Divine. Likewise, the self is a phenomenon which, like a rainbow, appears only from a certain perspective. If God is infinite, then by necessity, God is reading these words, writing them, and dwelling within them. Who else could You possibly be?

It was well understood by the Kabbalists that Ein Sof is not the same as what we conventionally refer to as "God." So, even if You are God, you are not the master of the universe. Sorry. On the relative level, you are still you. On an absolute level, however, the phenomenon of "you" is something that happens to God, and the temporary agglomeration of consciousness and matter to which you are so emotionally wedded is like a ripple on a pond. In the metaphor of the Tanya, the great nondual Jewish treatise discussed in the next chapter, you are like a sunbeam which appears to have separate existence only because you are surrounded by non-light. Returned to your source, the sun, you are seen as you really are: total naught and Nothingness (*ayin v'efes mamash*).

Again, for us today, to reason downward from a theistic premise may seem abstract, or ill-founded. Yet for those who do have a belief in God, it serves to move consciousness along from a simple anthropomorphic notion of God to Ein Sof, the "God beyond God," that which is arelational and omnipresent, a circle whose center is everywhere and whose diameter is nowhere.

PHILOSOPHICAL REASONING

Though nonduality is perhaps today most associated with mystical and nonrational modes of thought, it is also the ontological view of a number of different philosophical systems. In a sense, the classical philosophies of Plato and Aristotle, as well as their Jewish counterparts, notably Maimonides, in positing an unchanging One that is the true reality of all existent things, may be termed nondualistic, though they differ on the ontological status of those existents. The greatest Western philosophical influence on nondual Judaism, though, is likely Neoplatonism, which flourished from the third to sixth centuries and blended gnosticism, Judaism, Christianity, and Platonic thought into a mystical-philosophical synthesis. In the medieval period, Neoplatonism was transmitted into the Jewish world by Abraham ibn Ezra and others, and figured prominently, according to Gershom Scholem, in the Zohar.[16] Plotinus (204–270 C.E.), the leading expositor of Neoplatonism, is the first to identify Athens' philosophical One[17] with Jerusalem's religious God. The One of Plotinus does not admit of any change or generative action, since both would imply some lack in that which is posited as perfect. Thus the One emanates, like a full glass of water spilling over the edge, the Intellect/Intelligence (*nous*), and through the Intellect, the rest of the world.[18] For Neoplatonism, the world is an overflowing of God: God did not so much create the world as manifest it, become it; this moment is the act of the One seeing Itself.

As with Maimonidean Aristotelianism, religious Neoplatonism was as much a contemplative practice as theory. Plotinus's last words, recorded by his student Porphyry, were reportedly, "Strive to bring back the God in yourselves to the God in the All."[19] In the medieval period, Bahya ibn Pakuda's work *Duties of the Heart* became one of the first Jewish texts to insist on inwardness and emotional devotion as central to religious life. The essential attributes of God, Bahya wrote, are utterly unknowable by reason—but somehow knowable by love. But the secondary attributes may be known through reflection on the wondrous complexity of the natural world, the human body, and the other daily miracles we often ignore. Thus Bahya prescribes both the apophatic path of negation and the cataphatic path of affirmation: the former to "pierce the cloud of unknowing with a dart of longing love" (to paraphrase the anonymous medieval Christian mystic) and the latter to stimulate love and gratitude by means of reflection on the natural world. Love is the connection between the two: both the knowing-less love of the mystic and the love brought about by reflection on what is.

There are many other Western instances of philosophical nonduality. For example, German Romantic philosophers such as Johann Gottlieb Fichte and G. W. F. Hegel, and twentieth-century phenomenologists and post-phenomenologists Edmund Husserl and Martin Heidegger, are in part monistic.[20] However, our purpose in this chapter is only to identify possible avenues into a nondual Jewish perspective, and so expositions of these thinkers must wait. Before passing on, however, it would be wrong to omit perhaps the most famous Jewish nondualist of all: Spinoza.

Baruch Spinoza (1632–1677) is known by many Jews today chiefly as a heretic. Yet his tragic excommunication from the Jewish community was a response not to his monist philosophy (which was developed later) but to his claim that the Bible was the product of human authorship. Both were a consequence of Spinoza's rationalism, which, together with that of Descartes, Leibniz, and others, helped initiate political liberalism, the Enlightenment, the industrial revolution, the scientific revolution, and other foundations of the world we live in today. Writing in a precise, mathematical way, Spinoza attempted to prove that there could only be one substance in the universe—and whether we call it Nature, the universe, Being, or God, really doesn't matter.

Spinoza's argument is as follows. All things are made up of what Spinoza calls "substances." Substances are irreducible in definition, meaning that you don't have to understand something else in order to understand what a substance is. By definition, a substance has certain attributes. However, no more than one substance can share a single attribute, because if it did, it would in part reduce to the other substance. But this means that no substance can limit another, because substances with nothing in common cannot cause or limit one another (e.g., the body does not limit thought, thought does not limit the body). Thus substances must be infinite, and thus there is only one such substance in the universe,[21] that is, God, "an absolutely infinite being; that is, substance consisting of infinite attributes."[22] And so "there can be, or be conceived, no other substance but God."[23]

Famously, for Spinoza, God is the equivalent of nature: *deus sive natura*, "God or nature," in the felicitous phrase. This is certainly at odds with the traditional Jewish depiction of God as a personal being who rewards the good and punishes the wicked, and who loves Israel above all nations. Yet if Spinoza's speculation seems too remote, remember that as with the other philosophers we have mentioned, Spinoza is a lover, not only a thinker. As he observes, "the intellectual love of the mind towards God is part of the infinite love wherewith God loves himself . . . The love of God towards men, and the intellectual love of the mind towards God, are identical."[24] This is not quite atheism—compare Spinoza's statement to Meister Eckhart that "the eye with which I see God is the same with which God sees me."[25] Rather, nonduality may be said to be the place where mysticism and atheism shake hands. The cosmology may be identical, as there are no puppet-masters pulling the strings of our reality. Yet the stage is now a cathedral.

EXPERIENCE OF *CHAYAH*: UNITIVE MYSTICISM

Nearly every nondual sage will insist that only through experience can nonduality truly be known. Certainly, this makes sense; map is not territory, and reading a recipe is not the same as eating a meal. In the Jewish tradition, secret traditions are not secret because they are rarely disclosed. They are secret because they are experiential, and thus cannot be disclosed at all.

So it is no surprise that accounts of mystical experience, in all their classic forms, are present in nondual traditions: ecstatic raptures, contemplative insights, visions, and experiences whose very nature seems to defy description. Here we will look at five experiential ways of looking, mapped onto the five aspects of the soul according to Hasidic and Kabbalistic tradition: *chayah* ("soul"/mystical experience), *neshamah* (contemplative insight), *ruach* (love), *nefesh* (body), and most subtly, *yechidah*, that aspect of the self which is already enlightened, already at one with the One, for which "experience" itself is a misnomer.

Of the five, only the first category, *chayah*, contains the classic mystical experiences much studied by scholars. Generally, such experiences are described as possessing ineffability, a noetic quality, transience, passivity, unitary consciousness, timelessness, and a sense that the ordinary ego is not the real self.[26] One simply *knows* this, in a way that is impossible to communicate. One is not alone; one is one with the One. In nondual Jewish sources, such experiences often result from ecstatic prayer, which we will explore in chapter 7. For example, one Hasidic text, translated by Arthur Green and Barry Holtz, says:

> A person should be so absorbed in prayer that he is no longer aware of his own self. There is nothing for him but the flow of life; all his thoughts are with God. He who still knows how intensely he is praying has not yet overcome the bonds of self.[27]

Such peak experiences give a glimpse of that which cannot be communicated. They impart a kind of knowingness that is more certain than everyday knowing; that is to say, mystical experience is not less sure than ordinary experience, but more so. William James, for example, describes one mystical experience this way:

> There came upon me a sense of exultation, of immense joyfulness accompanied or immediately followed by an intellectual illumination quite impossible to describe. Among other things, I did not merely come to believe, I saw that the universe is not composed of dead matter, but is, on the contrary, a living Presence . . . that the foundation principle of the world, of all the worlds, is what we call love, and that the happiness of each and all is in the long run absolutely certain . . . I knew that what the vision showed was true. I had attained to a point of view from which I saw that it must be true.[28]

From my own experience, I can attest that if you follow the instructions of meditative, contemplative, and spiritual practices, the promised results do indeed occur: a dissolving of the sense of self; rapture in concentrated joy; transient feelings of immense bliss; and, for religious souls like me, a certainty that one is held and loved and engulfed by the Divine. It is worth the effort.

Yet if experience is essential, it is also problematic. First, it is difficult to conceive of an experience that is not an experience *of* something, a dualistic conceit. Even the idea that one experience is more an "experience of nonduality" than another is contradictory. What's more, the recourse to experience invites a critique that *all* one is really talking about is an experience of connectedness, wholeness, and so forth. How can such experiences be verified? Perhaps Freud is right that mystical experience is but a womb-memory, or the neurologists that it is solely an internal, neurochemical event. What then?

Moreover, it may be impossible to resolve the dispute according to purely objective criteria, because the only way to investigate the truth of a mystic's claims is necessarily subjective. Ken Wilber suggests that this is simply the nature of spiritual phenomena. Just as Galileo's interlocutors had to look through the telescope to evaluate his claims, and just as a logician must adhere to certain rules in order to evaluate a proof, so too must a critic of mystical experience look through "the eye of spirit."[29] Repeat the procedure, and see what happens. Similarly, Pascal, in his *Pensées*, notes that "we know the truth not only through our reason but also through our heart" and that, moreover, "It is through the latter that we know first principles, and reason, which has nothing to do with it, tries in vain to refute them . . . Principles are felt, propositions proved, and both with certainty though by different means."[30] God, being one of those principles, is known with the heart, and the procedures of rationality are simply the wrong methods to test it.

Two of the most important nondual Jewish Hasidic masters, R. Dov Ber of Lubavitch and R. Aharon of Staroselye, split the Chabad Hasidic world over this very question. For R. Aharon, experience was essential, and justified the inevitable admixture of perception, separation, and delusion; thus R. Aharon exhorted his followers to mystical experience. For R. Dov Ber, spurious experience was worse than no experience at all, and so he restricted ecstatic practice to the few. Surely both views can be defended; ecstasy may be close to *ayin*, but it is not *ayin*; there is indeed a mixture of multiplicity, even in an experience of unity. The tension is right there in the original sources.

However, we need not end in contradiction. In my own contemplative experience, I have observed what Wilber, following Abraham Maslow, helpfully labels as the distinction between prerational and transrational. If the skeptics are right that unitive experience is delusion, then it should be less than normal consciousness (i.e., prerational); it should be like getting high and not being able to think clearly. If the mystics are right that unitive experience is truthful, then it should be more than normal consciousness (i.e., transrational); it should transcend and include ordinary thought, not negating it but adding to it. (This accords with the Kabbalistic understanding that rational, discursive, dualistic faculties are associated with *binah*, or understanding; transrational, unitive ones with *chochmah*, or wisdom.[31]) The latter is, indeed, my experience; on retreat after retreat, I found my own *chayah* experiences to be—as the Jewish model suggests— "higher" and thus more inclusive than ordinary rational experiences. One does not see pixies during such experiences; one sees reality— including the rationalist critique of mystical experience, the logic of nonduality, and so on—more clearly. My experience is that *chayah* is more than rational, not less; it has the quality of clarity, not confusion. Such has been the experience of thousands upon thousands of careful meditators, joyful ecstatics, and spiritual journeyers, including many who hadn't read any spiritual books telling them that all is one. There is a certainty, a remembering, a sense of Self rather than self, that is as indubitable as love.

Of course, no experience is any more an experience of nonduality than any other one. Ultimately, all states must be let go, together with all images that would reify the ineffable. This can be a subtle matter. It is one thing to say that God is "just this"—just Being and Nothingness, and nothing more. Yet *chayah* experiences, during which such knowledge seems certain, also tend to occasion phenomena such as love, ecstasy, calm, bliss, and a perception of holiness. Thus many contemplatives suppose that God is in the fire, or the earthquake, or the storm, and mistake the states which occasion holiness for holiness itself. This can lead to all sorts of suffering, because all states pass, as well as to a kind of idolatry and delusion, in which any experience becomes associated with God.

Consequently, as the spiritual path progresses, peak experiences become more and more subtle. Gradually, contemplatives learn to let go of even the most cherished experiences, relinquishing even the holiest and most beautiful of sensations in favor of a *devekut* to that which does not come and go, that which is unformed and unconditioned. Consider: if whatever special feeling you are having has not always been with you, from the moment you were born, it isn't *it*. In this way the path progresses to *ayin*, true emptiness, which has no characteristics at all.

Of course, for most of us, *chayah* experiences are still precious; spiritual states are valuable teachers. So, along with discretion and negation, cultivating moments of proximity to the numinous—even if such a phrase begins to approach meaninglessness—remains essential to a life fully lived. These experiences are only brief uncoverings, but what the soul learns in such instants is deliciously hard to forget.

EXPERIENCE OF *NESHAMAH*: CONTEMPLATION

In the Chabad tradition of Hasidism, contemplation of the Divine omnipresence and unity is the primary form of meditation. Drawing on the Maimonidean tradition, the first two generations of Chabad—nearly alone among the Hasidim, who usually preferred devotional to philosophical practice—maintained that through contemplation, the intellect could become one with its Source. There is an ontological framework for this view: Chabad maintains the classical understanding of the Active Intellect (*sechel ha'poal*) and maps it onto the intellectual *sefirot* (*chochmah, binah,* and *da'at,* the first letters of which give Chabad its name), and R. Aharon in particular spends a great deal of time parsing the details. But for our purposes, these issues are of less concern than the method of contemplation and the experience of nonduality it purports to bring about.

As we will explore in more detail in chapter 6, *hitbonnenut,* nondual Hasidic contemplation, is more than mere thinking. It is a focused application of mental activity, coming back again and again to a single phrase or teaching, such as *Ein Od Milvado*—there is nothing besides God. This is not quite the same as mantra practice, in which a phrase is repeated in order to bring about a trancelike state, but it is meant to provide a depth of experience, a deeper "knowing" than mere understanding. Experientially, the result of focusing the mind on a single phrase, for perhaps an hour or more and to the exclusion of other thoughts, does indeed bring about a sense of profundity. More than that, however, I have found that insights arise during contemplation that, upon later and strictly rational reflection, seem quite solid and truthful. This, too, has its Kabbalistic basis—contemplation touches the depths of transrational *chochmah*, in addition to rational *binah*. And it suggests that the experience of *neshamah* is not only an experience, but a source of insight as well.

As we will also see in chapter 6, one may contemplate contemporary teachings as well as ancient ones. One that inspired me early in my own spiritual path is this paragraph from Rabbi Arthur Green's introduction to *Your Word Is Fire: The Hasidic Masters on Contemplative Prayer*:

> In all change and growth, say the masters, the mysterious *ayin* is present. There is an ungraspable instant in the midst of all transformation when that which is about to be transformed is no longer that which it had been until that moment, but has not yet emerged as its transformed self; that moment belongs to the *ayin* within God. Since change and transformation are constant, however, in fact all moments are moments of contact with the *ayin*, a contact that man is usually too blind to acknowledge.[32]

I remember reflecting on this notion one afternoon, sitting in the park twenty years ago. I had not yet learned how to meditate, and had no idea what nonduality was. I simply turned my mind, over and over again, to the persistent liminality of transformation, to the radical impermanence of all phenomena, the way they flicker in and out of being; to trees swaying in the breeze; to leaves budding, flourishing, and falling; to the currents of history, economy, and power. It was not all beauty—only a few generations down from the trees, and we humans have destroyed much of the earth. Yet in the flow of things, in what I would later conceptualize as Kali's dance or God's game of revelation and concealment, there seemed but one constant: the masquerade of Being itself.

Contemplation may also be so spare in its content as to ease the mind back upward from the insights of *neshamah* to the mystical experience of *chayah*. For example, following Genpo Roshi's Zen instruction, allow yourself a vacation from ego right now. Simply take a full breath, and as you release, drop into the non-seeking, non-desiring mind—what the Zen masters call the ineffable light, *musho ko*. Non-seeking, non-desiring. Don't try to accomplish anything, feel anything, know anything, understand anything. Definitely don't try to figure it out. Just let it go; relax; drop into the ocean.

It is possible, for a moment, to see from God's point of view, as long as no assumptions, no expectations, no intentions are maintained. And from the perspective of Emptiness, there's nothing that needs to be done, and nothing of note that has ever been done. Of course, mind states are transitory and conditioned, while the nondual is not, so let's not erect idols of our experiences. But the pressing concerns of the relative will return soon enough; if what we seek is balance, and the *ayin* is one half of the truth, can we really say that we devote proportional time to approaching it?

EXPERIENCE OF *RUACH*: LOVE

Isn't it true that, ultimately, we do what we do for love? Achievement, to attract love and learn to love ourselves; service, to love others; self-gratification, to try to feel love; the pursuit of justice, since out of love springs obligation; religion, to feel the love known as God's. Rather than ask, then, how love gives a glimpse of the nondual, one might do well to ask how nonduality brings about love.

The literature of nonduality is filled with words of love, from ecstatic Sufi poetry to the prayers of the Hasidim, from devotional *kirtan* to the erotic letters of medieval nuns. R. Aharon, for example, wishes us "to have the heart on fire with desire and passion to do the *avodah* [worship, service, practice] of YHVH and to connect to God's blessed unity, and to nullify himself through Torah and mitzvot to connect to God's wisdom and will, to extend God's will into real action, by means of deeds."[33] But more than that: for the greatest of nondual teachers, love is a necessary condition for realization; it is an ingredient of it, for God is experienced as love. R. Aharon elsewhere says that intellectual knowledge without emotional connection is mere imagination.[34] Likewise Ramakrishna, the founder of modern Vedanta and also a self-described *bhakta* (devotionalist), preferred God with forms to God without form, and likened pure nondual speculation to playing only one note of a flute.[35] And likewise, the spiritual text known as *The Cloud of Unknowing* says that "He may well be loved, but not thought. By love may He be caught and held; but by thinking never."[36]

In chapter 3, we will see how form and the formless interact in the life of the mystic, how the act of addressing this moment of Being as "You" yields an almost miraculous response from the One addressed as God, Christ, Krishna, the Beloved, *Shechinah*, Goddess, or Friend, and how none of this need depend on theology, faith, or belief. In chapter 7, we will explore four ways in which love may be practiced along the nondual path: ecstatic prayer that opens the heart, conventional prayer, the love of people as a nondual love of God in multiplicity, and the heart-rending path of *tshuvah*. Such movements make clear that what some people mean by "God" is equivalent to what others mean by "love."

Of course, the ebb and flow of wisdom and compassion is a cyclical motion in which one nourishes the other. I've told the story before, but I remember so clearly leading a meditation session on a two-week retreat, several years ago. Because, like the Dzogchen nondualists, I was meditating with my eyes open, the group of my fellow meditators filled my field of vision. At one point, I saw one of them move, which usually causes me irritation. This time, though, I felt only compassion—hoping her meditation was not disturbed, that she wasn't in too much pain—and immediately, I noticed how natural love appeared for me, when I am not clouded and confused.

This is the oscillation of my life. When I remember Who I am, I find it is easy to love almost everything, even the stupidity and wastefulness of our society, even those who have broken my heart. When my mind becomes distracted, I forget, and it feels impossible to love—least of all myself. And so much of my own spiritual work recently has been to submit to love always, to love myself unconditionally, and, as the Hasidim say, to extend that light as much as possible—to the legal papers as much as the poetry, the shopping as well as the dance. I fail more than I succeed, but I try to love the failure.

And what I have seen, occasionally, is that the love exists independent of subject and object; that it is a way into the nondual as much as a radiation from it. Devotion empties the self just as contemplation does, filling the mind instead with a love of the Absolute. The means is different, but the endpoint is the same: the heart loves what the mind knows.[37] Yes, in the ecstasy of eros, whether sexual or spiritual, made up of prayer or dance or lust, there is a sense of the lowering of boundaries, the merging of that which is separate. But even without consummation or rapture, even when the feeling of separateness arises, I have found that the path of love leads to a kind of relinquishment of ownership, a barrierlessness of lovingkindness. In the last year, I have suffered loss and rejection, and have felt betrayed, left alone, cast aside. I continue to grieve and rage and mend and heal. Yet this nondual love endures—not as a steely sort of determination, but as an endlessly pliant surrender, a gateless gate that leads to the presence beyond subject and object. It is unjustified, it is embarrassing, it is unsophisticated, and it is real. It inheres in the bud emerging from the branch, the erosion by water of rock. Humans are clinging animals; we yearn for the mother's embrace. But when the notion of externality is released somewhat, it is possible to discover a wider holding that contains all and is all and loves, finally, all. It is a thaw that eventually melts into liberation.

EXPERIENCE OF *NEFESH:* THE BODY

The Creator is found in every act of physical movement. It is impossible to make any motion or to utter any word without the power of the Creator. That is the meaning of "the whole earth is full of His glory."
—KETER SHEM TOV[38]

Since nonduality is essentially a proposition about how things are, most of the ways to know it are intellectual or emotional in nature—but not all of them. Western science now confirms that body and mind are far more related than Platonic/Cartesian dualism would suggest: mental attitudes can affect healing processes, and somatic conditions influence thought. Thus it is no surprise that body-oriented practices such as yoga, exercise, and diet can powerfully open consciousness to its essential condition by reducing the chatter of mental noise that ordinarily obstructs it. On one level, these practices simply relax the mind by relaxing the body—or in the case of diet, by purifying the body of toxicants. Yet it is also possible that spiritual work such as yoga and advanced forms of concentration practice enable subtle energies, of which we in the West still understand relatively little, to flow more freely and connect with their source as well. A belief in such energies is not necessary to apprehend nonduality: nonduality is not about which energies do or do not exist, but rather what all of them, and all matter, are in essence. Similarly, it is not that the experience of relaxation, energy, or connectedness *is* the experience of nonduality. Every experience is the "experience" of nonduality, expansion no more than constriction. However, these encounters with the numinous immanent in physicality create an aperture in the veil of self-concern and self-aggrandizement.

Yoga, tai chi, *qigong*—these are disciplines that are hundreds, even thousands, of years old. And all of them have nondual perception among their central goals: not a mental perception aided by the body, but perception by the body-mind as a whole. While this may seem radical to some, it makes obvious sense if situated in the context of a nondualistic ontology and an open-minded agnosticism regarding subtle energies. If such a path speaks to you, then, as the Jewish sage Hillel said, "Go and learn." If it does not, remember that simply being in nature, if the mind is quieted and the heart is opened, can provide an intimation of immortality, a melting away of the distinctions between self and other. As the American nondualist Ralph Waldo Emerson wrote:

> Standing on the bare ground—my head bathed by the blithe air and uplifted into infinite space—all mean egotism vanishes. I become a transparent eyeball; I am nothing; I see all; the currents of the Universal Being circulate through me; I am part or particle of God.[39]

Indeed, in our age of ecological devastation, the unification of body and mind may be the most crucial of nondual practices. In recent years, earth-based religionists, system theorists, holists, and ecofeminists have argued that the split between matter and spirit, body and soul, nature and culture, is the formative rupture that engenders the imperializing, dualistic outlook of oppression of the Earth, of the Other, and of women.[40] We are used to boundaries, and as Ken Wilber has said, every boundary is a battle line—the most intuitive is most destructive. The moment we establish a boundary between what is mine and what is yours, we at once fly in the face of ecological interdependence and perpetuate the objectification and exploitation that our hyperdualistic culture has brought about. For most nondualists, the "interbeing" (to quote Thich Nhat Hanh) of all life on earth is not the final step on the path—but for many, it is the necessary first one. Our human tendency to dualize, hierarchize, reduce, and despoil is where our delusion begins and ends. In terms of practical consequences, healing the divisions between human/nature, heaven/earth, male/female, and insider/outsider may be the most important aspects of the nondual path. Fortunately, nature abhors a binarism. If we sincerely disassemble the stone walls between body and mind, earth and sky, and male and female, then perhaps, like ivy, we might open cracks of life where light may enter.

Indeed, the "enlightenment of the body" is, as described in chapter 8, the most radical reorientation of who it is that gets enlightened, or what spiritual states are all about. Suppose the experience of the body, without *any* emotional or psychological correlate, were accorded respect; would our identification with the ego/mind not loosen as a result? The truth is, you are not your mind. Your mind is a sophisticated assemblage of countless programs, executing over and over again in an evolutionarily honed effort to keep you safe. It is marvelous—but it is not "you." Enabling the body to experience realization helps undo the notion that only what happens to the mind matters.

A dragonfly alights on my windowsill, its aquamarine body shimmering, its wings translucent and exquisite. I quickly forget errands and agendas, am opened to wonder, am rendered both speechless and effusive in the presence of grandeur. And then I remember.

EXPERIENCE OF *YECHIDAH*: JUST THIS

The truth is so obvious that it cannot be stated: because the Infinite *memaleh kol almin*, fills all worlds, it fills every particle of what you see before you now, every movement of mind, every stirring of heart. The nondual God is *yotzer or u'vorei choshech*: creator of light and former of darkness—and as a result, every experience is an experience of Ein Sof. Just this and nothing more; there is no need to look outside for anything, to seek anything, to find anything, to do anything. Desire seeks its own extinction; motion seeks rest; and the simple feeling of being, the mind resting in itself, can be sweeter than the most delightful of pleasures. Please, *shema*, try to hear these words not as prose on a page but as if they might be addressed to you directly, for You are all there is. The programs in your head are ripples on the pond. You are not them; you are the pond itself, the whole field of your awareness — not the person running around inside of it. And because What you see before you now is the Divine Indwelling, the ultimate mystical union is none other than ordinary experience. Just Being, with no special sense or pretense: this is the Zen ox-herder's "return to the marketplace," in which all is exactly as it was, yet somehow luminous, translucent, at once more real and more evanescent than before.

This is the experience of *yechidah*, the face of the soul which is union with God. Not rapture, ecstasy, or an altered state of mind, but a somehow inflected perspective on that which is before us all the time. Imagine: that God is in this place, but you somehow do not know it. Yet even the not-knowing is God. There is nothing else. As Adyashanti has said, "There is only life living itself, life seeing itself, life hearing itself, life meeting itself as each moment."[41] Or in the words of Rabbi Rami Shapiro:

God is the sole Reality. God is the Source of all things and their Substance. There is no thing or feeling or thought that is not from God, even the idea that there is no God! For this is what it is to be All: God must embrace even God's own negation . . . Thus we read "I am God and there is none else" (Isaiah 45:5). Not simply that there is no other god but God, as our Moslem cousins say, but that there is nothing else but God, which is what their Sufi masters whisper to the initiated.[42]

When I was younger, and an academic student of mysticism, I always imagined that mystical union would take place in some far-off place, under special conditions, probably to someone else. But when, on my first meditation retreat many years ago, the spark of God masquerading as me was blessed to recognize Herself at last, I was startled to realize the obvious: that since God is everywhere, mystical union would look perfectly ordinary, and would take the shape not of angels and clouds but of trees, walkways, bathrooms, and tables. I cannot describe for you the sanctity and joy I felt in those first hours of self-recognition. For a time, it was as if every object God/I touched was the delicate cheek of the Beloved, every taste was like kissing the lover's soft lips, and every gaze was into the eyes of God seeing Godself. All that was needed was quiet and concentration, an opening of the heart, a relaxing of the discursive mind. It was a kind of homecoming, a reunion with a lover who never had left.

2

SOURCES: THE ROOTS OF
THE ORCHARD

*All beings are words of God, His music, His art. Sacred books we are,
for the infinite camps in our souls. Every act reveals God and expands His Being. I know that may be hard to comprehend.*
— MEISTER ECKHART[1]

Everyone has their favorite way of arguing with God.
— ADYASHANTI[2]

What are the sources of nondual Judaism? For many of us, particularly
mystics, they are first and foremost experiential ones, known in prayer
or meditation, or deduced by reasoning. Such truths may be said to be
universal, as they depend on cultural and linguistic context only insofar as the ineffable requires definition and communication. Yet there
are two faces to nondual Judaism: the nondual, which is universal, and
the Jewish, which is particular. And when we turn to the particularity
of Judaism, we perforce turn to text as well as experience, the written
word as well as the directly perceived reality. To engage with Judaism as
a system of thought, practice, and people is necessarily to engage with
Jewish writing on God, Torah, and Israel. And that means text as well as
practice, word as well as spirit.

Historically, the clearest, most unmistakable statements of nondual
Judaism (until its recent revival) appear in the early stages of the Hasidic movement, from around 1750 to 1820. The movement's founder,
Rabbi Israel Baal Shem Tov, and his disciples clearly believed that God
filled every corner of the universe and that everything that seems to appear as a separate entity is actually a ripple on the ocean of the Divine.
This was no mere theological principle: the greatest good of human life,
devekut, "cleaving" or clinging or (some would say) merging with God,[3]

is realized by knowing that God is in front of you right now, inside of you right now, reading these words and thinking these thoughts. Some Hasidic rebbes emphasized the ecstatic realization of this truth, in fiery moments of unification with the Holy attained primarily in prayer, music, and dancing. Others emphasized contemplative meditation, focusing the mind on the great truths of nonduality, and criticized ecstatic practices as potentially deceptive ego trips. But the central goal of religious life was the same: *devekut—devekus* in Yiddish—being stuck to God like glue. We will explore these ideas later in this chapter.

But the Hasidim were not the first to hold these beliefs. As we will see, similar views are present at least two hundred years earlier, in the Kabbalah of Rabbi Moses Cordovero. Arguably, nondualistic theology is present even earlier, in the theosophical Kabbalah of the medieval period, especially as reflected in and transformed by the Zohar, the vast anthology of speculation, exegesis, and mystical narrative that appeared at the end of the thirteenth century.[4] It is not known how rigorously to interpret the Zohar's many nondual utterances or other Kabbalistic statements that "everything is in him and he is in everything" (Rabbi Meir ibn Gabbai—sixteenth century) and "nothing is outside of the Ein Sof" (Rabbi Azriel of Gerona—twelfth century).[5] Certainly, however, the very notion of the Ein Sof, which appeared in this period, is at the very core of nondual Judaism, depending on how it is understood.

What about earlier—what about the Talmud and the Hebrew Bible, the Midrash and Aggadah? The truth is that the sacred texts of the Jewish tradition at best admit of multiple interpretations. More likely, their theologies are different from the mystical theologies of Kabbalah, Hasidism, and contemporary nondualists. As we will see, biblical text does have a notion of a Divine "glory" (*kavod*) that fills the entire universe, and Talmudic commentators identified this with the omnipresent Divine Presence (*Shechinah*). Yet biblical text just as often regards God as a semi-anthropomorphic deity who created and rules the world, but stands apart from it.

How, then, do nondual Jewish sources work with those Jewish texts that are clearly dualistic in nature? There are multiple answers to that question. The most obvious "answer" is a fundamentalist one: that nonduality is what these ancient texts really mean, all appearances to the contrary. That is to say, since (1) nonduality is true and (2) sacred text is revealed and true, then (3) sacred text must be, somehow, really about nonduality. This may seem preposterous to us, but for many Hasidic rabbis, the truth of nonduality was the fundamental principle of the awakened mystical life, and so it had to be grounded in the Torah. Thus those biblical verses which could be interpreted to speak of it were elevated to great importance and given the nondual inflection that for them was so central. For example, R. Aharon reads *v'tmunat YHVH yabit*—the anthropomorphic statement in Numbers 12:8 that Moses shall see the image of YHVH—as meaning that Moses saw through the illusion of change and multiplicity to the reality that everything is actually the changeless One.[6] Such readings rest on the interpretive principle known by the acronym PaRDeS (literally "orchard"), that sacred writ may be understood in four ways: according to its simple meaning (*pshat*), as allegory and allusion (*remez*), as font for homiletical discourse and interpretation (*drash*), and according to secret meanings (*sod*), which may be conveyed linguistically, symbolically, or even by misdirection. This technique, which allows for a near infinity of meanings to be found, is standard mystical-hermeneutical practice and is the bedrock of traditional Kabbalistic and Hasidic readings of Torah.

For many readers today, however, this way of reading demands too much of our imagination. Unlike the Kabbalists, we tend to privilege the literal over the symbolic, and are troubled by texts which describe God as an angry father or fierce warrior. What then? As applied to nondual readings of the Bible, several interpretive strategies have emerged.

First, one might adopt a Maimonidean posture that "the Torah speaks in the language of human beings" and conveys the truth in concepts accessible to its audience. For Maimonides, that "truth" was Aristotelian; God is the One, the Knower knowing the Known, unchanging, perfect, and the ontological-metaphysical source of all manifestation. But since such a concept of divinity would have made no sense to the ancient Israelites, Maimonides reasoned that it had to be framed in terms they could understand. Thus the Torah describes God analogically, in anthropomorphic terms, because those are the terms that people can readily understand. (Maimonides's project in the *Guide to the Perplexed* is to decode the biblical cipher.) Likewise in the case of nonduality. It would be unskillful, unhelpful, and incoherent to speak of "God as All" to ancient Israelites, or to many people today who lack the privilege of philosophical or mystical education or the interest in pursuing it. So, we might suppose that, if the Torah is the product either of a Divine or an exceptionally wise human lawgiver, it may speak nondual truth in dualistic language.

Alternatively, and more radically, one could take the Kabbalistic approach that the Torah "contains everything." This principle was taken to great extremes by the Kabbalists: since the Torah was infinite, it could contain any innovation, and any new knowledge, that subsequently was discovered.[7] Of course, such a stance may let in too much—what *isn't* contained in the Torah, if such a view is to be adopted? Even today's so-called Discovery Program, which uses computers to "discover" prophecies in the patterns of letters in the Torah, makes sense in such a view. But it is not a plaything; for the Kabbalists, it allowed the secrets of the Divine to be unlocked.

In between these poles is my own view: that we can approach these sacred texts reverently, self-consciously, historically, and with an understanding that multiple interpretations are possible. When I read *ein od milvado*, I understand it to mean not merely that there is no other god but God but that "there is nothing else but God." Yet I do not claim that this is what the writer of those words meant, or that other interpretations are impossible. Nondual Judaism, after all, is but one form of Jewish thought and theology. Indeed there is plenty of disagreement as to what the cardinal principle of monotheism, that there is "one God," means: a God that is philosophically One, a God that is infinite and thus the only thing in the universe, or perhaps simply that there is but one God as opposed to two or three. Fortunately, if the Ein Sof is really infinite, it accommodates an infinite number of masks, iterations, and perspectives.

With this perspective in mind, there are three types of sources, or "roots of the orchard" of nondualism, with which we will engage here. The first are short, aphoristic statements that have been interpreted in a nondual way; these are sources that admit of multiple interpretations, and we will explore the nondualistic ones. The second are more extended texts from the Jewish mystical tradition that are explicitly nondualistic in nature. And the third are non-Jewish sources that have influenced nondual Judaism over the last few decades; Jews have looked to the other 99.5 percent of the world's population for theology, architecture, music, recipes, language, art, and culture, and in the information age, the rate of interchange has only increased. A handful of such sources are presented here.

SIGNPOSTS FROM THE PAST
YHVH

Perhaps the primary word of nondual Judaism is the ineffable name itself: YHVH. YHVH is sometimes thought of as the "name of God," but actually, "God" is but one name of YHVH. "God"—Elohim—is that face of the One which appears to us, from our relative and dualistic point of view, as the Divine; as powerful, caring, loving, creating. YHVH is Being and Nothingness, all that Is and all that Becomes.[8]

Linguistically, YHVH seems to be an agglomeration of Was-Is-Will-Be. Remember, though, the Hebrew language has no word for "Is." Usually no word is used at all—to say "David is a good boy" you simply say *"David yeled tov."* I like to think that YHVH is that missing word; that YHVH is "Is." *"Ehyeh asher ehyeh,"* YHVH says to Moses in Exodus 3:14: I will be that I will be (sometimes translated "I am that I am"). YHVH is this I-AM, the true Self reading these words and writing them, the true consciousness hidden, as it were, in plain view. YHVH is "The One Who Is": Consciousness, Being, Awareness. It is a verb, a process, Be-ing. As Rabbi Michael Lerner put it, "God is the totality of all Being and all existence that ever was, is, or will be, and more than that."[9] Or as Rabbi Arthur Green says, "God is both being and becoming, noun and verb, stasis and process. All of being is One in a single simultaneity in God, and yet God is at the same time process without end."[10] Lofty words, but what do they mean in practice? Simply that all is God, and that the highest mystical state is just the simple feeling of Being itself—what's left when everything transitory has been let go.

There's a traditional Kabbalistic meditation practice to "carve" the four letters of YHVH in one's inner eye using the power of concentration, and then, upon opening the eyes, to maintain the letters as you go about your life, seeing the world, as it were, through their lens. Everything you see—people and streets and forests—is YHVH, in essence and manifestation. Ultimately, it is simply Being, simply Is-ing, the verb of God, Emptiness dancing. This is the ultimate object of contemplation: simply what is, in the eternal present, the eternal relation.

It matters that YHVH is a verb, not a noun; a constant process of what Rabbi David Cooper calls "Godding."[11] "YHVH is a verb that has been artificially arrested in motion and made to function as a noun," writes Arthur Green. "'Being' is itself an abstraction, a concept; it does not represent the same flow of energy as 'is-was-will be.'"[12] Speaking in this way re-embraces What Is, Being, and Be-ing as a manifestation of the One, albeit differentiated in appearance. It transforms every *bracha* (blessing) and utterance of prayer, and reawakens scripture, not with a pretended return to original meaning but with an almost miraculous plasticity. And ultimately, its traditional ineffability mirrors the impossibility of speaking of the arelational. Perhaps the Divine name was banned from profane use merely out of an ancient totemic respect for kingship. Today, however, it acts as a metonym for the incapacity of language, and a gesture to that which lies beyond.

Shema Yisrael, Adonai Eloheinu, Adonai Echad

Nondual Hasidim transforms the conventional, monotheistic understanding of the Shema's command to "Listen, Israel, YHVH is our god, YHVH is One."[13] The ordinary understanding of the Shema is that there is only one God—or perhaps that God is "One" in the philosophical sense. But the nondual understanding is conveyed in these words attributed to the Baal Shem Tov: "When we say 'the Lord is One,' we mean that nothing other than God exists in all the universe."[14] Likewise, in the classic Hasidic commentary of the Sfat Emet (1847–1905), we are told, "The meaning of 'YHVH is One' is not that He is the only God, negating other gods, but . . . there is no being other than Him, even though it seems otherwise to most people."[15] That is to say, the Shema is not saying that there is only one God—"The numeric one can never,

God forbid, be used in reference to God," wrote one Chabad rebbe.[16] It is not even saying that God is One in the philosophical sense. Rather, it is saying that all is One, and thus that all is God. Thus the central truth of nondual Judaism is included in the central dictum of the Jewish people.

And another level: YHVH is here called "our Elohim," our God. To say this is to subjugate the ego, which sees itself as separate, to the immanent and transcendent Is. It is not that I bow before someone or something else, but rather that the sense of "I" is no longer the ordering principle at all. If YHVH becomes my Elohim, I see clearly that this "self" is actually an illusion, a ripple on the pond of Is. There is nothing there to bow down at all.

As with all these epigrammatic statements, when fed into the egoic mind, they are ideas to be evaluated, accepted, or rejected. But if the egoic mind, the *yetzer hara*, is itself called into question, a delicious yielding can occur.

Shiviti Adonai L'Negdi Tamid

"I have set YHVH before me always" (Psalms 16:8) is one among thousands of lines of the psalms, but it is a core teaching of nondual Judaism. If the Shema conveys the intellectual core of nondual Judaism, perhaps *Shiviti* expresses the emotional center: that What Is/Who Is/Is-Ing is always before us.

This is particularly true at those times which do not seem to merit the word. It's easy to be a mystic on warm, summer days, when one is well fed and rested. It's more profound to maintain enlightened consciousness when one is heartbroken, or ill, or confronting delusion in its destructive power. Likewise, it's quite easy to say "all is God" in the comfort of a retreat center, or at a shabbat dinner; can it be said in a hospital ward? In a prisoner-of-war camp? Or even in our own homes, when love is suddenly absent? Can we say that God is both light and darkness then?

Shiviti adonai l'negdi tamid ought not be an infantile, Panglossian attitude that all is for the best. Denial of darkness, stiff upper lips in the face of it, spiritual bromides, the self-fulfilling prophecies of rationale— these are but fideism and timidity. The courageous religious life is one which does not deny a thing: not science, nor war, nor the capacity of humans to do evil. Often, religion explains What Is in terms of what is desired; it puts a happy ending on everything. But to truly say *shiviti* is to invert that hierarchy, to insist that What Is, simply is, whether I want it to be so or not. We do not accept What Is because it is acceptable; we accept it because it Is.

So the nondual *shiviti* is a kind of challenge. There are so many things I have wanted over the years, and so many that I want still. But do I have the courage to see these desires merely as conditioned phenomena, and not as the standard of goodness in the world? Is it possible to look the present moment in the eye, as it were, and see it looking back? To at once maintain the truth of my own experiences and yearnings, and acknowledge that What Is, Is—*tamid*, always? And perhaps even to address it as "You"?

Ein Od Milvado

Perhaps Hasidism's favorite nondual biblical quote comes from Deuteronomy 4:35: *Ata hareita la'da'at ki YHVH hu ha'Elohim ein od milvado.* "For you were shown, to know it, that YHVH is the God, there is nothing [or none] else beside Him." (The non-gender-neutral language is preserved here to be as literal as possible.) How to read this verse has been disputed for centuries. Traditional monotheists translate *ein* as "none"—the verse then means "there is none else beside Him," that is, "there is no other god besides God." Monists, including most Kabbalists and Hasidim, translate *ein* as "nothing," which turns the verse into a watchword of nondual Judaism: there is nothing beside God.

Among the most influential nondual readings of this verse is in the pre-Hasidic text *Shenei Luchot HaBrit* by R. Isaiah Halevy Horowitz (1565–1630), a key inspiration for R. Schneur Zalman (the author of the Tanya) and his pupil R. Aharon Halevy, who was also R. Isaiah's direct descendant. In that book, R. Isaiah Halevy writes that *ein od milvado* means, "Not just no other God beside him, but nothing exists except God."[17] This was an enormously influential reading. The Tanya amplifies it:

> It was necessary for Scripture to warn, "And know this day and take it unto your heart" and so on,[18] so that it should not enter

your mind that the heavens and all their hosts and the earth and all that fills it is a separate thing in itself, but that the Holy One, blessed be He, fills the whole world like a soul clothed in a body.[19]

The principle is alive and well today. A *dvar torah* I found online teaches:

> We are taught that "*Ein Od Milvado.*" It is commonly understood that this means there is no G-d other than Hashem. Our Masora [tradition] teaches a deeper pshat [literal meaning]. "*Ein Od Milvado*" means quite literally that Hashem is the only absolute Existence in the universe. Everything in Olam Hazeh [this world] is transient. Hashem is the sole Being that has an absolute reality. This is the background to the pasuk [verse] that we recite during Kedusha—"*M'lo kol Ha'aretz kvodo*" [the whole world is filled with His glory/kavod: see discussion below]. Everything in the world can be viewed as an expression of the K'vod HaShechina that permeates the Creation. We tend to look at the world as separate from Hashem, but in reality He is absolutely immanent.[20]

This is how nondual Judaism is expressed in traditional sources: that God is the only absolute Existence in the universe, and that, consequently, all apparent phenomena exist only from a relative, conventional point of view, not absolutely.

Ein od milvado also has a personal intimacy to it, a power to inspire. No matter how the powerful waves on the ocean toss me back and forth, the ocean is all there is; there is nothing else beside God. Whether I am alone or beloved, sick or well; whether what is in front of me is beautiful or terrible, *ein od milvado*. The intimacy of "God" in these moments is one of the great gifts of nondual Judaism, as opposed to nonduality more generally. Yes, this "God" is a transparent God, a God beyond God, not the benevolent father figure familiar from bedtime stories. But there is nonetheless a sense of personality, perhaps half-projected but nonetheless embedded in the culturally conditioned subconscious mind, which provides solace, nearness, embrace. There's a story told by Rabbi Shlomo Carlebach of *ein od milvado* being recited even in the depths of concentration camps. The hero of the great heretical Hasidic novel *Chaim Gravitzer* (written in the 1920s by a cousin of the Lubavitcher Rebbe) maintains that *ein od milvado* even as he falls into perdition. Though our own lives rarely take on such extreme casts, *ein od milvado* is more than theology; it is assurance.

Likewise, as we turn from the realm of *bein adam l'makom* (between a person and God) to that of *bein adam l'havero* (between one person and another), *ein od milvado* reminds us that we have not turned at all. It is a powerful psychological corrective to the habit of seeing people as enemies, conditions as unsatisfactory, and the world as something that either does or does not cater to our desires. A difficult coworker? *Ein od milvado.* An illness? *Ein od milvado.* And, more seriously, in the larger tragedies and heartbreaks of our lives—then, as well, if the heart can be expanded, if the mind can be so full of love it resembles space, then also, *ein od milvado.* The lovely, too, is empty; the terrible, too, is nothing but God. The more we can separate the One from the thoughts of what we want, the closer we come to realization.

M'lo chol ha'aretz kvodo

A frequent corollary to *ein od milvado* is Numbers 14:21: *m'lo chol ha'aretz kvodo,* "the whole world is filled with God's glory." As we will see below, *kavod* (*kvodo* is the possessive form) might simply mean "glory," or "grandeur," as in Gerard Manley Hopkins' translation of *hashamayim m'saprim kvodo*: the heavens declare the grandeur of God. But Kabbalists understand the *kavod* as the immanent presence of God in the world. *Kavod* is often used as a synonym for *Shechinah,* which pervades the earth, is present in the earth itself, in the materiality and physicality of existence, including the many subtle energies of which we are often unaware. In words attributed to the Baal Shem Tov, "'The whole earth is filled with God's glory.' There is therefore absolutely nothing that is devoid of God's essence."[21]

As with *ein od milvado, m'lo chol ha'aretz kvodo* has devotional as well as contemplative value—but the tenor is different. *Ein od milvado* tends toward the transparency of God and the illusoriness of material phenomena. *M'lo chol ha'aretz kvodo,* in my experience, tends toward the affirmation of material phenomena as expressions of the Divine. When I see a sapling growing in the ground, *ein od milvado* reminds me that it is empty, that it is entirely a result of genetic information, laws of nature, favorable conditions of sun and soil. But the same sapling, viewed through the eyes of the *kavod*, becomes a kind of love song for God, in which She is singer and song as well. Perhaps the great innovation of monotheism is transcendence: that God is more than what is. But we have had thousands of years of this innovation, and its necessary counterpoint is immanence: that God is What Is.

OTHER BIBLICAL QUOTATIONS

There are many other biblical statements that are favorites of nondual Hasidim. Perhaps the essence of the spiritual quest is summarized in Jacob's words in Genesis 28:16, after his dream, when he says "God was in this place—and I, I did not know." God is already here; what is absent is only our remembering. Deuteronomy 4:39 repeats the *ein od milvado* of verse 35, but in a different context: "Know this day, and lay it upon your heart, that YHVH is God in heaven above and upon the earth beneath; there is nothing else." For Chabad Hasidim, this is a practice guide: "know this day" refers to contemplation, "lay it upon your heart" to ecstatic prayer.[22] Deuteronomy 30:14—*ki karov alecha ha'davar me'od, b'picha uv'lvavecha la'asoto*, "for the Word/Thing is very close to you, in your mouth and your heart, so you may do it"—is also given a nondual inflection in some Hasidic sources. The *pshat*, or plain meaning of the text, is that God's commandments are "not hidden from you, nor . . . far off" (Deut. 30:14). But the *sod*, or secret meaning, is that God's word is in our mouths and our hearts already; they are speaking God's Word, translated through us. Indeed, as God is present in the *Davar*, the Word, God is very close to you, in your mouth and heart.

The biblical books of the prophets and writings are also full of texts interpreted in a nondual way. "I, YHVH, have not changed" (Malachi 3:6) is often cited by Chabad Hasidim to support the Maimonidean notion that the transcendent God never changes—and thus that the world itself has no real existence, since if it did, God would change before and after creating it.[23] "I am God and there is none else" (Isaiah 45:5) is interpreted in a panentheistic way; that there is nothing else but God.

The Tanya cites "For YHVH Elohim is a sun and shield" (Psalms 84:12) to show that God is both the light and its concealment, expansion and contraction, absolute and relative. "You give life to all" (Neh. 9:6) hints at the omnipresence of the Divine life force. The injunction to "know the God of your father, and serve him with a perfect heart and a desirous mind, for God searches all hearts and understands desires and thoughts," (I Chron. 28:9) suggests Divine omniscience, and also repeats the imperative to know the Divine essence. And finally, the poetry of Psalms 139 embodies the omnipresence of God as well as the concept of *hashva'ah* (equivalence), which we will discuss in chapter 9:

> Where could I go to escape your spirit?
> Where could I flee from your presence?
> If I climb the heavens, you are there,
> there too, if I lie in Sheol.
> If I flew to the point of sunrise, or westward across the sea
> your hand would still be guiding me, your right hand holding me.
> If I were to say "Ah, darkness will hide me,
> and the light will become night around me,"
> even the dark is not dark to you, and night shines like the day,
> for darkness is as light to you.[24]

Naming the Immanence of God

Biblical, rabbinic, and medieval Judaism had several terms that denoted the immanent aspect of God, including *kavod* (literally, "glory"); the *Ruach HaKodesh* ("holy spirit"); and *Shechinah* ("presence"). These terms, the meaning of which evolved over the centuries, are not exactly equivalent to nonduality, but are close to it. All three are at first said to be aspects of the Divine which reside in specific places, such as the Ark of the Covenant, the Western Wall, or wherever the Children of Israel wandered in the desert. The *kavod* is generally that aspect of the Divine which is revealed to humans; it was said in the medieval philosophy of the Jewish scholar Saadia Gaon to be an entity created specifically for that purpose. The *Ruach HaKodesh* is a kind of spirit of prophecy that alights on human beings at propitious times.[25] And the *Shechinah*, which in Kabbalah became the feminine, indwelling aspect of God, is in biblical translations and Talmud sometimes simply the "Presence of God," the immanent "face" of God in the world,[26] and other times a personification of God, wandering from place to place, weeping with, and consoling, Israel.[27]

Sometimes, these revealed faces of God are said to be omnipresent, as in *m'lo chol ha'aretz kvodo* (the whole world is filled with God's glory), discussed above, or the midrashic statement that "every place has the *Shechinah* in it, even a humble bush,"[28] the Talmudic statements that the *Shechinah* is everywhere,[29] or the remark in a fifth-century Midrash that "everywhere is the center of the universe; every place is filled with the Divine Presence. There is no place on the earth that is void of the *Shechinah*."[30] At such times, immanentism slides into nondualism: God, or at least the *kavod* or *Shechinah*, fills the world, everywhere and at every time.

Memaleh Kol Almin u' Sovev Kol Almin

Moving from Biblical and Talmudic material to the Kabbalah, a classic Kabbalistic formulation of nondual Judaism is that God "fills and surrounds all worlds"—*memaleh kol almin u'sovev kol almin*.[31] This formulation is found in the Zohar[32] and other medieval texts, such as the twelfth-century *Shir HaYichud* ("Song of Unity") which says that God "surrounds all, and fills all, and is the essence of all; You are in all." The aspect of *memaleh*, filling, we have already explored: it is that every particle of being is filled with God. As the Zohar continues: "He fills all worlds . . . He binds and unites one kind to another, upper with lower, and the four elements do not cohere except through the Holy Blessed One, as he is within them."

The aspect of *sovev*, though, remains before us. It is a crucial part of the formula, and easily misunderstood. From a theological perspective, as described in the introduction, it supposedly distinguishes panentheism—the view that all is *in* God—from pantheism, the view that God is nothing more than the universe. But really, nothing—or rather Nothing—is added by the word "in." Try to imagine the transcendent aspect of God "surrounding" the entire universe. What does that even mean? If we imagine any kind of thing surrounding the universe (when I was a young boy I'd imagine a black rock wall, like the walls of a cave), we have erred, because whatever that thing is, it is comprised by aspects of the universe itself. So that's not it. Nor is "energy" or "space" or any other word in our language, because words refer to things that exist—and thus cannot "surround" all that exists.

Really, what *sovev* gives us is total ineffability, total Emptiness, total Nothing: *ayin*. It demands a cessation of thought, a renunciation of deduction. It is the great question mark enveloping our cosmos. And when combined with *memaleh*, it stands for the principle that all is empty; that form and emptiness are equivalent; that existence and nonexistence are two sides of a coin, two perspectives on the great nondual Is/Isn't of God and the world. It is the ultimate antidote to idolatry, because not just any image of God, but even any experience that sets itself apart from others, is error. We are no closer to God in the synagogue than in the mall, no nearer in meditation than in boredom. And, most radically of all, God is as immanent in evil as in good. It simply cannot be otherwise. *Sovev u'memaleh*, God fills and surrounds *everything*. Fills and surrounds; goddess and god; immanent and transcendent; form and emptiness; the great What Is of YHVH and the great void of *ayin*. We cannot make it cohere. If we could, it wouldn't be Is.

Leit Atar Panui Mineha

Another Zoharic passage favored by nondualistic Hasidim is the statement that *leit atar panui mineha*, "there is no place devoid of God." This phrase is found in the Tikkunei Zohar (57), a later addition to the Zoharic literature, but accorded great respect by subsequent generations of mystics. On a simple level, this sentence conveys the doctrine of omnipresence, and it was taken literally by Chabad Hasidism: "The meaning of 'He fills all the worlds and there is no place devoid of Him' is truly literal," says one text.[33] Yet perhaps the simple is not so simple—if omnipresence truly includes every particle of being, every synapse in the brain, every place of beauty and ugliness.

L'Shem Yichud Kudsha Brich Hu v'Shechintei

In theosophical Kabbalah, the transcendent and immanent aspects of the One are called, respectively, *Kudsha Brich Hu* (Aramaic for the Holy One, Blessed be He) and *Shechintei* (the feminine Divine Presence—the

Aramaic form of "His *Shechinah*"), respectively. The great work of Jewish ritual is to unite these two aspects, masculine and feminine, concealed and revealed, transcendent and immanent, heaven and earth, ultimate and relative, the one and the many. This formula is quite common in Kabbalistic literature and has become part of Jewish liturgy, recited before the performance of many ritual acts. It uses erotic language: *yichud* has the connotation of sexual union, and eros is not merely an analogy for the mystical path but an actualization and reflection of it. But what is meant when one recites the words before the performance of a seemingly ordinary *mitzvah*? Is this really the Divine lovemaking?

Let us consider an affirmative answer. The *Shechinah,* the Divine Presence, troped as feminine by the Kabbalists, is that which is present: the manifest, the real, the multiplicitous. She is the leaves on the trees, the earth nourishing the roots. She is precisely that aspect of the Divine which seems to be in exile, unredeemed; She is "the world" from which so many seek to escape. The Holy One, troped as masculine, is that which is transcendent: God removed from the world, perhaps God in search of the world. If the *Shechinah* is in exile from the Godhead, then the Godhead is in exile from us. The longing is reciprocal. If I yearn for God, God yearns for me.

In nondual terms, *Shechinah* corresponds to the introduction's long column of characteristics associated with two-ness, and the Holy One that of one-ness. For R. Aharon, *Shechinah* is the world as it appears in multiplicity; the Holy One is as it seems to God.[34] Recall, however, that the nondual mystic path is to understand both unity *and* multiplicity. Nonduality does not mean unity consciousness, no-mind, and *devekut* alone. It means marrying, uniting, all of those with the manifest world; to unify the *kudsha brich hu* and the *Shechinah.* Ours is not to flee the world to repeated, temporary islands of unity. It is instead to bring about the Divine lovemaking between *yesh* and *ayin*, nothingness and the all, a union delicious in its consummation.

NONDUAL TRADITIONS
The Zohar and Early Kabbalah

The Zohar, the great masterpiece of the Kabbalah, is a literary epic whose symbolic complexity is without rival in Western literature, and is at once a nondualistic and post-nondualistic work. Appearing in Spain in the late thirteenth century, but presented in the form of conversations among second-century rabbis, the Zohar is likely a product of a circle of mystics that was redacted into its present form by Rabbi Moshe de Leon. (Authorship of the Zohar remains controversial; for traditionalists, to suggest that it is anything other than the work of the second-century Rabbi Shimon bar Yochai is heretical.) The text is an infinitely absorbing amalgam of myth, commentary, mysticism, and theology, and it resists classification according to subject matter, philosophy, or even genre.

The Zohar takes as its beginning point the premise of the Ein Sof. And if one is serious about Ein Sof, then one must be a nondualist: one can't hold that there is something infinite and also that something else exists apart from it. We have already studied a few of the Zohar's nondual utterances above, and the text repeats over and over again, even in the midst of the most wild and anthropomorphic speculations, that *kula chada,* "all is One," and that "everything is unified in Him."[35] Mystics active in the circle of the Zohar made clearly panentheistic statements. Rabbi Joseph Gikatilla, among the most prominent, is recorded as saying "he fills everything and He is everything."[36] Moshe de Leon wrote that his essence is "above and below, in heaven and on earth, and there is no existence beside him."[37] And nearly a century before the appearance of the Zohar, R. Azriel of Gerona (1160–1238), arguably one of the founders of Kabbalah as we know it, presented one of the first clear expositions of nonduality in the Jewish context:

> If someone asks you "What is God," answer: He who is in no way deficient. If he asks you: "Does anything exist outside of Him?" answer: nothing exists outside of Him. If he asks you, "How did he bring being from nothingness, for there is a great difference between being and nothingness?" answer: He who brings forth being from nothingness is thereby lacking in nothing, for the being is in the nothingness after the manner of the nothingness and the nothingness is in the being after the manner of being . . . the being is the nought and the nought is the being . . . Do not take on too much in your speculation, for our finite intellect can-

not grasp the perfection of the impenetrable which is one with Ein Sof.[38]

The identity of being and nothingness is, as R. Azriel states, a confounding of logic. Yet as we will see in the next chapter, the dialectical interdependence of being and nothingness (the theme of *coincidentia oppositorum* that runs throughout mystical thought) can be understood as a matter of perspective; the All is, or is Not, depending on how you (or You) look at it. The principle, says R. Azriel, also applies to the *sefirot*: "The nature of *sefirah* is the synthesis of every thing and its opposite. For if they did not possess the power of synthesis, there would be no energy in anything. For that which is light is not-darkness and that which is darkness is not-light."[39] Elsewhere, R. Azriel states clearly that "if [the Ein Sof] is without limit, then nothing exists outside of Him. And since He is both exalted and hidden, He is the essence of all that is concealed and revealed."[40]

The Zohar emerges against this background. Once there is Ein Sof, there is nonduality. But the drama of the Zohar is contained not in the realization of absolute, nondual truth, but in the explication and revelation of the relative. Chiefly, the Zohar is interested not in the One, itself, but in how the One relates to the many: the emanation and relationships of the *sefirot*, the way human actions relate to the Divine realms, as well as the interplays of masculine and feminine, evil and good, human and heavenly, Jewish and non-Jewish, and a myriad of other dualities. As Scholem puts it: "the author of the Zohar inclines toward pantheism, a fact made even clearer by the Hebrew writings of Moses de Leon, but one would look in vain for confession of his faith beyond some vague formulae and hints at a fundamental unity of all things, stages, and worlds."[41]

Recall, though, that the nondual path is, essentially, a two-way street. In one direction, our goal is to transcend ordinary consciousness and realize that what seems to be real is not, ultimately, real; that you're not a wave, you're water. But in the other direction, the nondualist embraces manifestation: obviously, there are still people, trees, clouds, and sky, and all of them are luminous phenomena of God. Along the nondual path, there are elements of renunciation and otherworldliness, but at the culmination of the path, there is a re-embracing of the world, a re-enchantment of it, and a rededication, motivated by compassion and wisdom, to heal it. Perhaps none of this is real—but suffering still "exists," and beauty, and love.

The Zohar works in both of these directions. First, the real mysticism of the Zohar, as scholars and practitioners have explored, is not in its accounts of unusual experiences, but in the reading and re-enactment of the text itself. The "reader" of the Zohar becomes the mystic in her interpretation of the text, which itself records interpretations of text. Improvising and playing with the symbols of the Zohar, not unlike elaborating on themes in jazz, one gradually becomes enveloped in them. Colors are less themselves than the "sefirotic" referents to which they point; oceans are not oceans; mountains are not mountains. And since the *sefirot* are all emanations of God, the immersion into sefirotic symbolism becomes an immersion in nondual, panentheistic God-consciousness. By playing with multiplicity, the Zohar teaches unity.

Second, the Zohar can be read as an answer to a deceptively simple question: if everything is God, why does it appear as it does? Thus it begins from the premise of unity, and then spends thousands of pages inquiring into multiplicity. How does the relative relate to the absolute? What is the meaning of evil, of distinction, of binaries and pairs? How does the undifferentiated light of the Ein Sof become refracted, as it were, through the prisms of the *sefirot* and into the many hues we know from our experience? By answering these questions, the Zohar rebuilds the world. It becomes a kind of post-nondualistic science of manifestation, tying every aspect of the revealed world to its true Divine essence.

In this way, the Zohar is able to become the most outrageously anthropomorphic text in the Jewish tradition. As we will explore in the next chapter, nonduality leads to theological polymorphism, because all descriptions are but masks and approximations anyway, and the more, the better. The Zohar is the primary Jewish exemplar of this trend, with passages describing God's beard and hair, extended treatments of demons and angels, and an entire mythic cosmology, all the while insisting that all is one. And because it does this, because it meets us in duality, takes us through symbol to nonduality, and then returns us to a transformed world of apparent separation, it is a powerful tool for working with the duality we experience all the time.

For example, consider one of the first Zoharic passages, contained in Zohar 1:1b–2a. The passage begins with Isaiah's poetic exhortation: "Lift your eyes on high and see: who created these?" This is the quintessential moment of religious consciousness: we are awed by the stars, and wonder at how they came to be. In the Zohar, however, the sentence is transformed first into a mystical allusion, and then into a startling nondual theology. The first step is symbolism: "who" is here a name of Binah, the supernal Divine mother, womb of the world, the "End of heaven above . . . concealed and unrevealed." Her counterpart is "what," a name of Malchut, the *Shechinah*, the Mother here below. Like a mystical Abbott and Costello routine, these interrogatory words are now Divine names—but unlike comedy, they are reminders of nondual truth. "What" are you reading right now? In the Zohar's language, that is a statement, not a question: you are reading *what* right now, the revealed aspect of God. "Who" is reading? Yes, *who* is reading: understanding, consciousness. This is how the Zohar transforms us: not by unitive mystical experience, but by the textual resymbologizing of the world. Every *who* or *what* after which we inquire—is God.

But then the Zohar takes a second turn. Rabbi Shimon bar Yochai, the hero of the Zohar, interrupts these musings with a secret concerning another word in Isaiah's verse: "these," or *eleh*. In the Zohar, "Eleh" signifies those multiple powers which seem to be separate from the One. It is the symbol of polytheism, and thus idolatry, as when Aaron says in the book of Exodus, upon presenting the golden calf, *Eleh elohim Yisrael*, These are your gods, O Israel.[42] And yet, says the Zohar, only with *Eleh* can *Mi* become *Elohim*, God. In other words, God is only God when there is separateness as well as oneness, multiplicity as well as unity.[43] The world is not dual, a unitary God on the one hand and a multiplicitous world on the other. Rather, says R. Shimon, both the separateness and the mystery are God. The mistake of idolatry is not turning astray, but partiality; it sees the *eleh* but not the *mi*, the manifold but not the essential. And it is no more erroneous than the reverse.

This is a startling reversal. On the one hand, it suggests that idolatry is not so much wrong as incomplete—a far cry from conventional understandings of evil and "foreign worship." And even more outrageously, it says that monotheism is just as incomplete when it denies multiplicity. If we worship the One but not the Many, we are no less confused than the "pagans." No wonder the Zohar couches its theology in layers of symbolism and obfuscation; what it hides is radical.

Moses Cordovero

Moses Cordovero (1522–1570) was the great systematizer of Kabbalah—Scholem called him "undoubtedly the greatest" theoretician of Jewish mysticism[44] and the most panentheistic.[45] Cordovero's major work, *Pardes Rimonim* (The Orchard of Pomegranates), is a veritable encyclopedia of Kabbalah; it is long, complex, and remains untranslated to this day. Nonduality is the basis of the entire edifice, the foundational truth upon which all the others are built. Here is one passage, which in the last few years has become quite famous since it was translated by the scholar Daniel Matt (here provided in my own translation):

> The essence of God is in every thing, and nothing exists outside of God. Because God causes everything to be, it is impossible that any created thing exists except through God. God is the existence, the life, and the reality of every existing thing. The central point is that you should never make a division within God . . . If you say to yourself, "The Ein Sof expands until a certain point, and from there on is outside of It," God forbid, you are making a division. Rather you must say that God is found in every existing thing. One cannot say, "This is a rock and not God," God forbid. Rather, all existence is God, and the rock is a thing filled with God . . . God is found in everything, and there is nothing beside God.[46]

And here is another (again my translation):

> God is all reality, but not all reality is God . . . God is found in all things, and all things are found in God, and there is nothing de-

void of God's divinity, God forbid. Everything is in God, and God is in everything and beyond everything, and there is nothing else beside God.[47]

As a systematic theologian, Cordovero was not given to vagueness; he devotes many pages to the *keter* of the *keter* of *keter*, trying to bridge the gap between finite and infinite. He was well aware of contrary opinions within the Kabbalistic corpus and was at pains either to dispute them or to include them within his own theory. As such, Cordovero laid the conceptual groundwork for nondual Kabbalah and Hasidism, where it entered a new phase of development, to which we now turn.

The Baal Shem Tov

Rabbi Israel Baal Shem Tov (1700–1760), the charismatic founder of Hasidism, was a complex, half-mythical figure whose aphorisms are collected in many anthologies, some of them more reliable than others. Unlike Cordovero, the Baal Shem Tov (also known as the Besht, an acronym rarely used by Hasidim themselves) was not a systematic theologian and did not write down his teachings. But his spirit is almost palpable both in his recorded teachings and in the hagiographic tales about him. This was a man possessed of great joy, great reverence, and great power: his name is an audacious variation on "Baal Shem" (literally, "master of the name"), one who is adept at using angelic or divine names for magical purposes.

Whether the Baal Shem Tov was a nondualist is somewhat unclear, a determination complicated by uncertainty regarding which statements attributed to him are authentically his words. Certainly there are many statements that emphasize omnipresence and panentheism; for instance, in one text he asserts, "Nothing exists in this world except the absolute Unity which is God,"[48] and in another: "It is written, 'The whole earth is filled with His *kavod*.' This means that even the physical world is one of God's garments. The verse therefore says that 'the whole earth was filled with His glory'—even the physical."[49] These teachings are clear, and repeated often. And the notion that "even the physical" is filled with God's *kavod* is crucial, for it distinguishes Hasidism from dualistic notions of world-denial; everything is pervaded by Divinity.

Yet we must be honest with these and other Hasidic sources. First, the Baal Shem Tov never renounced the particularism of Judaism, the stories of the Bible, and the laws of the rabbis. His was a path that combined mystical fervor, popular in heretical circles of his day, with a conservative Jewish form: Hasidic literature is replete with traditional admonitions to follow the commandments and to repent of sins, traditional understandings of God creating the world and giving the Torah to Israel, and traditional ideas about prayer, people, and piety. At the very least, the Besht's panentheism is not one that says "all is God, therefore all is permitted."

Second, rather like Ramakrishna, the Besht had as much room in his religious worldview for personal, devotional, mythic, anthropomorphic, and dualistic conceptions of God as for nondualistic ones. Although for this book I have selected Hasidic sources that present the nondual view, they are not the only sources available. One could very easily write a book on "Hasidic dualistic Judaism"—indeed, using some of the same texts I cite here.

For example, when the Baal Shem Tov says that "the moment you separate yourself from God, you are worshipping an idol,"[50] the word "separate" could mean "have a notion of separateness," thinking of oneself as separate from the Divine. Thus, if you believe you are separate from God, then you are serving a projection, a myth, an idol. On the other hand, "separate" could just mean separate as in separating oneself from a lover, and the admonition is never to leave God's presence.

Even the central goal of Hasidic practice—*devekut*, which literally means "cleaving" or "attachment"—admits of multiple interpretations. Some contemporary nondualists propose that it means "merging" with the One. But more traditional scholars note that the metaphor is one of joining together two separate things, not melting one into the other. Practically speaking, there may be little difference; when one is truly in *devekus* (in the Ashkenazic pronunciation), one feels God within and without, surrounding and filling, inspiring and loving. Let the theologians figure out the details. Perhaps the very ambiguity is an invitation for the heart to lead.

Finally, consider this wonderful and ambiguous selection from the *Keter Shem Tov*, an anthology of the Baal Shem Tov's teachings compiled by R. Aaron of Opatow and published in 1784:

You should understand regarding the Holy Blessed One, that the whole earth is filled with his glory [*m'lo chol ha'aretz kvodo*], and there is no place devoid of it [*leit atar panui mineha*]. Wherever a person is, the Glorious Blessed One is found there. So why must his prayers be received by angels that go from heavenly palace to heavenly palace, and so on? A parable: . . . There was a wise and great king, and he built an illusion [*achizat einayim*] of walls and towers and gates. And he commanded that people should walk with him by means of the gates and castles, and commanded that treasures of the king be scattered at every gate, so one could walk to one gate and back, and so on. But when his beloved son tried hard to go to his father the king, he saw there was no barrier separating him and his father, because all was illusion. And the meaning is clear: that the Holy Blessed One fills the earth with His glory, and every movement or thought is from Him. Even the angels and the palaces all is created from his blessed essence, like the locust, whose garment is from it and of it.[51]

The meaning is clear, the text says, and yet it is deferred as well. We are told that the walls are illusion, but intercessionary prayer remains conveyed in the traditional angelic way. Moreover, the parable does not say that the illusion disappears when the beloved son cuts through delusion. Perhaps the form remains, but it is seen through—that is, seen as it really is. Notice too how the crucial ingredient here is effort: *hitametz me'od*, the original reads; "the son tries hard." Not a graduate degree, nor sweet intention, but hard work—only to find that no work is necessary at all. This is how the path to the nonlinear can itself be linear. Sometimes we have to work hard to surrender. And then, when we have exerted enough effort, the world remains in its full manifestation, but the sage is able to "see through" it to that which others believe it conceals. Really, there is no concealment at all.

The Tanya and Chabad Hasidism

The most important text of nondual Judaism, in terms of influence and clarity, is the Tanya by Rabbi Schneur Zalman of Liadi. Published in 1796, it is the founding text of Chabad Hasidism, which has a worldwide influence today. These days, Chabad is known for its assertive outreach efforts and messianic beliefs. However, when Chabad—an acronym for *chochmah, binah, da'at*, the three intellectual *sefirot*—was founded, it was regarded as the most philosophical of the Hasidic sects. And with good reason. The Tanya is, while not quite a work of systematic theology, close to it, and the Alter Rebbe's followers, his son and heir R. Dov Ber of Lubavitch, and his foremost disciple, R. Aharon of Staroselye, each produced multiple works of philosophical theology. And from the Tanya to the works of the last Lubavitcher Rebbe, Chabad has maintained the most rigorously nondualistic theology of any Jewish sect. On the surface, the telethons and tefillin-a-thons may seem rather silly. But underneath, the theology is radical and—largely via the activism of two maverick rabbis discussed below, Shlomo Carlebach and Zalman Schachter-Shalomi—has filtered through into movements such as neo-Hasidism, Jewish Renewal, Reconstructionism, and many other non-Orthodox sects. Its essence, according to the last Lubavitcher Rebbe? "The extension of the Ein Sof."[52]

The second part of the Tanya is called the *Shaar HaYichud v'HaEmunah*, "The Gate of Unity and Faith." Its stated purpose is to illuminate what the Zohar means when it says that the first line of the Shema ("Hear O Israel, YHVH is God, YHVH is One") is "higher unity" and the second line ("Blessed be the name of God's *kavod malchut* [glorious kingdom] forever") is "lower unity."[53] The Tanya's answer is that the first is the philosophical unity of the transcendent One, and the second is the union of that unity with the multiplicity of manifestation. It is precisely the nondual truth that transcends and includes both reality and appearance.

For the Tanya, the world is understood as a dialectic process between *yesh* and *ayin*, existence and nonexistence. Seen from one way, of course the world exists; this is the very meaning of the word "exist." Seen from another way—which for Rabbi Schneur Zalman and his disciples is God's way—the world does not have any ultimate existence, and would instantly revert to nothingness were the "Divine Word" to be removed. "With the removal of the power of the Creator from the thing created, God forbid, it would revert to naught and complete nothingness [*ayin v'efes mamash*]"[54] In fact, this would not be a change of state but merely a change of perspective, because nothing really exists from God's perspective anyway. As Rabbi Schneur Zalman writes, "every created, activated thing looks to us like something [*yesh*] and real because we cannot understand or see with our fleshly eyes the power of God and 'Breath of His Mouth' that is within it."[55]

The Tanya's metaphor for this is a ray of light, which appears to us as something, but "in its own place," that is, the sun, it is "naught and complete nothingness [*ayin v'efes mamash*], for it is absolutely nullified in relation to the body of the sphere of the sun which is the source of this light and radiance."[56] Likewise, Rabbi Schneur Zalman says, we and all other created things seem to exist only from a perspective distant from the Source; were we seen at our Source, it would be clear that, like a ray of sunlight utterly nullified in the body of the sun, the separate "you" simply does not exist when considered as part of its true Source, God. According to R. Aharon, expanding on the Tanya's ideas:

> In truth, the worlds do not have any essence of their own, because everything is God's blessed power alone, and in truth there is nothing devoid of God and nothing beside God whatsoever. And all the worlds which appear to be are only from the side of concealment in *yesh* which appears to be, but in truth everything is his power without any change.[57]

> God before the world and God after the world is the same: alone. Just as God was in Godself before the creation of the worlds, so the Blessed One is alone [*l'vado*] after the creation of the worlds, and all the worlds do not add to God (may he be blessed) anything that would divide God's essence (God forbid), and God does not change and does not multiply in them, and the worlds (God forbid) do not add anything additional to God.[58]

And yet, this is only the first step of the Tanya's argument. Rabbi Schneur Zalman next asks the question we saw earlier in the context of the Zohar: since, unlike the sun, God is omnipresent, why is it that we seem to exist at all? His answer is a nondual reinterpretation of *tzimtzum*, the Lurianic notion that the Ein Sof "contracted" itself to make room for the world. Obviously, a contraction of the Infinite is a flat contradiction, and the speculative Kabbalists of the Lurianic school devoted great effort to squaring the circle.[59] The Tanya, however, understands *tzimtzum* as being the very "shield" of separation itself—the principle of "contraction" that allows for the appearance of multiplicity. This the Tanya identifies with the Divine name "Elohim,"[60] which is numerically equivalent to *hateva*, or Nature,[61] and the *sefirah* of *gevurah*,[62] which has the characteristics of constriction and boundary. Nature—the laws of nature, the structure of the universe, all the principles of cosmology—is that which conceals, and yet also reveals, the Divine, YHVH.

The third step in the argument is the most important one: that YHVH and Elohim are two aspects of the same Unity: that YHVH *is* Elohim. YHVH, the tetragrammaton, is the ineffable, the *ayin*, the unitive truth. Elohim is that aspect of the Divine which shields us from that truth; it is the veil of illusion itself. Now, one might suppose that the teaching here is to get past Elohim to know YHVH—but while such unitive consciousness is an intermediate step, it is not the final one. The ultimate attainment is the seeing of the infinite *in* the finite itself; to know unity in multiplicity; that even delusion, suffering, pain, and separateness are but manifestations of the nondual, Being dancing as world, God donning the drag of us. The completion of the Infinite, for the Tanya, is precisely limitation; the completion of plenitude is privation. Thus, rather than perceive the energies of *tzimtzum* as obstructions between us and God, the Tanya sees them as enabling God to become us. The shadow is also light; indeed, for the Tanya, the shadow allows the light to shine.

This, finally, is the meaning of the upper and lower unity of the Shema. The upper unity, the Tanya explains, is YHVH, the first line of the Shema, Oneness of God from the Maimonidean perspective. Here God is totally one, perfect, and changeless:

> There is no change at all: just as God was alone before the creation of the world, so God is alone after it was created. And so it is written, "You were the same before the world was created; You have been the same"[63] without any change in God's essence or knowledge, for by knowing Godself, God knows all created

things, that are from God and nullified in God's essence from God's point of view.[64]

The lower unity, however, is the union of YHVH with the immanent. "Malchut," in the second line of the Shema, is that aspect of God which is throughout time and space[65] and which has the "aspect" of *tzimtzum, gevurah, and* Elohim.[66] In other words, the "lower unity" is the union of unity and multiplicity—the very essence of nonduality. This is the distinction between the highs of peak experience and the sanctification of the everyday. In practice, writes Rachel Elior:

> Higher unification is the focus of spiritual worship [*avodah*], and it means *the annihilation of the world* and its inclusion within the godhead . . . This unification is called the transformation of *yesh* into *Ayin* . . . The lower unification means the *influx of divinity* from upper realms to lower ones, from *Ayin to Yesh*, and its infusion into the world.[67]

Nonduality reaffirms the world as we find it, only now it is transformed into divinity.

By way of comparison, let us return to *Mi Chamocha*, the 1869 tract by Rabbi Shmuel Schneersohn, which, of course, builds on the Tanya. In the passage quoted earlier, R. Shmuel showed how any thing reveals itself, upon contemplation, to be made up of non-thing elements. And yet, it's not that a piece of wood "is" earth, air, fire, and water; there seems to be some essential "wood-ness," yet, like the Platonic forms, it can never really be found. For a Buddhist, this shows the emptiness of "wood." For R. Shmuel, it shows its Godliness: God is that which is the true reality of every thing. And yet, R. Shmuel continues, it is not only that God is the truth of the wood—God is also the illusion of the wood. Nonduality is not just the truth hiding behind the appearance, it is both the truth behind, and the appearance itself. In R. Shmuel's words:

> In truth the power of concealment is as Divine as the power of revelation, as it is written "And I have hidden my face . . ." (Isaiah 8:17) . . . The power of concealment and limitation are as

Divine as the power of boundlessness, as it is written in the *Avo-dat Hakodesh*,[68] that if you were to say that Godliness is a limit-less power, but without the power to limit, you have detracted from its wholeness.[69]

In Mahayana Buddhist language, liberation is not an escape from sam-sara to nirvana; it is recognizing that samsara *is* nirvana. In nondual Jew-ish language, truth is not running from the world to God; it is knowing that God is both the world and its negation, both essence and existence, both truth and illusion. The mask is of the same Divinity as the Divin-ity it conceals within. This is no small point, and we will return to it in the next chapter. It is the link between enlightenment and love, wisdom and compassion. The shadow, too, is light.

Other Hasidic Masters

There are numerous other Hasidic masters who taught nonduality. For example, one of the most popular texts of Hasidism, the *Kedushat Levi*, by R. Levi Yitzchak of Berdichev (1740–1809), prefigures the way im-manence and transcendence are discussed in the Tanya. For example:

God has two aspects, distance and nearness. The aspect of dis-tance is that we believe that the Light of the Blessed Ein Sof is utterly primordial [*kadmon l'chol kadmonim*], and that nothing in the universe can comprehend It, because it is impossible for thought to comprehend God, since thought is conditioned, but the Holy One is unconditioned [*machshavah mechudash v'ha Ka-dosh Baruch Hu Kadmon*][70] . . . This is the aspect of distance, that is, distant and apart from comprehension. The aspect of nearness is that we believe that the Blessed Creator fills all worlds, and is contained in all worlds, and surrounds all worlds, and no place is empty of God, because "the whole earth is filled with God's glory." (Isaiah 6:3). This is the aspect of nearness. And we Children of Is-rael must believe in both of these aspects.[71]

Both transcendence and immanence; nothing and everything. Like-wise, consider this teaching from another of the earliest Hasidic texts, the *Ben Porat Yosef* of R. Yakov Yosef of Polonnoye: "Man is obligated to believe that the whole earth is full of His glory, may He be praised, and there is no place devoid of Him, and that all a man's thoughts contain his presence."[72] Or this from the Maggid of Mezrich, the second leader of the Hasidic movement:

> The whole earth is full of His glory, and there is no place devoid of Him, and wherever one is, there he will find devotion to the Creator, may His name be praised, from the place where he is, because there is no place devoid of Him . . . and in every place there is divinity.[73]

Or the Maggid again: "God is called the Ein Sof. This means that there is nothing physical that hinders God's presence. God fills every place in all worlds, both spiritual and physical, and there is no place empty of God."[74]

Another nondual Hasidic master, Rabbi Menachem Nahum of Chernobyl (1730–1797), preached nonduality in his masterpiece *Meor Einayim* ("The Light of the Eyes") with teachings such as, "The whole earth is filled with this presence; there is no place devoid of it. There is nothing besides the presence of God; being itself is derived from God and the presence of the Creator remains in each created thing."[75] In another passage, he writes:

> All is one: Divinity above, Israel, Torah, the world-to-come, and this world. All bring forth the flow of His Godliness, this world in a more external way, but containing within it that inward self of the world to come. These must be joined into a total oneness, such that will allow body to be translated into soul, just as happens within a single human person.[76]

The letters of Rabbi Meshullam Feibush Heller of Zbarazh, written in the 1770s, are among the earliest of Hasidic texts. In one, translated by Miles Krassen in *Uniter of Heaven and Earth*, R. Feibush says "There is really nothing in the world other than God and His emanated powers which are a unity. Other than that, nothing exists. Although it seems there are other things, everything is really God and the divine emanations."[77]

R. Feibush also compares the mystic with the ordinary person. In one passage he writes:

> Things are exactly the opposite of the way people imagine. For when they cleave to the world rather than the blessed Creator, it seems to them that they exist and are great. But in what sense are they great? One day they are here and the next they are gone . . . But if one considers himself as nothing because of *devekut* with the Creator . . . one mentally causes all his powers to cleave to the blessed Creator, as before creation. Hence such a one is very great. For the branch comes to its root and is in a state of complete unity with its root. Since the root is Ein Sof, the branch is also Ein Sof. For its existence has been voided like a single drop that fell into a great sea. It returned to its root and thus is one with the water of the sea and cannot be distinguished at all.[78]

In another passage, R. Feibush uses erotic language to make the same comparison. A mystic is like someone who, when he sees a beautiful woman, lusts for the woman underneath the fancy clothing, whereas an ordinary person is one who is distracted by the glittery clothes.[79]

Finally, one cannot discuss contemporary Hasidism without mentioning R. Nachman of Bratzlav (1772–1810), among the most original, idiosyncratic, and revered Hasidic masters. Today, the streets of Israel are filled with Rebbe Nachman enthusiasts, who chant the rebbe's name (in a magical formula) and celebrate the reality that *ein od milvado*. In the original sources, however, the genius of R. Nachman of Bratzlav lies not in nondualism but in the experience of duality. R. Nachman cries out to God, prays to God, struggles with God; although he has his moments of ecstasy, his is a Hasidism of striving, yearning, and devotion. In sharp contrast to R. Schneur Zalman, R. Nachman ridicules any attempt to know God by way of philosophy, and he argues that theology is often an obstacle to pure and simple faith.

At the same time, it should be noted that even in Bratzlav, which so emphasizes these dualistic modes, the underlying theology remains consonant with the rest of Hasidic nonduality. For example, in his *Lik-kutei Moharan*, R. Nachman repeats the familiar Hasidic quotations from earlier sources, and gives them his own distinctive spin:

> Every individual must realize that "the whole earth is filled with his glory" and "there is no place empty of him" and that "he fills all worlds and surrounds all worlds." Even someone doing business with nonbelievers cannot excuse himself by saying, "It is impossible to serve God because of the mundane, godless work that falls to me because of my business and business partners." Our sages of blessed memory have already shown us that in all material things, and in all foreign languages, it is possible to find Godliness, as it is written, "You give life to them all" (Neh. 9:6).[80]

Notice here the combination of a nondualistic theology with R. Nachman's distinctive notion of struggle. God is everywhere, but, R. Nachman emphasizes, it often takes effort to recognize It. The easy way out is not an option; it is incumbent upon all to find Godliness in every thing. In Bratzlav, nonduality becomes a gateway not to acceptance and surrender, but to effort and devotion. In the same chapter, R. Nachman continues:

> This is the meaning of the lesson in the Jerusalem Talmud.[81] If a person asks, "Where is your god?" you should say to him, "In the great city of Rome," as it is said, "He calls to me from Seir."[82] Clearly, the person who asks, "Where is your god" has fallen in the realm of the husks [*klipot*] . . . and it seems to him that in his place there is no God. Thus you say to him, "Even in your place, in the realm of the *klipot*, even there it is possible to find Godliness, because God gives life to everything, as it is written 'You give life to all.' And from there, you can attach [*l'davek*] yourself to the Blessed One, and return to him fully. Because God is not far from you,[83] only in your place there are many garments."[84]

As we have already seen, this Kabbalistic view of evil is radically different from traditional dualistic ones. In the Kabbalistic model developed here, the term *klipot* refers to the realm of evil; the Tanya identifies this realm with *elohim acherim*, other gods.[85] Literally, however, the term means "husks," or "shells." For all their negative associations and characteristics, the *klipot* are ultimately just garments covering the Light, and, R. Nachman continues, as one progresses, the shells eventually drop away. Even in the realm of shadow, God is present, albeit clothed. This is quite different from the naive dualistic model of good guys and evildoers, God and Satan. Here, as in earlier Kabbalistic sources, that which we regard as evil is actually that which awaits incorporation into the Divine; the content of evil is the mistake of thinking that it exists. Would that today's fundamentalists, in whatever religious community, were so confident in the omnipresence of light.

Contemporary Teachers

There are today more teachers of nondual Judaism than at any previous time, primarily in the "Neo-Hasidic" world of non-Orthodox Jews strongly influenced by traditional Hasidism. Perhaps the patriarch of neo-Hasidism is Rabbi Zalman Schachter-Shalomi, or Reb Zalman, as he is called by his followers. The founder of the Jewish Renewal movement, Reb Zalman has an academic background (he was a professor at Temple University), Chabad Hasidic training, and a lifetime of spiritual epicurianism, having sampled and learned from Hinduism, Buddhism, Sufism, and a dozen other traditions (he even created a tongue-in-cheek "table of in/compatibility" between Judaism and other religions[86]). The neo-Hasidism promoted by Reb Zalman and his fellow Chabad maverick Rabbi Shlomo Carlebach has had a wide influence: hundreds of thousands of American Jews now go to synagogue for Hasidic-style ecstatic davening, with *niggunim* and rousing melodies, and books such as the one you are reading right now are products of the view that Judaism is enriched, not impoverished, when it comes into contact with other traditions.

Reb Zalman has maintained a nondualistic theology throughout his career. Here he is in typically radical, yet logical, fashion, in *Wrapped in a Holy Flame*:

We are in the shift to the place where everything is God, pantheism. The understanding that has come from mysticism and from people on the cusp of periods moving from past to present, people talking about primary experience, is that the body and the soul cannot be separated. It shouldn't be that they should be fighting one another, that you have to get rid of one in order to get the other. We want Wholeness, a holistic understanding, now. I believe that people are moving from theism to pantheism. There are some who don't like the word *pantheism*, the idea that God is everything. They prefer the word *panentheism*, which means that God is *in* everything. I, however, don't think that the distinction is real. What was the objection that people had to pantheism, God is everything? "Are you going to tell me that the excrement of a dog is also God?" And the answer to this would be—"Yes." What is wrong with that? It is only from the human perspective that we see a difference between that and *challah*. On the submolecular level, on the atomic level, they all look the same. And if you look from a galactic perspective, what difference is there between one and the other? So if "God is everything," why are you and I here? Because we are the appearance of God in this particular form. And God likes to appear in countless forms and experience countless lives . . . deep down, the deepest level of the pattern is that God is everything. So it's not that God *created* the world but that God *became* the world.[87]

If Reb Zalman is the spiritual patriarch of contemporary nondual Judaism, then Rabbi Arthur Green is its leading systematic exponent— Moses Cordovero to Reb Zalman's Isaac Luria, if you will. Like Reb Zalman, Green is both an academic—he taught at Brandeis University for many years and wrote his dissertation on R. Nachman of Bratzlav—and an innovative Jewish rabbi and theologian in his own right, as well as a key player in numerous alternative Jewish cultural movements since the mid-twentieth century. His nondual, perennialist view is made clear in his 2004 book, *Ehyeh: A Kabbalah for Tomorrow*: "The basic teaching of mystics, dressed in the garb of many traditions, is essentially this simple message: There is only One. All multiplicity of beings and their sense of separateness or distance from one another are either illusion or represent a less than ultimate truth."[88]

Green's major theological work, *Seek My Face: A Jewish Mystical Theology* (1994), is heavily influenced by Chabad theology, in particular the doctrines of upper unity (annihilation into the transcendent Divine *ayin*) and lower unity (experiencing the Divine unity in *yesh*), which we have already reviewed. In Green's presentation, the two unities are described this way. Upper unity means "all is one as though there were no many. Nothing but the One exists. God after creation and God before creation are one and the same . . . The world makes no difference. Its existence is wholly unreal or totally inconsequential from the point of view of the One."[89] And lower unity is experienced "in and through the world, not despite it. Each flower, each blade of grass, each human soul, is a new manifestation of divinity, a new unfolding of the cosmic One that ever reveals itself through multicolored garments, ever taking on new and changing forms of life."[90]

Yet for all his engagement with Hasidism and Kabbalah, Green maintains an overtly non-Orthodox approach to questions of covenant, law, and the revelation at Sinai, which he regards as scandalously particularistic. For Green, "YHVH speaks in thunderclaps; it takes a Moses to translate God's thunder into words."[91] And thus,

> because I know of the human role in the origin of the commandments, and because I know that all human creations are fallible, I never hand myself over entirely to them. I know that they are but a means, and an often arbitrary one, to the greater end of spiritual awareness. Out of my love for our ancestors and the divine spirit that dwelt within them, I choose to live in faithfulness to the religious discipline they created. I will do so wherever this discipline does not bring me into conflict with more deeply held religious principles: awareness that YHVH is One, manifest throughout the world, recognizing all humans as bearers of the divine image, and the seven Noahide commandments, as I understand them.[92]

Other contemporary nondual Jewish teachers span the gamut from traditional to radical. Rabbis David Cooper (*God Is a Verb*) and Rami Shapiro (*Open Secrets*) have each published books in which nonduality is a central theme and in which it is carefully distinguished from other theological positions. Shapiro, for example, writes:

> Some would argue that God is a divine spark inside each being, some would say only within human beings. Others would argue that God is above and outside creation. But I teach neither position. God is not inside or outside, God is the very thing itself! And when there is no thing, but only empty space? God is that as well.[93]

Likewise in the work of other contemporary nondual teachers, including Rabbis Dovber Pinson (*Toward the Infinite*), David Aaron (*The Secret Life of God*), Marcia Prager (*The Path of Blessing*), Arthur Waskow (*Godwrestling*), Michael Lerner (*Jewish Renewal*), David Ingber, Miles Krassen, Ohad Ezrachi, and many more. Some, like Cooper, Shapiro, and myself, deliberately draw from multiple religious traditions. Others, like Pinson and Aaron, remain committed to an Orthodox view of God, Torah, and Israel. In between are a myriad of variations — as well as many teachers who do not publish or publicize their work. Today, we are blessed with many more than the *lamed vav tzaddikim*, the thirty-six righteous ones whose work sustains the world. And our righteous are building new ones.

NON-JEWISH TRADITIONS

There are, of course, nondual traditions around the world, and one cannot understand nondual Judaism without understanding them, their influence on Jewish thought, and their points of similarity and difference. Whether all mysticism is ultimately unitary or not (this is the debate between Aldous Huxley's "perennial philosophy" and scholars such as R. C. Zaehner, Steven T. Katz, and others), it is certainly the case that Hinduism, Buddhism, Islam, Christianity, Taoism, and indigenous traditions around the world all have their nondualistic traditions, including Vedanta, Zen, Vajrayana, Sufism, mystical Christianity (in its medieval forms, and in those of more recent expositors such as Pierre Teilhard de Chardin and Matthew Fox), and many more. For considerations of space, we will focus only on three traditions that have most directly influenced nondual Judaism: Vedanta, nondual Buddhism, and twentieth-century spirituality generally. To be sure, Sufism, particularly in its contemporary, Westernized form, has also exerted a powerful influence, as have popularizations of Taoism; the Christian writings of Meister Eckhart, John of the Cross, Thomas Merton, and Teilhard de Chardin; earth-based traditions from all continents; and many more. But Vedanta, Buddhism, and twentieth-century spirituality are arguably as important for the development of contemporary nondual Judaism as Jewish sources are. We will thus spend a brief moment on each.

Advaita Vedanta

Advaita Vedanta—literally, the "nondual end of the teachings"—is arguably the world's most elaborately constructed, radical, and influential iteration of nonduality. The most important Advaita sage was Shankara, who lived in southern India from 686 to 718 C.E. Shankara's view, which rested both on philosophical exposition and contemplative experience, is a straightforward one: "Brahman—the absolute existence, knowledge, and bliss—is real. The universe is not real. Brahman and Atman (the ultimate Self) are one."[94] This is as radical as it sounds: all the universe is like a dream in the Divine consciousness, which is your consciousness. The whole world really is all in your head—only, it isn't your head, it's God's.

Really, this was not Shankara's innovation. It is contained already in the Mahavakyas (the four "Great Sayings") of the Upanishads: *Prajnanam brahma* (Consciousness is Brahma),[95] *Ayam atma brahma* (Atman is Brahma),[96] *Tat tvam asi* (You are that),[97] and *Aham brahmasmi* (I am Brahman).[98] However, Hinduism, like Judaism, has its many branches and agendas, some of which emphasize the acosmic and unitive aspects and others of which emphasize the devotional and theistic ones. Shankara made the recognition of nonduality central. As he restated the famous utterance of *tat tvam asi*:

> The scriptures establish the absolute identity of Atman and Brahman by declaring repeatedly: "That art Thou" [*tat tvam asi*]. The terms "Brahman" and "Atman," in their true meaning, refer to "That" and "Thou" respectively . . . "Brahman" may refer to God,

the ruler of Maya and creator of the universe. The "Atman" may refer to the individual soul, associated with the five coverings which are effects of Maya. Thus regarded, they possess opposite attributes. But this apparent opposition . . . is not real . . . "The apparent world is caused by our imagination, in its ignorance. It is not real . . . It is like a passing dream."[99]

For Shankara, and for most Advaita Vedantins, knowledge of the nondual is liberation: "The state of illumination is described as follows: There is a continuous consciousness of the unity of Atman and Brahman. There is no longer any identification of the Atman with its coverings. All sense of duality is obliterated. There is pure, unified consciousness."[100]

Advaita is more stark than most other traditions, including Judaism, in its presentation of nonduality, acosmism, quietism, and its radical insistence that Mind is all there is. Advaita is insistent; it demands an awakening from the illusion of separation. It is a rigorous philosophy, argumentative, logical, and fierce.[101]

In the last century and a half, there has been a remarkable resurgence in Advaita Vedanta, in both India and the West. For example, Vedanta philosophy influenced the American transcendentalists Ralph Waldo Emerson and Henry David Thoreau; Emerson's "Over-soul" is essentially Hinduism's Atman. But the growth of Vedanta in the West is largely the legacy of, on the one hand, Ramakrishna (1836–1886) and Swami Vivekananda (1863–1902), and on the other, teachers such as Ramana Maharshi (1879–1950), Nisargadatta (1897–1981), and others, who have inspired a "neo-Advaita" that is popular, and sometimes controversial, today. Led by figures such as Muktananda (1908–1982) who founded the Siddha Yoga global community (and who is the root guru for Elizabeth Gilbert, the author of *Eat, Pray, Love*), Satchitananda, Meher Baba, and, in our times, Deepak Chopra, popularized forms of Vedanta and have attracted hundreds of thousands of Western followers.

Ramakrishna was not unlike the Baal Shem Tov: charismatic, devotional, unorthodox, and regarded as a saint by his followers—although unlike the Baal Shem Tov, Ramakrishna was both an ascetic and an erotic-mystic, often experiencing the Divine in powerful, devotional, and sensual ways. As reflected in the collection of his oral teachings known as the *Gospel of Sri Ramakrishna*, Ramakrishna was a god- and goddess-intoxicated mystic whose mind soared to the abstract heights of Advaita Vedanta and whose heart loved the Divine personalities. Both perspectives were essential:

> When I think of the Supreme Being as inactive—neither creating nor preserving nor destroying—I call him Brahman or Purusha, the Impersonal God. When I think of Him as active—creating, preserving, and destroying—I call Him Shakti or Maya or Prakriti, the Personal God. But the distinction between them does not mean a difference. The Personal and the Impersonal are the same thing, like milk and its whiteness, the diamond and its lustre, the snake and its wriggling motion . . . The Divine Mother and Brahman are one.[102]

Vivekananda, too, was a remarkable figure whose life included periods as a monk, political leader, galvanizing orator, transmitter of Hinduism to the West, and prolific writer. Vivekananda's Western Vedanta also influenced such figures as the writers Christopher Isherwood and Aldous Huxley, who in turn greatly influenced the 1960s spiritual revival and thus contemporary nondual Judaism, a history discussed in chapter 5. Vivekananda produced a huge volume of work, and tended toward the *jnani* (wisdom) rather than the *bhakti* (devotional) side of Vedanta. A few representative quotations are included here, taken from an anthology of his teachings called *Living at the Source*:

> The whole universe is one. There is only one Self in the universe, only One Existence, and that One Existence . . . Everything in the universe is that One, appearing in various forms . . . The Self when it appears behind the universe is called God. The same Self when it appears behind this little universe, the body, is the soul.[103]

> You, as body, mind, or soul, are a dream, but what you really are, is Existence, Knowledge, Bliss. You are the God of this universe. You are creating the whole universe and drawing it in.[104]

There is but One, seen by the ignorant as matter, by the wise as God.[105]

Ramana Maharshi and Nisargadatta, two independent Advaita masters who were far more quietistic than the globe-trotting Vivekananda, taught similarly. In Ramana's worldview, "there is no inside or outside for the Self. They are also projections of the ego. The Self is pure and absolute."[106] There is no greater mystery than the following: Ourselves being the Reality, we seek to gain reality. We think there is something hiding our Reality, and that it must be destroyed before the Reality is gained. That is ridiculous."[107]

Nisargadatta's views are similar:

In the ocean of pure awareness, on the surface of the universal consciousness, the numberless waves of the phenomenal worlds arise and subside beginninglessly and endlessly. As consciousness, they are all me. As events they are all mine. There is a mysterious power that looks after them. That power is awareness, Self, Life, God, whatever name you give it.[108]

I do not negate the world. I see it as appearing in consciousness, which is the totality of the known in the immensity of the unknown. What begins and ends is mere appearance. The world can be said to appear, but not to *be*. The appearance may last very long on some scale of time, and be very short on another, but ultimately it comes to the same.[109]

As can be readily seen, these Vedanta texts have a clarity and forthrightness absent in the Jewish ones. Why do Advaita sages speak so directly, while Jewish ones seem to talk in riddles? One answer may be that nondual Judaism evolved over time, and was at first a secret, marginal tradition, whereas in Hinduism, nonduality is present right from the beginning and was the subject of enormous philosophical speculation. Moreover, Judaism's rigorous monotheism invites a certain reticence when it comes both to theological polymorphism and to monism, whereas Hinduism is at home with both.

Notice, too, a certain paradox of Advaita teaching. If all really is Mind, what is the difference between what we conventionally label an enlightened mind and an unenlightened one? What is the difference, if all mental phenomena are just ripples on the same pond of consciousness? This is why the contemporary teacher Ramesh Balsekar says there is no use seeking enlightenment—"Don't make it, as you say, a federal case. Let the seeking take its own course!" he has said[110]—and why neo-Vedantin books have titles like *Doing Nothing* and *This Is It*: because the very notion of spiritual search can reinforce wrong ideas such as the existence of a separate searcher and the imperfection of the "unenlightened" mind. Really, God is everything, unfolding everywhere, and all minds are objects of the Divine process.

Nondual Buddhism

All three of the "vehicles" of Buddhism, Theravada, Mahayana, and Vajrayana, contain nondual teachings, though they vary in emphasis. Naturally, in a book on nondual Judaism, it is not possible to discuss these traditions in any depth. Instead, I will focus on how nonduality is presented in those traditions which have had the greatest impact in the West generally, and on contemporary Judaism in particular.

Perhaps surprisingly, the tradition which has most shaped Buddhist-Jewish syntheses in our day is Theravada Buddhism, the "way of the elders," based primarily on the Pali Canon of Buddhist sutras. In a sense, this tradition should be the least appealing to Westerners, as it is primarily monastic, and can often seem disinterested in the cares of householders. Yet this path has been the primary entry point for many Jews exploring Buddhist practice, including this one—I have sat six-week, nine-week, and twelve-week *vipassana* (insight) meditation retreats in the Theravadan tradition, in both Asia and the United States. One reason for Theravada's appeal, I think, is the dichotomy between contemplative and devotional practice. Vipassana is primarily contemplative; its central objective is *jnana*, wisdom, not *bhakti*, devotion. Thus it is compatible with secularism, atheism, and also with religions such as Judaism, because it has relatively little emphasis on worship, ritual, and faith in the religious sense of the words. As transmitted to the West—in large part by secular Jews—Theravadan Buddhism is scarcely a religion at all.

Yet it is resolutely nondualistic. First, as we have already seen, the principle of nonduality flows directly from the insight into *anatta*, or non-self, one of the three characteristics of all conditioned phenomena. The insight into *anatta* is necessarily an insight into nonduality; if every thing lacks separate reality, what else is there? If Vedanta dissolved the "object" of the world into the ultimate Subject—You are All—the doctrine of non-self dissolves the subject entirely, leaving only the All.[111] (Judaism has a bit of both: *bittul ha'yesh* is more like the Buddhist model, *memaleh kol almin* is more like Vedanta.) Likewise the realizations that all things are *anicha*, impermanent, and *dukkha*, unable to ultimately satisfy us. As these insights take hold, not intellectually but intuitively, a letting go of the unreal naturally evolves. And for a nondualist, this subtraction of the illusory is the most important step toward realization of the true.

In the Pali Canon, these doctrines are of relatively little interest as ontological principles. The Buddha's teaching in these texts is primarily about suffering and the end of suffering, not the nature of reality, and as such is conveyed in relative terms, not absolute ones.[112] However, the two subjects are of necessity intertwined, for what we call the "ego" is where suffering occurs, and when the delusion of a soul is erased, then phenomena like pain, sadness, and anger are merely phenomena which arise and pass, often in an instant. Look closely, and you will never see the "self" doing anything at all; you will only find mental factors and material forms—never a self.

The notion of *anatta*, non-self, may seem diametrically opposed to Vedanta's conception of the Atman, or Self. However, the two are more alike than they seem, because in both cases, the small self—you, me—is more illusion than reality, and that is what matters. For Theravadan Buddhism, what's left when the self is taken away is Nothing. For Vedanta, it is Everything. For Nondual Judaism, it is God. But it is the subtraction that really matters.

In a sense, the only question dividing these nondual traditions is whether everything is One, or Zero. And despite years of intensive practice in all three of these traditions, I am hard-pressed to tell the difference.

The traditions' conceptions of the "problem" are similar as well. In

Theravadan Buddhism, the problem is the illusion of the ego and its grasping onto impermanent and selfless phenomena. In nondual Judaism, the problem is the illusion of the ego (*yetzer hara*) and its turning away from the truth, i.e., grasping onto the unreal. It's not that the absolute is any more real than the relative—but there's a lot less suffering in God's point of view. Consequently, the solution to the problem is similar as well: in Theravadan Buddhism, the three trainings of wisdom, concentration, and virtue; in nondual Judaism, the three paths of contemplation, ecstasy (which brings about bliss states quite similar to the Pali canon's concentrated absorptions), and fulfillment of the commandments.

In Mahayana and Vajrayana traditions, the parallels become even more acute. For example, the Heart Sutra of Mahayana Buddhism introduces the dichotomy—and identity—of emptiness (*ayin*) and form (*yesh*):

> ... form is emptiness and the very emptiness is form; emptiness does not differ from form, form does not differ from emptiness; whatever is form, that is emptiness, whatever is emptiness, that is form, the same is true of feelings, perceptions, impulses and consciousness. ...

> In emptiness there is no form, nor feeling, nor perception, nor impulse, nor consciousness; No eye, ear, nose, tongue, body, mind; No forms, sounds, smells, tastes, touchables or objects of mind; No sight-organ element, and so forth, until we come to: No mind-consciousness element; There is no ignorance, no extinction of ignorance, and so forth, until we come to: there is no decay and death, no extinction of decay and death. There is no suffering, no origination, no stopping, no path. There is no cognition, no attainment and non-attainment ...

> Gone, gone, gone beyond, gone altogether beyond, O what an awakening, all-hail![113]

If we were to translate the Heart Sutra into Hasidic language, boldly and ahistorically, I think it would run something like this:

SHAMAYIM: THEORY

yesh is *ayin* and *ayin* is *yesh*. Everything that appears to be Yesh is actually Ayin. From the perspective of the Ein Sof, there is nothing: no creation; no body, heart, mind, or soul; no *sefirot* and no worlds; no life or death; no sin or righteousness. Higher, higher, higher even than the idea of higher, YHVH, *halleluyah*.

As with the Hasidic view, the "emptiness" of the Heart Sutra refers to the intrinsic emptiness of all things. For example, as we saw in chapter 1, while a table certainly exists according to our usual definition of "exists," there is no intrinsic table-ness. All its properties come from without: strength, color, shape, atomic structure, whatever. Take these "other" things out, and nothing is left. "Table" is really a convenient label only for a temporary set of conditions which, in the Buddhist view, are impermanent, empty, and ultimately unsatisfying.

From the perspective of nirvana all of these formations look like nothing. Yet from the perspective of samsara, nirvana looks like nothing; it has no characteristics, and while it is present right now, it goes undetected except by those who have let go of delusion.

Compare this perspective with that of the Tanya and R. Aharon. From God's point of view, all of what we see as *yesh* (something) is actually *ayin* (nothing), whereas the only real Something is what we see as nothing—it has no characteristics, and it goes undetected except by those who have transcended delusion. This isn't similar to the Buddhist view; it is functionally identical to it.

In both traditions, realization is not merely the "going beyond," for that concept still bespeaks a dualism of liberation and nonliberation, attainment and nonattainment. Thus the sage must go beyond even the idea of beyond, beyond even the notion that there is any going beyond at all. As R. Aharon says, from the perspective of Ein Sof, there is no distinction between the world before it was created and the world after it was created: both are totally empty. And yet, the Absolute transcends and includes the relative; it is not the complement of the relative but the totality of the relative and its opposite. Especially in Mahayana and Vajrayana Buddhism, one does not escape from samsara so much as reinterpret it. A similar understanding is essential to Tantra, in which, as David Loy describes it, the "ultimate goal . . . is the perfect state of union—union between the two aspects of the reality and the realization of the nondual nature of the self and the not-self."[114] As a Kabbalist might put it, *l'shem yichud* . . .

As we will explore in more detail in chapter 6, these theoretical and philosophical parallels become truly transformative when put into practice. Like nondual Judaism, all forms of Buddhism emphasize the importance of meditation, for a variety of reasons: to concentrate the mind, to acquire insight (direct, experiential knowledge) into reality, to break the identification with the ego, to rest in primordial awareness, to short-circuit the dualistic and rational mind, to purify the mind, and many other purposes. Today, Buddhist-Jews, or "Bu-Jus," apply these practices to Judaism in a variety of ways. Some divorce the practice from the theory, applying Buddhist technology for Jewish ends such as appreciating the holy or praying with *kavvanah* (intention). Others take expansive approaches to "insight," and use meditation to gain deep and powerful understanding of their minds. Some find parallels between meditation and Torah study. And some, like this writer, spend considerable amounts of time living in the Buddhist world, making Buddhist meditation a central part of their spiritual paths.

Some Jews (nondual and otherwise) have responded with caution or even outright fear to these developments. Yet given the importance of meditation to traditional nondual Judaism, learning meditative techniques from a culture which has systematically developed them for thousands of years is of immense value to the Jewish path—and no less "Jewish" than bagels or falafel, both learned from other cultures. The Buddha, after all, did not teach Buddhism, a religion just like Judaism, with rites and rituals and beliefs; he taught the dharma, a system of discovering the truth of things. And while the relative paths differ—and, for me at least, the Jewish one resonates with those factors of mind we conventionally call the "soul"—the truth to which they lead, if it is worthy of the name, does not.

1960s Spirituality and the "New Age"

Lastly, contemporary nondual Judaism is nourished by the amalgam of spiritualities that flourished in the 1960s and 1970s and that have come to be referred to collectively as the "New Age." Not all of the New Age's excesses have to do with nonduality, of course. But many contemporary teachers place it at the center of their messages, and have influenced nondual Judaism as a result.

Of the hundreds of contemporary teachers expounding doctrines of nonduality, let us choose a single illustrative example: Ram Dass. Born Richard Alpert to a prominent New England Jewish family in 1931, Ram Dass was a successful Harvard researcher until his psychedelic work with fellow professor Timothy Leary caused him to be expelled from Harvard. Finding his way to India, Alpert met his guru in 1969, who gave him the name Ram Dass ("servant of God"). Upon his return, Ram Dass became one of the most important figures in the New Age, penning the 1971 classic *Be Here Now* and spreading the truth of nonduality in accessible, extremely popular ways. He continued along his own spiritual path as well, and continued to teach into the twenty-first century, albeit slowed by a stroke he suffered in 1997.

Ram Dass was once asked for advice about relationships. He told the following story in reply, which I heard from one of his students, Eliezer Sobel. Imagine, he said, that you're on a rowboat out on a lake on a foggy summer's evening. You're enjoying the sound of the crickets, the sensations of floating. And then you see, in the fog, another boat, and notice it's coming toward you. So you shout out, "Hey! There's another boat here—be careful!" Still it gets closer. Now you're getting upset, shouting and cursing. But just as the boat is about to hit, you see that it's empty.

This is our situation, says Ram Dass. Imagining myself to be a real, separate self, and seeing others the same way, I get upset when these others don't act as I think they should. But there really is no one minding the store (or the boat), no one to be angry with. We are all just the effects of causes. Anger, selfishness, generosity, forgiveness—these are phenomena caused by other conditions. Thus there is no difference, really, between an empty boat and a boat with someone in it; in either case, effects are following their causes, and there's no one there to blame.

Another Ram Dass *meise*: Imagine two waves, a smaller one and a larger one, traveling across the ocean. Suddenly, the larger wave sees land approaching, and gets upset. He cries to the smaller wave, "Oh no! Up ahead—waves are crashing and disappearing! We're going to die!" The smaller wave, somehow, is unperturbed. So the larger wave tries to convince her, to no avail. Finally the smaller wave says, "What would you say if I told you that there are six words, that if you really understood and believed them, you would see that there's no reason to fear." The bigger wave protests, but as the land approaches, he becomes desperate. He'll try anything. "Fine, fine, tell me the six words."

"Okay," the small wave says. "You're not a wave, you're water."

And so we are. As the poet James Broughton said:

This is It
and I am It
and You are It
and So is That
and He is It
and She is It
And It is It
and That is That.[115]

Now, just because we are It, God, Consciousness, Infinite Bliss, does not mean we are any of those things on the relative level. As Ramakrishna said, from the point of view of the nondual, each of us is Divine—but really that term cannot even be used from such a "point of view." From our relative perspective, in which the word "God" applies, Ramakrishna said that "I look on myself as a devotee of Krishna, not as Krishna Himself."[116] We are all God in the Absolute, but none of us is God in the Relative.

The wave, the named self, the relative ego is not that which gets enlightened. In the words of the contemporary writer Jan Kersschot, "the person you think you are will never find Liberation. You have to disappear first—so to speak—before the understanding appears that you are Beingness."[117] Or in the words of the Hasidic masters, one must think of oneself utterly as *ayin* in order to attain higher consciousness. Or in the words of the contemporary teacher Jean Klein, "awakening happens when we are convinced that there is no one who awakens."[118] Yet it does happen sometimes.

In the meantime, the great work remains.

3

GOD: THE GOD BEYOND GOD

I have divided myself into God and me; I become the worshiped and I worship myself. Why not? God is I. Why not worship my Self? The universal God—He is also my Self. It is all fun. There is no other purpose.
—Vivekananda[1]

Hashem is here, Hashem is there, Hashem is truly everywhere. Up, up, down, down, right, left, and all around. Here, there, and everywhere, is where He can be found.
—Jewish nursery rhyme

I don't believe in the same God that you don't believe in!
—Rabbi Zalman Schachter-Shalomi[2]

What is the relationship of nondual Judaism to "ordinary" Judaism? The first two chapters of this book have explained the nondual view and its roots—but how does it relate to (and transform) Judaism as it is conventionally understood today? The next three chapters will attempt to answer this question, focusing on the three pillars of Jewish life: God, Torah, and Israel. In this chapter, we will explore the meaning of "God" in the nondual Jewish context and question whether the word should be used at all. In the next chapter, we will explore the "Torah" of nondual Judaism; namely, if everything is God, what's the point of Jewish practice, of following a Torah, whether understood traditionally or not? And then in chapter 5, we'll look at nondual Judaism in relation to Jewish community, history, and messianism—to "Israel" writ large.

Throughout these chapters, there are two important basic principles: first, that nonduality is one among many possible Jewish theologies, and second, that nondual Judaism does not dictate a single Jewish practice. The first principle we have already explored: there are dualistic Jewish theologies, agnostic Jewish theologies, and many others; nondualism is but one view among many. The second principle will become clear in the chapters to come: nonduality is compatible with many forms of Judaism, from Hasidism to Reform, from cultural/nationalistic to spiritual/universal; it is compatible with atheistic Judaism, with notions of Judaism as an ethnicity, and with many forms of Judaism with which I personally may disagree. One of Judaism's great strengths is its focus on "deed rather than creed." One can remain entirely within the Orthodox fold, for example, while holding all sorts of seemingly heretical notions, because with only a few exceptions, "Orthodox" describes practice, not doctrine (despite its literal meaning of "right belief"). Conversely, one may hold very traditional conceptions of God and Torah, while practicing as a very progressive Conservative Jew, or Reform Jew, and so on.

Likewise, the nondual "creed" is compatible with many philosophies of "deed." Some nondual Jews practice the *mitzvot*, and others do not. Some are liberal, egalitarian, and progressive, and others are conservative, nationalistic, and traditional regarding gender roles. Some are Jewish particularists, emphasizing the unique role of Israel, while others see the Jewish path as but one among many. Some are pious Hasidim, and some heretics, even antinomians. The nondual view does not compel one particular view of Jewish tradition, practice, or purpose.

It does, however, demand certain questions be asked. If the world of phenomena is but the surface level of an ultimately nondual Reality, what is the point of busying oneself with meat and dairy dishes, or reading from the Torah? If the phenomenal world is illusion, what significance could there be to the *mitzvot*, or, for that matter, to ethics? Conversely, if YHVH is the reality of our lives, is a religious life required? What changes, and what remains? How are dualistic statements of Jewish texts to be understood? And what of God? We'll start with the last question first.

THE APOPHATIC WAY: NEGATIVE THEOLOGY
AND THE GOD BEYOND GOD

Far or forgot to me is near;
Shadow and sunlight are the same;
The vanished gods to me appear;
And one to me are shame and fame.
—RALPH WALDO EMERSON, "BRAHMA"[3]

So what about God? If the God we want is the benevolent Parent who cares, then it would seem that nonduality denies this God, replacing It (or Him, or Her) with a kind of transparent, pantheistic, and even useless concept. This may well be a "fortunate fall," since naive, limited God-concepts may seem, at best, to be quaint and outdated, or at worst, dangerous and infantile (consider the work of Franz Kafka, Philip Roth, Shalom Auslander, or, for that matter, the theological writing of Rachel Adler, Daniel Boyarin, or Jerome Segal; I return to this question in chapter 5). But in fact, things are not as they seem, for two fundamental reasons: first, the nondual God is not useless at all, and second, it is only half of the story.

Let's explore, first, the "uselessness" of the nondual God, as expressed in terms of negative ("apophatic") theology. There is a tendency for nonduality to seem intellectual, as if it is purely a theological enterprise. As I will return to again and again in this book, however, this is not so. "The truth will set you free"—spiritually, emotionally, even physically. It can revitalize how life is experienced. And if there's one thing nondual theology is useful for, it's negative theology: telling us that we don't know what we think we know. Think you know the purpose of life? You don't. Think you know what God wants, or is, or what the word even means? You don't. And as soon as you don't have to know anything, two things happen: first, the dangers of dogma and religious oppression disappear, and second, the world opens up.

Try it. The promise-keeper of Israel, the smiter of enemies, the Judge, the Father, the Mother, the peacemaker, the ethical voice—not It.

How about that wonderful sense that you get when you make the world a little less painful for someone who is suffering? No, that's not God either; what about the sense you get when you've done something awful? Isn't that part of Ein Sof too?

Maybe the sacred feeling you get in meaningful spiritual ritual—nope.

Or the joy of victory when your team/nation/army/tribe wins its battle—not that either.

All these are myths, projections, hopes, and yearnings. Some are beautiful, others quite hideous, but none is "It" because "It" is all of these and none of them, everything and nothing. "God is not light nor life nor love nor nature nor spirit nor semblance nor anything we can put into words," says Meister Eckhart.[4] Asked to describe Awareness, Nisargadatta replied, "Only by negation, as uncaused, independent, unrelated, undivided, uncomposed, unshakable, unquestionable, unreachable by effort. Every positive definition is from memory and therefore inapplicable."[5]

Here's a simple way to remember it: As long as God is everything and/or nothing, we are doing fine. It's when we think God is something that we've gotten into trouble.

Good? Powerful? Male? Ineffable? Concepts, projections. Even "Being" is only half of the picture. In the Kabbalistic understanding, attributes (including the name "God") belong to the realm of the *sefirot*, not the Ein Sof. *Tiferet* is the Holy One, Blessed be He, the God of Israel. But the Ein Sof is refracted in that mode and nine (really ninety-nine) others. And if we ask carefully what it is we actually know, we disabuse ourselves of all the lofty, lousy, and divisive ideas we project up into the heavens. How do you know that God wants a gentler world, but doesn't want child sacrifice? You don't: you just want it one way and not the other. How do you know that God loves Israel, and not the Palestinians—or, alternatively, that God loves all people equally, regardless of nationality? You don't. How do you know that God did or didn't write the Torah? You get the point.

Thus the non-knowledge of negative theology is really something. Suppose you went through the day holding every conceptual idea a bit more lightly: politics, fashion preferences, how people are supposed to behave. It's not that you wouldn't have these ideas, and act on them sometimes—it's just that you'd not be so sure. Would that lead to more conflict, or less? Would you be more open to the impressions of the world, to the daily music of humanity, to the power of Nature, or less? Would you be more detached, or more engaged? Surrendering assumptions about God yields a much-needed surrender of certainty.

Experientially, this transparent God is similar to the notion of the "Witness" one cultivates in meditation, which simply sees and observes everything. The Witness is not a commentary on life, not a story about how things should be, not a judge or a character. It is an antidote to the ego's endless stories and commentaries: I want to be like this person, I want to be loved in this way, that person is wrong, I like this, I don't like that. Indeed, the basic, animal response of like it/dislike it/don't care (what Buddhism calls *vedana*) arises with every perception we have, however subtly. All animals do it; it's a basic survival mechanism. But we take it to extremes. Like the food, don't like the sauce; like his shirt, but the pants are wrong. No percept is too insignificant to be imbued with a pointless note of preference.

Preference is like a cloud, occluding the reality of things, and it leads to the delusions of the ego and to suffering. It's not that the selfish ego, the *yetzer hara*, is bad; it's necessary to survive, as the rabbis say.[6] But it distorts the world. Good is what meets my desire, bad is what doesn't. And worse yet, not just Good—but God.

Here is another way to express it, seemingly banal but in fact so radical that it may overturn monotheism itself: Everything happens as it must—not as it should.

Traditional theism posits a governor of the universe, who causes things to be as they should. This immediately leads to all the old problems of theodicy. Did God "intend" for the earthquake to kill innocents? For a child to be born with disease? In the traditional monotheistic frame, such questions must be reconciled with a conception of God as good, and since the days of Job, the project has been an arduous one. Presumably, it must once have provided great solace to imagine a God who judges. Indeed, the Hebrew psalms rhapsodize about the rivers clapping hands and the forests rejoicing because God is coming to judge the earth. In a world of moral anarchy and religions of might, the yearning for rectitude must have been more intense than we postmoderns can imagine. And the god of this yearning? An all-powerful, all-just Father, who would set right the wrongs of earthly existence.

That this god is a projection of our deepest wants and fears is not to belittle it: after all, what is deeper than these stirrings of the heart? To say that God is a father figure perhaps smacks of Freudian reductionism—but only if one has never explored the recesses of consciousness, the dark places in which the self is built. Father figures, among others, are essential to our lives. But such projections will always run afoul of reality. The wicked are not always punished, the good not always rewarded. No wonder the principle of *schar v'onesh* (reward and punishment) became a signal definition of faith in the Jewish tradition: only faith can maintain it.

Because this Father God is so dearly beloved, generations of theologians have labored to square the circle. Perhaps, as in Job, all evil is but a test of the righteous. Or perhaps we are rewarded and punished after death, in invisible heavens and hells. Who knows, maybe "everything really happens for a reason," as the Panglosses and Pollyannas of both religion and New Age spirituality tell us. Or, maybe, as Harold Kushner's best-selling and confessedly heretical *Why Bad Things Happen to Good People* suggests, God is good, but not all-powerful after all. And of course, the righteous Father God is only one of many images. God/dess is also the Compassionate Mother, the sensualist, the ethical stirring of the soul, and reality is edited accordingly.

Human beings provide such explanations not only despite the facts, but often directly because of them. Studies such as *When Prophecy Fails*[7] have shown that religious faith often increases, rather than decreases, when a theology or prophecy fails to accord with reality. Now the faithful can be tested; now there is a creed, an orthodoxy, a sect of true believers. This, too, has its nobility; the Jewish theologian Franz Rosenzweig once observed that if the Sambatyon, the mystical river which is said to cease flowing on the Sabbath, flowed through Frankfurt, then obviously everyone would be religious—and piety would have no value. God, Rosenzweig said, desires only the free.

Freedom, though, means growing up religiously. Popular religion tends to have very basic theological ideas of reward and punishment, right and wrong; it takes its myths seriously, and often concludes that only one version of the story can be correct. It meets very basic needs for comfort, meaning, and ethical guidance. But at some point, we ought to outgrow it.

But there are more reflective alternatives: monasteries instead of megachurches, Sufi rituals instead of fundamentalist fatwas, meditation instead of superstition, and, in the Jewish tradition, a variety of forms including Talmudic text study, Biblical exegesis, philosophical reflection, contemplative practice, and Kabbalistic speculation, and institutions like the yeshiva, mystical fellowships, the *kloiz*, or contemporary intentional communities. Contrary to the ludicrous and uninformed generalizations of some of today's "neo-atheists," these forms have been part of religion since the beginning. They are ill-suited to popular consumption, because they require investments of time and effort, not to mention the interest to do the work, and the financial circumstances to enable it. But they do exist, and they always have.

So, yes, the nondual God-concept is different from that of popular monotheism, just as Teilhard de Chardin's "cosmic Christ" is different from televangelism and Ramana's Self is different from the Hindu pantheon. This is just as one would expect; until very recently, nondual Judaism was an elite form of Jewish thought, not a popular one. It afflicts the comfortable more than it comforts the afflicted, and as we will see in part 2, its form of liberation takes work (*avodah*) to cultivate and maintain.

Today, however, the myths and creeds of popular religion have come under increasing (and deserved) attack, and many people have rightly left them behind. If religion is to survive for the benefit of mankind, and not for its destruction, reflective religious forms such as nonduality can no longer be confined to the elite.

Notice, too, that while nondual Judaism may take more *avodah* in some respects, it also lightens the burden considerably: when the nondual Ein Sof is understood, much of the convoluted labor of religion simply fall away. All the religionist's explanation and justification, from the ridiculous to Rosenzweig, results from the monotheist's positing of an external moral or aesthetic order, which cannot be demonstrated and which flies in the face of reality. And all of it vanishes in the nondual moment. From the nondual perspective, What Is is What Is, and the religious question becomes not why God has done or allowed a certain thing to come to pass, but how we as human beings are to relate to what has come to pass. "What's going on right now, and can I be with it," said Eckhart Tolle on *Oprah*, when asked, like Hillel, to summarize his philosophy. Most of the time, this maxim carries with it a rather predictable contemporary consciousness: being more present, more alive, more awake. But take it to its logical extreme, and it is a radical demand. What if "what's going on right now" is a hospital visit with a child? What if it is confronting AIDS in Africa? What if it is even the simplest sadness, which nonetheless slams our pretensions to the floor and devastates us, despite all the spirituality in the world?

Now "can I be with it" is an imperative to look reality clearly in the eyes, not a platitude. Can I truly see this, not accepting it morally, but accepting its truth, with the perspective of: yes, God, yes, you are here as well; yes, in this darkness; yes, in this injustice; yes, in this evil. To repeat Surya Das's similarly pithy encapsulation of his philosophy, the imperative is "to see the light in everyone and everything, in every moment."[8] Everything—not just summer days, but dark nights of the soul. Everyone—not just friends and family, but also those who cause harm to others and to the planet. Everyone means everyone. Wittgenstein said that what we are really saying when we say that "God is X" is "I value X." How profound, then, to say that God is everything.

Profound—but not easy. The apparently beatific aphorisms of nonduality actually conceal great spiritual labor. Nondualists are relieved of the monotheistic burden of explanation, but we take on the burden of integration. I cannot ascribe this random, terrible occurrence to Satan. I cannot explain it away by saying that God works in mysterious ways. And I do not possess a cosmology that makes everything all right in the world to come. No: this happened, life is random, and fairness is a human ideal, not a natural law. Now, what do I do next?

As a personal matter—for religion can only be personal, if it is to be authentic—I find it somehow inhuman to explain away the reality of evil and suffering, and far more honest to see it for what it is. Thank God, I have so far experienced only a small amount of death and suffering among my loved ones, but that which I have experienced, I don't want to ascribe to any kind of purpose or plan whatsoever. I don't seek a "should" to distract from the "is." When the "is" is lovely, I celebrate it; when it is tragic, I cry. Sometimes I maintain equanimity, and sometimes I don't—and this, to me, feels human.

In the *Hanhagot Yesharot* ("Upright Practices"), R. Menachem Nahum of Chernobyl asks us to:

> Believe with a whole and strong faith that God both fills all the worlds and surrounds them, that God is both within and beyond them all . . . Believe with a whole and strong faith that "the whole earth is full of God's glory" and that "there is no place devoid of Him" . . . His divine Self wears all things as one wears a cloak, as Scripture teaches "You give life to them all" (Neh. 9:6). This applies even to the forces of evil, in accord with the secret of "His kingdom rules over all" (Ps. 103:19). All life is sustained by the flow that issues forth from God. Were the life-flow to cease, even for a moment, the thing sustained would become but an empty breath, as though it had never been.[9]

All the world is but a cloak for God—including the forces of evil. What R. Menachem Nahum calls the "life-flow" of God, a nontheist might simply call the system of causality and the laws of the universe. The point is that there is nothing that is not part of the system. This is not a flaw, not an aberration; this, alas, is what Is.

Everything happens as it must, not as it should. This happened; it happened because the causes and conditions were present to cause it to happen. When I drop a stone to the floor, it must fall, and it must make a sound. When the conditions are present, the person must fall in love, or fall ill, or fall from grace. Life happens, shit happens, joy happens, anger happens, and all of it happens exactly as it must. There are no uncaused phenomena, no quantum misinterpretations rescuing the illusion of free will; everything happens simply and exquisitely as it must.

This understanding is a significant shift from monotheistic conceptions of God ordering the world. And now the spiritual work is different. When something unfortunate happens, the monotheist explains what has taken place with recourse to some higher purpose. The nondualist does not offer any such explanation, but instead invites a deeper kind of acceptance. Inside, outside, nothing is happening without conditions, nothing is not happening despite conditions; everything is God unfolding. Can I be with it, and not run away into explanation or rationale?

As we will see in chapter 9, this is not a lazy "acceptance"—I am also charged with moral imperatives to continue my work of pursuing justice. "Shoulds" remain in the world of the relative, and some are more praiseworthy than others. But the normativity of "should" applies only to our ethical decisions. Our usual tales of "should"—I am right to be angry, I am entitled to be disappointed—are seen through. There is nothing justified or unjustified; there is only what happens due to conditions. And, I have noticed, with the loosening of the bounds of explanation comes a taste of the world to come. There is a wonderful Zen story about an enlightened master who learns that his son has died, and who is seen by his students to be crying. The students, knowing that their master has transcended desire and does not suffer, ask why he is crying. The master answers, "Because I am sad."

Sadness is present, tears flow. Everything happens as it must. This is a taste of liberation.

The "should" is a wish, transcendent but not immanent; the "must" is truly omnipresent. The "must" can be uttered at any moment, as a mantra or a *zikr*, a reminder. "This happens as it should" seems often to be obscene. It reinforces my ego, my judgments, my evaluations of good or ill. It adheres to just and selfish desires alike, without discrimination, and with the bombastic potency of authority. It can deify desire as much as inspire justice. But when I remember the "must-ness" of any moment, traffic jam or symphony, bliss or frustration, I remember in the holy sense of remembering: I remember Who is really here, and What is really happening. I remember what my work is in the world: to relate to the One in wisdom and love. I remember, and while nothing has changed, everything has changed; the how, not the what.

This is the liberation of nonduality: not that anything changes in the world, but that the inflection of perception shifts; there is a relaxation of demand, and an abiding joyfulness in the simplest, most mundane experiences of breathing, sitting, eating. Perhaps such spirituality really is hedonism, because there is no finer pleasure, and none more accessible, than the everyday intercourse with Being itself. This is the God beyond the God of our projections.

How little time we spend being honest that we want to love. What a misdirection, to mold these yearnings into "shoulds" and "oughts" about the world. What is important about petitionary prayer, to God or Christ or Krishna, is the soul-stirring authenticity it may evoke, not the theology it implies. What is wrong about cruelty is suffering, not a violation of some Divine order.

Seeing what Is enables this honesty. The Witness doesn't try to shade the truth; it only notices, and asks whether we can accept the truth or not. Holocausts, wars, earthquakes, and famines; from the perspective of nonduality, all of them simply *are*. What are you going to do about them? Likewise in our own lives: births and deaths, romances and separations, all of them just *are*, without elaboration or explaining away. In this bare observation, the Witness enables a response unclouded by the smoke of philosophy. It is not apathy; it is clarity, vision. And from that place of balance, love and compassion arise naturally, without any effort. By seeing clearly, we allow love to unfold.

But now let us allow the pendulum to swing back. For I love not only the Ein Sof; I also love God, the Compassionate One, the Friend, the Father, the Mother. Must I part with these images and archetypes, in the name of "growing up"? In fact, in the nondual view, they are all right here.

THE CATAPHATIC WAY: POSITIVE THEOLOGY AND THE RETURN OF GOD

Monotheism is not the whole picture.
 —RABBI DAVID AARON[10]

The unspeakable is only one half of God. In Kabbalistic language, it is the *ayin*: nothingness, empty, featureless, transparent, unknowable. But recall that emptiness is the starting point, not the endpoint. The Ein Sof births the *sefirot*, the God of attributes and characteristics.[11] Nirvana appears as samsara. And thus, in Ramakrishna's words, "God with form is just as true as God without form."[12] That All is One is only an intermediate stage of the spiritual path. In Chabad language, the next step is the return to the "lower" from the perspective of the "higher," the samsara that is one with nirvana, the multiplicity that is one with unity.

Skillful religionists know that at different times in our lives, we need different faces of God. On a meditation retreat, for example, it is often good to discard all images of the Divine, even the notion of "Divine" itself, and approach the ineffability of nonduality. In a hospital, however, this can be extremely unhelpful; there we may need God as healer, as listener, as rock of strength. And in times of emotional pain, we may need some of each. I love that my religious consciousness allows my heart to pine for the God of my ancestors and connect with Him (and Her) through ritual and the body.

This is how God returns—not as It, but as You. Ontologically, there is perhaps no difference between the two. But as Martin Buber most famously explained, the difference between It and You is a fundamental one of attitude. Buber began as a rigorous nondualist, compiling an anthology of unitive mystical experiences (*Ecstatic Confessions*) and writing his own essays on nonduality (such as *Daniel*). Later, though, he came to see that unitive mysticism was insufficient.[13] It failed to account for multiplicity, and for the fact that the phenomenon of the self is constituted by relation. When I encounter You, "I" am formed; "I" emerge in the encounter itself. And when I choose to regard you (or You) as merely an It, as an object, a thing, "I" harden, "I" objectify, "I" dominate.

The attitude of It-ing is the materialist reduction of beings to quantities and commodities. The attitude of You-ing is to recognize their sanctity, their uniqueness, and, perhaps paradoxically, their otherness. Not a dualistic otherness, exactly—but an otherness when You are viewed from the perspective of the I. The You is not about characteristics or quantities; You are not European, or female, or tall, or smart. You are precisely the You which cannot be so demarcated and described. And, as the capitalization suggests, "You" is the only way we can properly address God. God as "It" involves some attribution of characteristics to the infinite, a theology and projection. But God as "You" is a mode of relation to Being. By choosing to address the world as You, by seeing fit to label Being as God, as the Beloved, as the Friend, the primal "Yes" is uttered. Yes to the world, and Yes to myth and to image. The No of negative theology remains—No to the reality of image, No to projection, No to definition, No to limit. But it is accompanied by the Yes, the re-embrace of image, projection, definition, limit, intimacy.

Perhaps you have noticed the irony that the traditions which most embrace nonduality also embrace polytheism. Hinduism is the greatest example, accommodating within itself both the rigorous philosophical nondualism of Advaita Vedanta and an effulgent pantheon of deities, incarnations, and mythological figures.[14] But in the Jewish tradition too, precisely those mystical strands which most emphasize the Ein Sof as the totality of all existence also depict the dynamic *partzufim* (countenances) and *sefirot* of the Divine realm, mythologizing the latter not merely as Neoplatonic emanations but as characters in the heavenly novel, with personalities, narratives, sex lives, and names which multiply these prisms of Divine light into a radiance of infinite permutation.

On first blush, this would seem to be a contradiction. Why would precisely those traditions which emphasize that all is one multiply into infinity the faces and manifestations of God, gods, and goddesses? Surely these traditions should be the most iconoclastic, denying, in Zen-like form, every predicate attached to God, insisting on pure transcendence, pure otherness, and the ineffable oneness of the absolute, correct?

The resolution of this apparent contradiction is the crux of nondual Judaism as Judaism. It is no less than the most radical endpoint of nondual contemplation itself: that samsara *is* nirvana, that apparent is real, that God and the world interpenetrate, and are one. So let us explore it.

Presumably the first step along all of our spiritual paths is becoming aware, however dimly, of the numinous elements and experiences of our lives. Perhaps these insights occur in the context of religion, or perhaps of family, art, or activism. But the form is less important than the content: we experience wonder, awe, and love; we are outraged at suffering, injustice, and evil. Eventually, we come to cherish these experiences, understand our values, and, perhaps, interpret our lives according to myths and symbols inherited from our culture. Thus is born, in myriad different ways, the most basic forms of religious consciousness.

At this first stage, religion may take on many forms. It may not have a theology at all; it may simply be a love of life, or an appreciation for spirits and magic. Or it may evolve into polytheism, or a primitive monotheism that praises one god over others. In all cases, certain objects and places are sacred, certain myths are held to be true, and certain values are upheld.

Eventually, a second, more reflective stage arises—and comes to reject the earlier stage. Now, the philosophical theology of a Maimonides or an Aquinas comes to critique and reinterpret the old myths. This is a good thing: the unreflective religiosity that still holds sway in much of the world today, which posits a father figure in the sky who gets angry, judges, and forgives, has been the cause of great unreason and great violence. As today's "new atheists" have pointed out, the old beliefs, held in an unreflective way, are often as unwise as they are untenable. So reflective religion audits our theologies: God does not have a body, God does not change, God does not have any attributes at all.

Over time, the second stage matures into the *via negativa*, denying all attribution to God, and forcing us to let go of even our most cherished images. This is crucial work, even though along the way the notion of "God" becomes entirely empty of content. This is God as *ayin*, Emptiness alone. It is absolutely essential to do this work before progressing onward; only in this way can the omnipresent be truly everywhere, rather than just in the places we like. If you have an idea of God, God negates your idea. If you have an image with limits, prepare to surrender it. Thus, gradually, reflection and discernment lead to a radical letting go, a total surrender which melts our idols into light. God becomes the All, and the Nothing, and becomes the One looking through your eyes right now.

And yet, there is still one further step, in which the "God beyond God" circles back to God, because "God" is seen as but another mask, just like your or my sense of self. To be honest, I think most of us rush here too quickly—I know I do—but it's understandable. After all, God-as-Emptiness seems to deny our lived experience, and the reason we got involved in religion in the first place. I love resting in Being, identical with Emptiness—but I don't pray to it. The Ein Sof doesn't "hear" or "not hear"—it is everything and nothing! The reason I use the word "God" in the first place is because it captures a way of relating to the world. So there is a tendency to want our images back, even though we have not yet fully seen through them.

Yet logic, and perhaps Spirit, still draws us on. If Ein Sof is infinite, then does that not also include all of the manifest, finite world? Is not the very veil of illusion also Ein Sof? Or, in Kabbalistic language, isn't the *tzimtzum* also God—is not Elohim also YHVH?

Yes, every concept is a mask, and all masks are illusory, but many are helpful in translating nonsense into sense. And since all masks are illusory, all masks are permitted. From the perspective of nonduality, polytheism and polymorphism become not theological propositions, if they were ever intended to be so, but representations of the variety of experience, the plurality of modes in which the world presents itself to consciousness. Now "God" appears as judge, conqueror, creator, gardener, nursemaid, lover, and king, because "God" is known in all those ways and more. Even the most traditional of prayers recognize the many faces of the One, because, as the individual soul becomes more attuned to the tempos and tenors of existence itself, the modes of divinity multiply.

With this understanding, polytheism and theological polymorphism are more consonant with nonduality than traditional monotheism is, because they recognize that whatever the ultimate is, it cannot be expressed in a single manifestation. Again, this is not necessarily radical: the psalmist knew this, the ancient Israelites knew this, and anyone who is willing to be curious about spirit can know it as well. The pious may label some of these instantiations of the divine as demons, or foreign gods, or worse, but to the nondualist, they are all, from the sublime to the sinister, pathways of knowledge of the one.[15] As Vivekananda wrote:

> If the buffaloes desire to worship God, they, in keeping with their own nature, will see Him as a huge buffalo; if a fish wishes to worship God, its concept of Him would inevitably be a big fish; and man must think of Him as man. Suppose man, the buffalo, and the fish represent so many different vessels; that these vessels all go to the sea of God to be filled, each according to its shape and capacity. In man the water takes the shape of man; in the buffalo the shape of the buffalo; and in the fish the shape of the fish; but in each of these vessels is the same water of the sea of God.[16]

We have at our disposal thousands of myths, symbols, and other linguistic technologies that enable us to speak obliquely of the unspeakable. And the more deeply we know ineffability, the more amenable we are to multiple forms of approximation. So nonduality and polytheism exist not in uneasy tension, but as complements of one another. Ein Sof dances as God, YHVH, Christ, Vishnu, Kali, Astarte, Beloved, and King, precisely because the Ein Sof transcends all of these appellations. God is everything precisely because God is nothing.

Every time we ascribe an attribute to God—including pleasant ones such as good, creative, holy—we make a mistake, limiting the unlimited. Yet every time we deny an attribute to the Infinite, the same error appears. The error of idolatry, as it is traditionally understood in Jewish texts, is less one of attribution than of separation: to suppose that God is this but not that. God is in the fire, but not in the water; in the stone of the idol, but not in the stone cast aside. The error is at once presuming too much (i.e., this image is of God) and too little (i.e., this image, but not that one). And it is one that arises all the time, when we say, "God is in the heavens, but not in the earth," or "God is in the feeling of peace, but not the feeling of anger."

Naturally, which images we use will depend upon our cultural conditioning. I recall one visionary experience, during which I perceived something dimly like a wing, or the ear of an elephant—who knows what the mind or inner eye had really seen—and then proceeded to "fill in" the whole rest of the elephant head, and enjoy a long (if Jewishly troubling) communion with Ganesh, the Remover of Obstacles. Hours later, after the experience was long over, I reflected that the same image might easily have been interpreted as one of the *kanfei Shechinah*, the wings of the Divine Presence, or the wing of archangel Gabriel, or any number of other mythic structures. I had only "seen" Ganesh because Ganesh had been on my mind. Experientially, the act of interpretation was instant, barely divorced from the perception, but conceptually, it was distinct from the experience itself. Even "wing" or "ear" is concept, overlaid on the bare perception by a mind eager to make sense of the insensible. *Kal v'chomer*—how much more so—the other great error of idolatry: experiencing power, and then believing the power to be one's own.

So, yes, mystics around the world report different things, different experiences, different visions. But these differences do not deny an under-lying unity precedent to reported experience, which of necessity includes interpretation. Even the most sublime of theophanies is an interpretation as well as a revelation. In mysticism, all concept is symbol that exists not to represent the known but rather to stand in synecdoche for the unknown.

Consequently, the Zen ox-herder's "return to the market" from the ex-perience of nothingness is an embrace of manifestation necessarily more deeply ecumenical than any naive religion that precedes such knowledge. As I return to my cherished symbols, to challah and wine, candles and songs, I do so with no pretension or desire that they are in any way supe-rior to other symbols, or more accurate, or more holy. Yes, some symbols are better than others, relatively speaking; better candles than guns. But their worth is evaluated in a consequentialist way, in terms of the kinds of life they engender. In terms of the absolute, they are all technologies, nothing more; they are fingers that gesture at the moon, and also, if I may extend the metaphor, reflect the moonlight into hand and home. Could challah and kiddush be communion wafers and wine instead? Of course. Are they in fact descended from loaves baked for Astarte? Most likely. But it doesn't matter. This is an antifoundationalist religion, as the postmod-ern pragmatist Richard Rorty would describe it: one without claims of priority, but with an affirmation of utility. I take up these tools not because they are God-given or superior to others, but because these tools work, especially for someone who grew up with them. They work because they have been used for thousands of years, refined by tradition, and imbued with value and mystery I cannot understand. For many people, they do not work, and ultimately that is fine as well. I choose these tools because I love them, and nothing more. No theology, no history, and community only, for me, in a secondary role. I love them; that is enough.

Likewise images like the Friend and the Lover and the Father. These concepts are powerful. Yes, as described in the last section, they are pro-jections; but they *work*. Of course "God" is a projection of a father (and Goddess a mother), with all the baggage that entails. But what could be more valuable, more powerful, or more accurate, than such fundamen-tal psychological realities?

With the deep ecumenism of the nondual view, it becomes clear that what animates so many of the religious conflicts of our time is less the religious experience than the mythic way in which it is understood. These are not fingers pointing at the moon, the fundamentalist insists; this is the moon, and something else is not.

But the boundless does not know such lines.

THE SANCTIFICATION OF THE WORLD

Earth's crammed with Heaven,
And every common bush afire with God
—ELIZABETH BARRETT BROWNING, "AURORA LEIGH"

When someone asks me who they are or what God is, I smile inside
and whisper to the Light: "There you go again pretending."
—ADYASHANTI[17]

So, while nonduality ultimately effaces images of the Divine, it re-embraces even more of them. Nonduality does not posit that "God" is a character in the play of life. Recall, God does not exist—God is existence Itself. And then all masks return.

There is one final step of the path: the re-embrace of the manifest world itself, of multiplicity. Many nondualists, including some Hasidim, have tended toward "acosmism," the view that the material world simply does not exist, or is at least of no significance. Many Chabad texts speak of *bittul b'mitziut*, or annihilation in (or of) existence, and as we saw already, R. Aharon insists that God after the creation of the world is exactly the same, and just as alone, as before it.[18] In this regard, nondual Judaism is not unlike the many religious views that "understand everyday life to be disvalued with reference to some ultimate reality."[19]

But it does not end there. Nonduality eventually re-embraces not just the masks of God, but the very material world itself. *Bittul b'mitziut* means seeing both *ayin* and *yesh*, holding both contradictory perspectives simultaneously: *ḥibbur shenei hafakhim*, the coincidence of opposites.[20] What the scholar Rachel Elior calls the "paradoxical ascent to God" could also be termed as the "paradoxical descent of God" into multiplicity: God as both/and, both ultimate and relative. For the distinction between ultimate and relative is, itself, relative.

As we will see in chapter 8, this is how R. Aharon understands *ham-shachat or Ein Sof*, the extension of the light of the Ein Sof into the material world: all continues as before, only now it is only God doing it. It is how the Chabad sages understand *dirah b'tachtonim*, the dwelling of God "below." And it is the nondual inflection of *l'shem yichud kudsha brich hu v'shechintei*, which is to see unity in plurality, emptiness in form, God in the world. In all these formulations, nondual Judaism is a panentheistic re-wonderment at the world. As Rabbi Shlomo of Lutsk says in his introduction to the *Maggid Dvarav L'Yaakov*:

> It is important to know that the whole earth is full of God's glory and there is no place empty of Him, and that God is in all the worlds, etc. This idea can be sensed in everything, for the life-force of the Creator is everywhere.[21]

Historically, scholars debate whether more Hasidim were this-worldly, as Martin Buber wished to claim, or other-worldly, as Gershom Scholem maintained; that is, whether they were pantheistic or acosmic. But experientially, seeing that "the life-force of the creator is everywhere" enables a simultaneous embrace and annihilation, a re-appreciation and re-valuing of precisely those energies which monotheism sought earlier to displace. As the Zen saying goes, "Before zazen, there are mountains; during zazen, no mountains; after zazen, there are mountains." The mountains return, as mountains *and* as emptiness. In the conjunction is nonduality's affirmation of the world.

In other words, God is not in heaven—God, when nondual Judaism is done right, is right here, right now, just as it is, only perhaps a little more luminous. The world as it appears is God's erotic play (Kabbalah), Indra's Web (Hinduism), Kali's dance (Hinduism again), the amorous hide-and-seek game of Lover and Beloved (Sufism). Identity is not to be privileged over difference; multiplicity is as much a dance of the Divine as unity.

This is the Tanya's "lower unity," the seeing of the world as God. It is similar to how Mahayana and Vajrayana Buddhism emphasize that "nothing of samsara is different from nirvana, nothing of nirvana is different from samsara . . . There is not the slightest difference between the two."[22] This is not simply paradox. It is to understand that existence and non-existence are two ways of seeing the same reality.[23] The incarnation of the spiritual as the physical, in what Chabad texts call *hit'asqut im hahutzah be-ofen shel hitlabshut,* engagement with the external in the manner of garbing, or even *hitlabshut mohin de-gadlut be-mohin de-katnut,* the garbing of expansive consciousness in diminished consciousness.[24] Confusion is enlightenment! The very mind you have, right now, is enlightened mind—God is doing the dance of you.

To hold both of these perspectives, nirvana and samsara, absolute and relative, in a dialectical relationship, is the goal of *hitkallelut,* the incorporation of all things in the infinite essence, and *hashva'ah,* total equality or equanimity of view. One of the Kabbalistic symbols of *hitkallelut* is that of the circle (*iggul*) and line (*yosher*).[25] The circle knows no boundary, no distinction, no polarity, no duality. The line is that which divides, into left and right, light and dark, true and false, sacred and profane, ultimate and relative. The circle has no history, no time; it is the sacred eternity of the liminal. The line is all linearity, direction, history—but also ethics, memory, and self.[26] Most of us live most of our lives in linear time, and so the necessary work is to enter the realm of the timeless, the eternal now, the sacred circle. But true *hitkallelut* is the circle and the line combined. Nonduality is the union of union and duality.

Thus nonduality brings back the everyday sensuality of surfaces, touches, smells; the feel of fabric, rough or smooth, the contact of finger with tabletop, *kal v'chomer* with flesh. Of warmth and of cold. And, too, of the play of manifestation in our own human conditions: the sadnesses and joys of human experience, loving, losing, surrendering.

In its other-worldliness, Western religion can, at times, devalue the world of phenomena. It is so focused on God that it forgets the world, and it criticizes those who love it as "pagan," as too entranced by the world of appearances. But from a nondual perspective, this world, in its particular phenomena, embodied, emotioned, and ever new in its complexity, *Is.* Thus the nondual is at home with sucking the marrow out of life, with drinking from the well of life's blessings while cultivating a gratitude so rich it can ache, with the sensual, the pagan, the atheistic, and the orgiastic. It is with Henry Miller, himself both a sensualist and, in his later years, a nondualist who helped found Esalen in California. It is with William Blake's *Marriage of Heaven and Hell*, the union of rational and sensual, ordered and chaotic. It is with Oscar Wilde, who reveled in surface and deplored piety and "substance." It is with Zen iconoclasts from Ikkyu to Leonard Cohen, both of whom embrace both enlightenment and sensuality. It is with the stage manager in Thornton Wilder's *Our Town*, who rejects both the ephemeral distractions of the living and the fatalism of the dead, insisting on a productive tension between the two perspectives. And it is with the sculptor, the painter, the artist, and the poet, who find mystery not in the abstract but the concrete. This is nonduality: a re-embrace of the world as ripples on the pond—ripples only, perhaps, but ripples, beautiful, reflecting light.

As with eros, so too with ethics. Sometimes the Light is awful; it denies, oppresses, despoils. The Light is also in darkness, and it is easy to call it evil. If we take seriously the meaningfulness of this world, we must own its injustices and horrors, not only the delights of touch and taste. This is why nondual Judaism is so irreducibly *Jewish*, because in its reappropriation of the world of relativity, it finds Judaism's ancient and historic priorities: social justice, righteousness, and this-worldly ritual. Yes, God is in the world, but as Heschel articulated more poetically than anyone (especially in his early poetic work, such as the anthology now available as *The Ineffable Name of God: Man*), that means God suffers with those who are suffering, God's face shines and is hidden, God's revelation is contained in the interpersonal. Heschel's humanism is a nondual one: it begins with the intoxication of God in All, and progresses to its consequences.

One of the biblical verses quoted often by nondual Hasidim is the Divine exhortation to "make a tabernacle [*mishkan*], so that I may dwell within them."[27] In the Hasidic reading, this *mishkan* is not the historical tabernacle in the desert, but any dwelling place for the infinite which we make here in finitude. In general, Judaism is a householder religion concerned with the proper ordering of society; it is nearly (though not entirely) univocal in its affirmation of this-worldly experience and the importance of sanctifying that experience for divine service (*avodah*). The Jewish revelation spends but a few words on theophany, yet offers chapters on tort law and hygiene. The Jewish paradise is a community that cares for its needy. Thus, while renunciation and solitude remain indispensable steps along the spiritual path—one must not "integrate" too quickly—and eventually, nondual Judaism leads to a re-embrace of the world.

By way of parallel, consider the Buddha's first noble truth— that suffering exists—not as a pre-emptiness notion, but as a post-emptiness one. Yes, nothing is "real." But to the extent anything is "real," suffering exists—and our work begins there. Just as there is action without an agent, enlightenment without one who gets enlightened, there is suffering even if there is "no one" to suffer. As in Buber's turn to dialogical philosophy, to multiplicity and relation, which came after years of monism and mysticism, there is the understanding that we are all one; but in our manifestation, we are two, we are many, we are responsible. *Bittul b'mitziut*: both nothing and everything, and in "everything," differentiation.

In erasing the notion of essential difference, nonduality transcends; it denies the mythic God, effaces the world, sees everything as a dream of the mind. But in erasing *all* difference, it returns to all of these and more. The masks of God are seen anew, and the play of emptiness dancing is celebrated with joy, clarity, and responsibility. Not for the nondualist the life-denying, eros-repressing hierarchies and authoritarian systems which claim that the sacred is only accessible by a single means—usually one mediated by authority. Eros is everywhere, and nowhere, and each moment is an opportunity for the uniting of immanent and transcendent, the goddess and the god, and in that uniting, a transcendence even of the notion of transcendence. To call the entirety of existence a cosmic dance is an invitation, not a negation: Come and Dance with Me.

May it be that the re-embrace of the world is also the speedy redemption of the *Shechinah*, for so many generations thought of as other than God, wandering in the exile because of our mistaken notions of separation. May it be so—and what better way than asking Her to dance?

4

TORAH: JUDAISM AS A NONDUAL DEVOTIONAL PATH

i thank You God for most this amazing
day: for the leaping greenly spirits of trees
and a blue true dream of sky; and for everything
which is natural which is infinite which is yes

(i who have died am alive again today,
and this is the sun's birthday; this is the birth
day of life and of love and wings: and of the gay
great happening illimitably earth)

how should tasting touching hearing seeing
breathing any—lifted from the no
of all nothing—merely human being
doubt unimaginable You?

(now the ears of my ears awake and
now the eyes of my eyes are opened)
   —E. E. CUMMINGS[1]

So, my brothers and sisters, our whole business in this life is the healing of the eye of the heart, that eye with which God is seen.
   —ST. AUGUSTINE[2]

In the classic Jewish triad of God, Torah, and Israel, it is the middle term which most refers to the texts, traditions, and practices of Judaism. Thus the turn to Torah is one from philosophy to law, legend, and above all "religion"—as well as from the absolute to the relative, from the universal to the particular, from *nondual* Judaism to nondual *Judaism*.

Of course, narrowly speaking, "Torah," which literally means "teaching," refers to the Five Books of Moses, or, somewhat more broadly, to the textual tradition which embraces the Bible, the Talmud, and the vast bodies of Jewish legendary, legal, ethical, philosophical, and mystical material. "Torah" is that which is studied, learned, and lived. And it is primarily, though not entirely, intellectual in its orientation.

But "Torah" is also used in a broader sense—as a particular religious outlook on life. Different teachers, for example, are said to have different "Torahs," not in the literal sense, of course, but in the figurative one: different perspectives, different ways of life. Indeed, a Torah in this sense is often quite the opposite of a literal Torah: it is more emotive, more devotional, more personal, and less intellectual, less philosophical, and less associated with beliefs and opinions. The turn from theology to Torah is thus a turn from mind to heart. This is nondual Judaism as a lived, communal tradition, and, I submit, essentially a devotional practice—essentially a matter of love.

The contemplative is what we know; the devotional is what we feel. The absolute is what we are, but the relative is who we are. Wisdom is unchanging, but love changes as we do, throughout our lives and throughout the year. The general is universal; the particular is not. And whatever our choices of lifestyle and circumstance, each of us lives in the dance between the two. Purely from a cognitive perspective, there is no distinction to be made between forbidden and permitted, sacred and profane, body and mind, divine and mortal, dark and light; this is why elite traditions such as nondual Judaism have been so carefully guarded from misuse. But from the emotive perspective, the naming is all.

The nondual, itself, demands no response, no action, no community at all. One might even argue that, following today's neo-atheists, by causing us to think that certain ceremonies, rituals, and mind states are closer to Goodness than others, religion in particular is actively unhelpful. Beliefs in rites and rituals are for intellectual children, they say; when we grow up, we leave such childish things behind. Many contemporary nondualists agree, though for a slightly different reason: because neither the dogmas of religion nor the beloved mind states of spirituality are any closer to the Infinite than the greatest of heresies.

The more you think there is something you have to do to be enlightened—keep kosher, be compassionate, make money, whatever—the less enlightened you are.

And yet, the heart knows two even when the mind knows one. We are Ein Sof, but we are also the *sefirot*, also human, also animals. My theology is nondual, but I am not so "advanced" as not to be moved by a sunset. And so, following my heart and my Jewish karma, I choose to address Being not only as It but also as You; not only as Ein Sof but also as God. "You" is to the heart as "Is" is to the mind.

When there is no sense of the self, then religion is of no purpose; but when there is, and when there arises the need to love and be loved, then religion becomes relevant again. And because the religious response is voluntary, and because it springs from the yearning of the heart, being religious, in the sense that I understand the term, is not a matter of opinion. It is a matter of love.

This is not, of course, a radical position; as we will see, Judaism, like all religions, places love at the very center of religious life. But today, confused as we are by the notion that religion is about what you believe, it may seem odd to describe it in terms of what you feel, or how willing you are to be open to love. Yet even a traditionalist who follows the rules because God commanded them is still motivated by the heart's desire to be in accord with God's will, rather than run afoul of it. Of course, there may well be opinions intermingled with this yearning: notions of reward and punishment, for example. But opinions are secondary; love, fear, yearning are at the root. *Kal v'chomer*, a fortiori, for those of us who do not hold such beliefs. Beneath the many layers of rationale, we do religious things because we deeply want to do them, and we believe religious ideas because we want to believe, because the belief does something for us, or enables something to happen. Motive is always present, even—especially—among those who say they have no motive. To obey God's command; to feel all right; to feel like I'm doing the right thing, or that there is a right thing to do in the first place—these are powerful, even primal motives. Nondual Torah is born of love, for God is a name that lovers give to Being.

In my case, love of life preceded any spefically religious response to it. I still treasure my dreams and aspirations from the days when I first heard of Thoreau, Whitman, Ginsberg, and Heschel, when I yearned in college and the years right afterward to be one of—Kerouac here—

> the mad ones, the ones who are mad to live, mad to talk, mad to be saved, desirous of everything at the same time, the ones who never yawn or say a commonplace thing, but burn like fabulous roman candles exploding like spiders across the stars and in the middle you see the blue center light pop and everybody goes "AWWW!"[3]

I have more in common with an atheist who dances than with the supposedly pious men who are asleep in their lives. And so, for me, non-dual *religion*, as opposed to nondual philosophy, is about being in love with the world. I don't care about the God you don't believe in; I want to know only if there is something sacred for you. Here is Friedrich Schleiermacher, the consummate German Romantic, writing in 1799:

> The universe exists in uninterrupted activity and reveals itself to us every moment. Every form that it brings forth, every being to which it gives a separate existence according to the fullness of life, every occurrence that spills forth from its rich, ever-fruitful womb, is an action of the same upon us. Thus to accept everything individual as part of a whole and everything limited as a representation of infinite, is religion.[4]

For Schleiermacher, religion is about cultivating and expressing our intuition of the infinite—that inchoate yearning that has been expressed as animism, paganism, polytheism, monotheism, and monism, and which is often more present among the "cultured despisers" of churches, hierarchies, and dogmas than those who uphold them. There can be no authentic system of religion, Schleiermacher wrote, any more than there could be a system of intuition. Surely those of our contemporaries who eschew all religion but call themselves "spiritual" are making a similar distinction.

That being said, my own religious path has many traditional elements in it. I still keep Shabbat in the halachic way, still am so *shomer kashrut* that I won't eat most foods in a nonkosher restaurant. But I see these ritual practices as acts of love. I abstain from bacon not because I am afraid of punishment, not because I think it unhealthy, and not because it is part of the folkways of my people. I do it because I love God, and when you love someone, you do stupid things for them. There is nothing essentially sensible about bringing your lover flowers. So I don't mind that avoiding bacon makes no sense either.

To surrender the notion that the laws make sense is to relate to Judaism as a devotional practice—what a Hindu would recognize as *bhakti*—and to put an end to the hyperrational "wrestling" that characterizes many attempts to rationalize Jewish text and practice. On the one hand, it admits fully that these traditions are derived from ancient, human sources and reflect their concerns. On the other, it affirms a love of the forms of life that result from them. We do these things because we deeply want to do them.

Now, when faith is combined with ideas about how the world should be, it turns into dogmatic religion—and as such has been heavily attacked in recent years. Unfortunately, many religionists have responded with ludicrous exercises in false consciousness, such as pseudo-philosophical defenses of the God idea, or the risible inconsistencies of "intelligent design." These are wrongheaded, primarily because they come from the head. The real reason the believer believes has to do with her heart, not the argument from design. Would she really stop believing if quantum mechanics didn't bolster her religious claims? If not, why pretend that physics is relevant? Proofs are beside the point. They are games, often played unconsciously, which demean both head and heart by masquerading the latter as the former. Anyway, with a little practice, it is easy to argue any Jewish position: pantheistic atheology and traditional halacha, traditional theology and egalitarianism, agnostic theology and purely cultural Judaism, agnostic theology and fundamentalist halacha—if you know how to argue, you can square any circle you like. The philosophy is decoration, layered atop a fervently held desire.

Yet if religionists layer belief atop unexpressed desire, atheists often ignore the desire entirely. What is the significance of the yearning of the religious heart? Is it contemptible, adolescent? Or is it noble, not unlike the appreciation of painting, dance, or music? Some atheists treat religion the way a bad junior high school teacher treats a poem:

as being about the facts it seeks to convey. Whereas a connoisseur of poetry or of religion knows that the informational content of words is often less important than how they are said—and in the case of religion, the way myth functions in a self-examined life. I care about the trauma of Abraham's leaving for Canaan, or the trauma of Isaac submitting to his father's violence, not because of pseudo-history, but because of the power of myth. And from a nondual perspective, which dispenses with the fundamentalist's need to establish facts, these myths retain all their attraction to the relative self. They tell us nothing about the ultimate— but then, nothing can tell us about the ultimate. What they do tell us about is how "I" struggle, prevail, surrender, and fail in "my" relationship with it.

For some of us, these tales are told in the language of God, and of Judaism. Reciting the Ashrei prayer is my way of buying a bouquet of roses for the universe. After all the tragedies of the world, I can't say what God hears and doesn't hear. I just know I want to express love. Of course, for others, a nontheistic devotional practice, through art or yoga or meditation or some other form, can better express that love. But for me, relating to God often feels fuller, from an emotional perspective, than resting in Being alone, not least because of the different modes and masks which God assumes. To once more quote Ramakrishna:

> God with form is as real as God without form. Do you know what describing God as being formless only is like? It is like a man's playing only a monotone on his flute, though it has seven holes. But on the same instrument another man plays different melodies. Likewise, in how many ways the believers in a Personal God enjoy Him! They enjoy Him through many different attitudes: the serene attitude, the attitude of a servant, a friend, a mother, a husband, or a lover.[5]

Or, as Arthur Green puts it:

> Because we feel the relationship with God as one of great intimacy, we cannot help but depict it in images of the sorts of hu-

man intimacy that we know best: God as our spouse, God as our parent, God as our loving friend. The process of seeking and of growing in faith requires an opening and making vulnerable of the self that usually happen to us only in the intimacy of human relations.[6]

In just this way, devotional nondual Judaism complements the Ein Sof of *ayin* with the God of *yesh*, and complements contemplation with prayer, ritual, study, and the dance of manifestation. It provides a communal and ethical frame for how the "individual" relates to the community. It is a language of people, spirit, righteousness, and, finally, of connection. And, as David Loy describes it, religious devotion "is the path of purifying my emotional response to the world—or, less dualistically, the 'emotional tone' of my being-in-the-world. Such devotion cuts through the web of negativity that perpetuates my sense of separation from others."[7] Love of God, and love of other people, lead to a sense of oneness between lover and beloved, a lowering of boundaries. Thus universal love leads to a similarly universal unveiling.

It does not make sense. Whether one updates the language of prayer or not, for example, its core dualistic assumption, and of course its dualistic language—God, please help me; I need you; I want to be close to you—are as philosophically problematic as they are devotionally powerful. However you modify it or don't, none of it makes sense.

But would we demand that someone praying for her sick child "make sense"? Sense is not the measurement of devotion. So, as I approach ancient texts of Judaism, I accept that they have their cosmology, and I have mine—and we are united by love, not theory. Let's allow the heart to have its place and the mind its. Let's not have the mind pretend to have anything to say, really, about the essence of religion; let's allow the heart to soar. And, conversely, let's not pretend that the heart's yearnings about God have anything to say about how the world should be—let's leave that to calm and rational reflection, coupled with human moral sentiment. Wouldn't we all get along better, and be more honest with ourselves, to boot? Or would it be just too terribly embarrassing, to admit that we choose God out of love and not reason?

GETTING SERIOUS ABOUT LOVE

Human things must be known to be loved; but Divine things must be loved to be known.
—PASCAL

If nondual Judaism is a path of the heart, how is it expressed in practice?

As we have said, nondual Judaism may be quite traditional or quite radical. For traditionalists, the realization that all is God is carried into every aspect of our lives by the physical performance of the commandments. For nontraditionalists, the commandments may be only one means toward the twin ends of realization and expression, and they may be accompanied, or even displaced, by others. Both perspectives are accommodated, so long as both understand themselves as working with the relative, and with the aspirations of the heart.

But perhaps "the path of the heart" is insufficiently specific, for surely we do not mean by this phrase the path of yielding to all the heart's desires—that is, doing whatever one wants. Thus there must be some distinction among "wants," between those which are ennobling and those which aren't. For example, all of us on the contemplative path have had, at some time, to place our own deep needs above the expectations of our society, to follow our own voices against the din of materialism, mainstreams, and modernity. Yet that same inner bravery can lead to egotistic indulgence, placing "my needs" above fairness, responsibility, and maturity. "This is what my heart tells me" can be a watchword of spiritual growth, or one of avoidance, delusion, or worse. This is the complaint many skeptics have against the "New Age": that it is just about serving one's own needs, a selfish, boomer-inflected movement of treating, not transforming, the self.

So, then, the path of the heart is not merely about listening to what we think the heart is saying, but about cultivating a heart of compassion, righteousness, and openness, and discerning profound from profane. This implies a task, an obligation. If we are serious about a religion of love, then what begins with love must lead to commitment. For those of us who remain god-intoxicated but clear-eyed as well, cultivating authentic, reflective love, and discerning that love from mere fancy, must become a serious religious priority.

In the Jewish tradition, the two poles of religious emotion are *ahavah* and *yirah*, love and fear. (*Yirah* is usually translated as "awe" in politically correct circles, but for reasons I'll explain, I think "fear" might be better.) In the classical structure, love of God, theologian Rudolf Otto's *fascinans*, is the pull toward the holy, the beautiful, and the good. As one feels love for another person, one wants to be with that person, to hold them, and, yes, to serve them and make them happy; likewise with love of God. Fear of God, what Otto called the *mysterium tremendum*, also responds to the holy, beautiful, and good—but with a sense of humility, awe, and trembling. The awesome, infinite power of the universe—and the fleeting, puny nature of human life. The responsibility to alleviate suffering and act justly—and the selfishness and cruelty of the ego. *Yirah* also leads to service, but out of a sense of obligation and noble servitude, not desire.

Traditionally, both *ahavah* and *yirah* are deeply connected to theology—particularly *yirah*, which stems from beliefs about reward and punishment. However, *yirah* does not actually require theology. When I learn of the genocide in Tibet, I feel a sense of outrage, and an obligation to do more than I do. When I ponder the images from the Hubble telescope, I remember that I really have no idea what the universe is like and have no business making propositions about it. When I reflect upon my own privilege as a relatively wealthy white male, I remember that I have been given a leg up in the world that comes at the expense of others. And when I visit a place of natural sublimity, it takes my breath away, and I lack the words to describe the wonder. All these are *yirah*, sacred awe, or fear, and all arise without any notions of reward or punishment. Likewise *ahavah*, which arises whenever my mind is quiet enough to appreciate the silence that grounds all sound, the miracle of a string bean, the beauty of the humblest of houseplants, precedes theology. Indeed, theology itself might well be defined as the attempt to give intellectual form to these twin emotional movements.

Yet neither *ahavah* nor *yirah* arises on its own, and neither can be immediately trusted. We fear many things which turn out not to be fearsome, and we often love that which cannot receive our love. If you ask me what I want when I'm in the middle of a hectic and stressful work-day, I'll give you an ill-considered answer. And it's all too easy to change the channel from the Tibet documentary, blow off the space pictures, ignore one's own privilege, and just take a snapshot of the pretty view of nature. As Rabbi Zalman Schachter-Shalomi says, the mind is like tofu—it takes the flavor of what it marinates in. (The original source for this metaphor is Ramakrishna: "The mind will take the colour you dye it with. It is like white clothes just returned from the laundry."[8]) Marinate in front of a Bloomberg machine all day, and it's hard to experience much awe or love—unless you make a special point of doing something for your heart, every day, as a religious obligation.

What's necessary, then, is a process of refinement and reflection that clears the mind and opens the heart. That process is the business of contemplative practice; in Hebrew, *avodah*, "service of God." As I'm using the term, it means something we *do* to enable the heart to make the kind of serious religious decisions in the absence of theology or dogma. If I'm going to be so audacious as to determine for myself, on a case-by-case basis, what religious practices are working for me, I need *avodah* to ensure that my discernment is as clear as it can be, and that the ego isn't inventing rationalizations for laziness. Otherwise I really am deluding myself. If deciding not to keep Shabbat is to be anything more than preferring to go to the mall, *avodah* is required first.

Contemplative practices are technologies of becoming the people we want ourselves to be. If our hearts speak the Jewish language, then it is this language which becomes the most skillful means both for ascending the mountain from multiplicity to unity (the upward-pointing triangle of the Jewish star) and for descending the mountain back into daily life (the downward-pointing triangle). This is so not because of any cosmic reason or ontological priority, but because the yearnings of the heart matter, and cannot be described.

The specific nature of this *avodah* is the subject of the second part of this book. There, following the nondual sage R. Aharon of Staroselye, we will explore nondual practices for the mind, the heart, and the body—roughly speaking, meditation, prayer and acts of love, and performance of the *mitzvot*. But of course, there are plenty of other such practices as well. Working with myth, ritual, and symbol can activate the imaginal faculties, and illuminate one's own narratives in the light of timeless, power-ful archetypes that bring insight, love, and wisdom. What Thomas Moore calls "care of the soul," which may include viewing or participating in art, theater, food, music, dance, or other forms of culture; spending quality time with children; conscious sexuality, body practices like yoga or exer-cise, special diets and nutrition—all of these can wake up the body, which in turn wakes up the heart. There's no shortage of practices, and no one practice that will be right for everyone. The point is that it's the practice and the diligence that separates "I do what works for me" said in a serious tone from "I do what works for me" in a dismissive, casual, or lazy tone.

Some regard these kinds of spiritual practices as indulgent fads that bourgeois Americans do to make themselves feel good. I've tried to sug-gest that, when done with serious intention, the opposite is the case. Spiritual practice is not to feel good, but to feel, period. Who can really say, honestly, that they're making decisions based on a clear-eyed view of what their deepest feelings are, when we've all got a hundred e-mails in the inbox? No wonder "doing what we want" has led to chain stores and strip malls. Without quiet and reflection, "what we want" is just ap-petite. But in the context of spiritual practice, "what we want" is the question, not the assumption.

It is also sometimes alleged that spiritual practice is divorced from the affairs of the world and from the Jewish imperative to pursue justice. All that meditating—what about *tikkun olam*, repairing and complet-ing the world? We will explore these objections more deeply in chapter 9; suffice to say for now that in my own experience and, *l'havdil*, that of Jewish spiritual activists from Abraham Joshua Heschel to Arthur Waskow and Michael Lerner, opening the heart inevitably awakens us to suffering and to the mandate to alleviate it. But more than that: in Heschel's nondualistic cosmology, God is resident in all faces; God suffers through the sick, languishes through the impoverished, and, in the bodies of all who are stricken, demands a response of us. Love of God inexorably leads to love of people. Indeed, given the ineluctability of that causal nexus, one wonders at the consequences of fear.

Accepting the Torah of nondual Judaism is an act grounded in love, rather than intellection. From that acceptance can spring many different forms of *kabbalat ol malchut shamayim* (accepting the yoke of heaven), from traditional study of sacred text and performance of the *mitzvot* to secular social justice and ethical refinement, to spiritual hybrids like the Jewfis, BuJus, and HinJews. In all cases, though, the love beneath the form must be cultivated and discerned, not taken for granted. Only after the mind has been quieted and the *yetzer* seen for what it is can I presume to say something about what religious moments bring me closer to what matters most, and what do not. Like the children of Israel said, *na'aseh v'nishmah*—when I do the work, I hear the voice. But only then.

FETISHIZING THE TRIGGER

There was once a prisoner who yearned for freedom. One day, the prophet Muhammad appeared to him, and gave him a set of keys to his cell, saying, "Your piety has been rewarded. Allah has set you free." So the prisoner took the set of keys, mounted them on the wall, and prayed to them five times a day.
—SUFI TALE

As I was writing this book, I took a short trip to Israel, where I had earlier lived for three years. As a longtime resident of Jerusalem, I was not interested in the tourist track of ruins and holy sites, yet I felt drawn to the Kotel, the Western Wall. This despite my own misgivings, and despite the fact that my friends and I hardly ever visited the place when we lived there. In fact, it's fashionable, in progressive circles, to dismiss the Kotel: some find what goes on there idolatrous, others sexist; some see it as a cliché, still others find it oppressive, and to many it's simply irrelevant. But the Kotel, like so many places around the world, is a kind of energy vortex; it oozes what Pacific Islanders call *mana* and what many languages call *baraka*, the mysterious life-energy that seems somehow concentrated, perhaps by the attention of the devoted, in some places more than others. Jewish tradition holds that the Divine Presence never left the Western Wall, and I feel I can sense Her whenever I approach.

This time was no different. The plaza was busy: there was some kind of military ceremony going on, Chabad missionaries were laying *tefillin* on a large group of Birthright Israel kids, and there were *schnorrers* asking for money and tourists snapping pictures. But—I'd like to say "And"—all of it was suffused with holiness. Despite the cliché of an American having a spiritual moment at the Kotel, I did so, not forgetting the political and social issues in play, but swimming in the tension between them and the holiness I felt. And when I got distracted one time, a Hasid, as if on cue, shouted, *"Ein od milvado!"* reminding me both how nondual Judaism is so much a part of the religious mainstream today and, of course, that there was nothing besides God in that moment. It was a wake-up call from the Absolute.

We are defined, Rosenzweig memorably wrote, by our first and last names; by our personality and our family, by our independence and autonomy, and our interdependence and relationship with others. Indeed, one of the great struggles of postmodern spiritual communities is to rebuild the networks of commonality that premodern religions constructed over centuries. Theoretically, of course, sacred spaces and groups should not matter. Isn't the whole point that God is everywhere? And yet, we approach the Absolute from the Relative, the universal from the particular. These are my people, my family—which is doubtless why I sometimes can't stand them.

As many critics have pointed out—with renewed vigor in the post-9/11 era of Islamic, Christian, and Jewish fundamentalism—these ties of kinship come at an awful price: intolerance, ethnocentrism, hatred, and demonization. Indeed, there seems never to have been a human social grouping (religious, national, ethnic, or other) that has not sought to elevate itself above others. Add God into the mix, and the result is predictably toxic. As Vivekananda said, "Each religion brings out its own doctrines and insists on them being the only true ones . . . This is not through wickedness, but through a particular disease of the human brain called fanaticism."[9]

In the Jewish world, fundamentalism and ethnocentrism are present even among the spiritual Left. Some of Israel's most ardent nationalists are pot-smoking, guitar-playing neo-hippies who love nature, their fellow Jews, and God. Many are nondualists, many meditate, and many are committed, in a serious way, to spiritual practice. Nor can I prove that they are wrong according to sacred text. I can quote Isaiah, but they can quote Joshua. I can talk of love of all humankind, but they can talk about the Chosen People.

What happens in so many of these cases is that the fundamentalist finds a trigger that brings about an authentic and powerful spiritual experience—and then fetishizes the trigger, convinced that it and only it is the path to truth. It's this land, this Torah, this Kabbalah, this people. And then the trigger must hold everything: any insight gleaned from another tradition must somehow be shown to be indigenously one's own. And the sphere of moral consideration contracts: no longer all people, but just my people. Worse, the more zeal, the more enthusiasm, the more fetishization. Precisely those who are the most afire with love for God can become the most ardent, zealous, and dangerous.

So the turn to devotion and particularity is not without its perils. Personally, I am a pluralist and a radical ecumenicist. I love the Torah, but I don't need to make it say everything I believe. I love that the Jewish path can lead me to *devekut*. But I don't need to prove that *devekut* is better than *samadhi*. I'm happy to share Oneness with the rest of the world's religious traditions, to learn from them, and not to assume that the choice I've made to follow the Jewish path is necessarily the right or the best choice. Yet at the same time, I don't want to fall back into a mushy universalism either. I don't want to fetishize the trigger, but I do want to pull it. These are still my folkways, my first and last name.

Ultimately, identity of any kind must be surrendered in the sweet consummation of the mystic quest, not only for these essentially political reasons, but in order for the dissolution to be complete. If one is holding on to ethnic or tribal identity, one is still in the realm of the relative. Indeed, this is one of the blessings of nonduality: that a deep recognition of it must efface the sense that only one's own path is just. Many channels bring the flow of blessing—and even our beloved notions of God, angels, spirits, lands are but channels for that which cannot be expressed. "We dance round in a ring and suppose / But the secret sits in the middle and knows," writes Robert Frost.[10] All these names, these holidays and rituals and ceremonies—all are tools, technologies only. Surely one of the great gifts of nonduality is the deep ecumenism that results from it.

To feign transcendence is delusion. Some particularism is ineluctable, because we are products of our cultures, our "selves" constituted by cultural practices and culturally defined terms. But just as the Jewish heritage is a gift, it is a burden. We cannot ignore the suffering our own self-actualization causes to others, or fall back on tribalism as a defense against the imperatives to justice. The truth of *ein od milvado* does not flatten our responsibilities to one another. Just as it is upon us to erase division in the ultimate, so it is upon us in the relative world to render it a blessing.

5

ISRAEL: COMMUNITY, HISTORY, AND NONDUAL MESSIANISM

I appeared unto Abraham, Isaac, and Jacob as El Shaddai but by my name YHVH I did not make myself known to them.
—EXODUS 6:3

The contemplative path often seems solitary, but nearly every mystical tradition emphasizes community as one of the pillars of spiritual practice. Mystical fellowships appear in Christian, Jewish, Sufi, and Hindu orders. Sangha (community) sits aside Buddha and Dharma in the Buddhist triple gem. And in the Jewish world, "Israel" complements "God" and "Torah" as a foundation of Jewish life. Indeed, as Judaism is predominantly a householder religion, concerned with society, it may be argued that the community of Israel, construed narrowly or broadly, is its fundamental concern. One teacher of mine told me that to be a good Jew, you need only believe in one God or fewer. But you still need nine other Jews to pray.

What is the significance of community from a nondual perspective? First, and most obvious, it is an essential part of the spiritual path. Of course, human beings seek love, support, and the primal power of the group, and for spiritual seekers, finding common ground and common cause is of enormous value, notwithstanding the dangers of community and ethnocentrism discussed in the previous chapter.

In this chapter, though, I want to explore a deeper significance of community: history—the history of consciousness specifically. So far, we have explored nondual Judaism rather ahistorically. But the concept of nonduality does not simply appear on the stage without precedent or consequences; it is a historical development. As we saw in chapter 2, we know that nonduality is probably not "what Judaism has said all along." So what does it mean that Judaism is "saying" it now? As we'll see, the answer to that question implicates Judaism's most radical historical pronouncements: that history has a direction, and that the dawning of nondual consciousness is a form of messianic realization.

A SHORT HISTORY OF NOTHING

Conceptions of nonduality evolve historically. As a philosophical notion, it is most clearly found for the first time in the West in the second century C.E., in the Neoplatonism of Plotinus and his followers. As a Jewish religious notion, nonduality begins to appear unambiguously in Jewish texts during the medieval period, increasing in frequency in the centuries thereafter and peaking at the turn of the nineteenth century, with the advent of Hasidism. It is certainly possible that earlier Jewish texts may suggest nonduality—as, of course, they have been interpreted by traditional nondualists—but, as we also explored in chapter 2, this may or may not be the most useful way to approach them.

Since the middle of the twentieth century, however, nonduality has entered the Jewish mainstream in an unprecedented way. During this time, a variety of scholars, teachers, and teacher-scholars have rekindled interest in nonduality and created new forms of Judaism, such as neo-Hasidism and Jewish Renewal, which incorporate it to some extent. There are at least five important sources for this historical development.

First is the first wave of "neo-Hasidism," led by Abraham Joshua Heschel, Hillel Zeitlin, and Martin Buber, who drew on the wellsprings of Hasidic teachings for their own twentieth-century Jewish worldviews. Heschel, for example, united the theological nonduality of Hasidism with its ethical and personal emphases, crafting a theology that, rather like Catholic liberation theology, sees God in the faces of human beings, waiting to be redeemed. Buber, as is well known, was inspired by Hasidism and existentialism for his dialogical philosophy of "I and Thou," and, as we remarked in chapter 2, began as a nondualist and moved from there to his post-nondual philosophy of relation.[1] This first wave of neo-Hasidism incorporated traditional Hasidic teaching into contemporary social, political, and spiritual thought, and nonduality was one of many Hasidic teachings brought into the Jewish mainstream.

The second historical source of nondual Judaism is the second wave of neo-Hasidism, led primarily by two renegade Chabad Hasidim, Rabbi Zalman Schachter-Shalomi (b. 1924) and Rabbi Shlomo Carlebach (1925–1994). This second, more popular, more egalitarian neo-Hasidism has had a significant impact on the ritual, political, and social structures of American Jewry. Contemporary neo-Hasidism is mystical, progressive, and postmodern in its approach to sources; it proposes not a reconstruction of a lost Hasidic ideal but a renewal of Hasidism and mystical Judaism for the modern period. It is self-reflexive, its leading proponents standing at the juncture between academics and practitioners. And, as discussed below, nonduality is often of primary importance.

Neo-Hasidism is not confined to progressive American communities, however: the third source for nondual Judaism is traditional Hasidism itself. In Israel, "Ein Od Milvado" bumper stickers are common among Bratzlav Hasidim and the enthusiastic neo-Bratzlavers who, like many Krishna devotees, celebrate God's presence by constantly cultivating a state of joy and simplicity. Around the world, Chabad continues to teach the Tanya and its rigorous nondualist view, although, as is well known, this teaching has been often eclipsed in recent years by messianism. And the Carlebach community in Israel, more religiously and politically conservative than its counterparts in America, remains a potent force, particularly among *baalei tshuvah*, those "returning" to traditional Jewish practice.

Outside the realms of Hasidism and neo-Hasidism, there are two additional historical sources of contemporary nondual Judaism. One is the academic work of Gershom Scholem (1897–1982) and his many disciples. Through Scholem's vast work, Kabbalah became regarded for the first time as theologically serious, and the Kabbalah's theology of the Ein Sof and the *sefirot* entered academic parlance and, eventually, wider Jewish awareness. Scholem and his immediate successors, including Joseph Dan, Isaiah Tishby, Moshe Idel, Rachel Elior, Elliot Wolfson, and Yehuda Liebes, are avowedly nonreligious (at least in the traditional sense), but their work brought nondual Judaism to an academic and scholarly audience which otherwise would never have encountered it. This work continues today.

Fifth and finally, as we have already had occasion to describe, nondual Judaism has been nourished by many traditions outside of Judaism, particularly Vedanta, Buddhism, and the conglomeration of spiritual traditions known as the New Age. As we will see, nondual systems of thought were crucial in the development of this form of American spirituality. While the notion that "all is one" may seem like a cliché, it actually emerged historically, with influences including Advaita, Zen, Tibetan Buddhism, American transcendentalism, the Theosophical Society, "new thinking," the Vedanta Society, gurus of the 1960s, the psychedelic movement, and the human potential movement.[2] The Jewish Renewal movement and contemporary neo-Hasidism grew out of the 1960s, and reflect the ecumenical, experiential, experimental, spiritual, and social values of the times.

Today, most expositors of nondual Judaism bring together many of these five aspects. Rabbi Arthur Green, for example, is both a professor of Jewish thought and a Jewish theologian in his own right, and he has found inspiration in both traditional and mystical Judaism, as well as in the cosmopolitan spiritualities of the 1960s. Rabbi Michael Lerner has been nourished both by neo-Hasidic roots and by left-wing social activism. Rabbi David Cooper is a student of Reb Zalman who also spent ten years practicing Theravadan Buddhism and ten years as a Sufi practitioner.

As a student or friend of all of these teachers, I have a similarly hybrid background: I am an academic scholar of Kabbalah and Hasidism, but also someone whose soul is nourished by them; I keep Shabbat and kashrut in the traditional way, but am also a dedicated *vipassana* practitioner, as well as an activist on behalf of sexual and gender minorities; and I am at once a spiritual explorer and, as a legal scholar, someone accustomed to the rigors of philosophical argumentation. Like my teachers, I approach nondual Judaism as integrating the gifts of sense and soul, history and introspection, particular and universal.

Nondual Judaism's relationship to non-Jewish traditions, however, is often fraught with controversy. To some, any relationship with a non-Jewish source (presumably excluding East European *shtreimels*, cuisine, and music, not to mention Aristotelianism, ancient Near Eastern contract law, and Enlightenment philosophy) is problematic, and neo-Hasidim is simply dressing up Buddhism or Hinduism in Jewish clothing. The implicit narrative is of a Jewish spiritual seeker being entranced by "Eastern" ashrams and meditation, and then creating "Jewish" versions of these other traditions. Indeed, Reb Zalman himself has criticized some Jewish meditation as being "Buddhism in a *tallis*," and it is well-known that many leading Western Buddhist teachers are of Jewish origin.

In fact, however, the historical narratives of neo-Hasidic nondual Jewish leaders are quite different. Some, indeed, are seekers, finders, and returners. Others, such as Rabbi Aryeh Kaplan, were traditionalists concerned about Jews wandering "off the *derech*" and who promoted Jewish alternatives to 1960s spirituality. And some, like Reb Zalman and Rabbi Arthur Green, were knowledgeable "insiders" taking inspiration from how other traditions presented spiritual, experiential aspects of their religions. "I was very excited," Reb Zalman told me, "to find out how they were dealing with spirituality and the questions that Ramakrishna raised about how to deal with monism and dualism, and everything that he had to say really made a lot of sense to me." Green reported:

> I marveled at the way the Indian teachers coming to the West seemed to be ready to shed so much of their particularity. I remember meeting Satchitananda and realizing that he was not interested in making people Hindus or teaching them Sanskrit. He said, "Close your eyes and chant *om shantih om* with me, that's all you have to do—be present in the moment." But [in the Jewish community,] it was, "Keep *shabbos* and *kashrus* and fifteen years later we'll talk to you about mysticism." The Jewish way in was an arduous way in.

Satchitananda's method was no accident. Contemporary Vedanta, one of the primary sources of 1960s and New Age spirituality, was itself a "renewed" tradition. Vivekananda presented Vedanta for Western audiences, stripped of Hindu particularism, ritual requirements, and technical language, and deliberately positioned as a kind of post-religion religion. Christopher Isherwood, Aldous Huxley, and others translated Vedanta texts and teachings, adapting them for Western ears and concerns. In fact, by the time Vedanta encountered the 1960s, we may speak of a "neo-Vedanta" as much as a neo-Hasidism. Neo-Vedanta presented a popular, accessible form of mysticism, which emphasized the nondual core of Vedanta teaching, and which resonated with both contemplative and entheogenic experiences of the time.[3] Reb Zalman called it "Vedanta for export."

Nondual neo-Hasidism adapted this model. Where Kabbalah was obscure and text-centered, neo-Hasidism became experience-centered—like neo-Vedanta. Where Kabbalah insisted both on outward performance and inward intention (shell and kernel), neo-Hasidism emphasized the latter over the former—like neo-Vedanta. Where Kabbalah (and even Hasidism, for most of its history) was elitist, neo-Hasidism was populist—like neo-Vedanta. And where Kabbalah was particularist and even ethnocentric, neo-Hasidism was universalistic and ecumenical—like neo-Vedanta.

The embrace was not total, however. Today, neo-Hasidism regards engagement with the this-worldly as a kind of litmus test of right spirituality, often projecting a quietistic, monastic "Hinduism" to serve as a kind of foil—notwithstanding Vivekananda's intense social and political activism. Neo-Hasidic sources sometimes describe Judaism as "hot," theistic, and devotional, in contrast with a "cool," nontheistic, and contemplative Vedanta—notwithstanding Ramakrishna's insistence on devotion. ("Cry to the Lord with an intensely yearning heart and you will certainly see Him," he says at one point.[4]) And neo-Hasidism has never fully embraced acosmism—even though it is found in some Hasidic sources—again ascribing it to an imagined Hinduism, notwithstanding Ramakrishna's similarly "both-and" theological stance:

> Brahman is neither "this" nor "that"; It is neither the universe nor its living beings . . . What Brahman is cannot be described . . . This is the opinion of the *jnanis*, the followers of Vedanta philosophy. But the *bhaktas* [devotees] . . . don't think the world to be illusory, like a dream. They say that the universe is a manifestation of God's power and glory. God has created all these—sky, stars, moon, sun, mountains, ocean, men, animals. They constitute His glory. He is within us, in our hearts . . . The devotee of God wants to eat sugar, not to become sugar.[5]

So perhaps nondual Judaism resembles these other traditions more closely than we even suspect. Really, this should not be surprising. If one believes that all of us are gesturing toward the same ineffability, then it makes sense that the modes of gesture will resemble each other the closer to the Source one gets. Obviously, the external forms are quite different, as are the mystical experiences themselves, colored as they are by culture, notions of the self, and religious teaching. But nondual Judaism is by nature an integral Judaism, one which seeks to bring the world's contemplative, scientific, personal, and philosophical wisdom to the table and which seeks to touch all aspects of the self. In its progressive forms, the community of Israel to which it belongs is not merely those people born of Jewish mothers, but all those who are god-wrestlers, in every religious tradition. Yet as nondual *Judaism*, it stands for the proposition that there are some uniquely Jewish verses which may be contributed to the ongoing play of life. Paradoxically for a system which holds all to be God, it grows and evolves over time.

This is not, however, the end of the story.

NONDUAL MESSIANISM: INTEGRAL JUDAISM AND THE TRANSFORMATION OF CONSCIOUSNESS

Judaism is both a historical and an ahistorical religion. Ahistorically, our time is cyclical: the Sabbath comes every seven days, and our agriculturally timed cycle of holidays renews itself each year. Historically, though, our sense of time is linear. We tell stories of an ancient creation and hold hopes for a future redemption. We involve ourselves in history, in collective enterprises such as Zionism and individual ones such as righteous action on behalf of the less fortunate. For the Kabbalists, the cyclical and linear aspects of time represent the feminine and masculine aspects of Divinity, the power of Now and the trajectory of temporality.

The Ein Sof does not, in essence, evolve. But manifestation does, and with it our best efforts at gesturing toward the wholly inexpressible. So, while the fundamentalist imagines a divinely-written text expressing nondual philosophy in the language of war gods and judgment, such an imaginative enterprise denies the beauty, otherness, and genius of the biblical writers (or Writer). These were men (we presume) possessed of religious insight, and of categories of religious thought wholly different from our own, concerned with antinomies of purity and contamination, order and disorder, justice and anarchy, civilization and chaos. They saw in their sky god a great king who had ordered creation and who demanded an ordered society to reflect it. They made a pact with this king, who would lead them in war and sustain them in life if they would maintain his commandments. Can we not appreciate the religious genius of these ancestors, rather than demolish it so that it fits our own theology? Personally, I find it much more uplifting to let this religious genius speak on its own terms than try to fit it into mine.

In the beginning, our ancestors were animists, and polytheists. They believed in power gods, nature spirits, warrior deities, fertility goddesses. Eventually, some came to venerate one sky god above all others, insisting that all the Divine energies in the world were from a single source alone. Later, philosophical thinking refined these notions of this single source, away from an anthropomorphic deity and toward an impersonal Oneness. Mystics experienced the One in love, and in so doing resacralized the whole world as the veiling and unveiling of the Beloved. Everything became seen as the costume of God. When we gaze into the mirror of the Infinite, we cannot help but project the contents of our minds onto It.

Yet if we remain stuck at an adolescent understanding of Divinity, then we will naturally abandon the concept of God as we progress beyond adolescence. As Moses Cordovero wrote:

> Now, the poor person thinks that God is an old man, as it is written, "the ancient of days sits"; and he has white hair because he is old, as it is written, "the hair of his head like clean wool"; and he sits on a great wooden throne, glittering with sparks, as it is written, "his throne was fire"; and that his appearance is like fire, as it is written, "For YHVH your God is consuming fire." And the result of all these images, which the fool thinks about until he corporealizes God, is that he falls into some trap, and abandons his faith . . . But the wise, enlightened person knows God's unity, and his essence that is completely devoid of material boundaries . . . And from this he will add strength to his awe . . . and a great love in his soul.[6]

Compare Cordovero's words to these of Vivekananda:

> It is good to be born into a church, but it is bad to die there. It is good to be born a child, but bad to remain a child. Churches, ceremonies, and symbols are good for children, but when the child is grown, he must burst the church or himself. We must not remain children forever.[7]

These are strong words, in both cases. They both suggest that traditional notions of God are not merely partial but immature, and eventually destructive: at some point, one must leave behind either the church or one's dignity.

What Cordovero feared has indeed come to pass. Today, as we observed in chapter 3, not just a few shrill neo-atheists but a seeming majority of Western elites has come to regard religion as childish, dangerous, or worse. Yet such critiques are often reacting to an adolescent form of religious expression and supposing that there is no more advanced alternative. Of course, the mythic religionist really believes the substance of her tradition's tales. But religion has always had its elite and popular forms, and it is foolish to assume one is reducible to the other. Bashing "religion" because of the excesses of fundamentalists is like rejecting "music" because of the vapidity of a teen idol.

But let us take a further step, and observe that our God-concepts evolve not only as we mature individually, but as we mature collectively as well. Indeed, there seems to be a provocative directionality to the evolution of our God-concepts across cultures: "God" is a concept that evolves by disappearing. Primitive gods on most continents were very personal, very present, and represented in images. Beginning with monotheism in the West, God began to take on a new, less visible form: One God, whose humanlike image cannot be represented. Philosophy pushed the One even further away, to an unchanging, formless perfection—closer to the One Being of Vedanta and Buddhism in the East, which also supplanted a rich pantheon of personal deities, or transplanted them into a new cosmology or theology. Within the last five hundred years, even the concept of the One has been eclipsed by the lack of God altogether. And within the last two hundred years, the joining of East and West in some philosophical and spiritual circles has spread the doctrine of monism. As Rabbi Zalman Schachter-Shalomi has said, we have moved past the stage of deism (which he associates with *ein aroch*, there is no measurement to God) and even past theism (*ein zulatecha*, there is no God besides You), and into monism (*efes biltecha*, there is nothing besides You). Does this evolution have a meaning?

If we assume that the One is ultimately unknowable, these developments are welcome indeed. The gods are idols. Concepts of "God" are idols. Even the "belief in God" is a concept. So the most accurate picture we can have of God is no picture at all, which is precisely what many people today hold. Yet the less clear the picture, the further the distance feels. A philosophical Jew who believes in the One is likely to have a less rich emotional-religious life than the pious Jew who prays to the God of Abraham, or the Catholic who addresses the Virgin. This is the critical difference between atheism and monism: that for monists, God is right here, now, in the fingers typing these words, the plants on my desk, the thoughts being sensed by the mind. God is bathing me in love, if I admit it.

And so we are seeing a turn to spiritual practices (or to more self-aware artistic or cultural ones) on the part of people in the West for whom "God" has ceased to be a tenable concept. Of course, most Westerners are still quite happy with mythic religion, thank you very much, while many others are happy with egotism. But there are some who are deeply engaged with the Good, be it aesthetic or intellectual or ethical, and who are rediscovering God, but without the concept of God. Ironically, while many "spiritual" people define themselves in explicit opposition to God, they are in fact, closer to God than most of the religious.

So "God" has reappeared, divested even of the word. What is the significance of this development, the appearance of a nondual God so refined it is almost transparent, in the context of the Jewish notion of history?

One of Judaism's central historical tenets is the belief in a messiah, a redeemer who in some future time will change, or even end, history. Jewish beliefs about the messiah have themselves evolved over time. Initially, the messiah was seen as a purely military/political leader who would bring independence back to Judea. Later, the messiah became seen as a cosmic figure who would change the entire nature of reality.

Likely under the influence of Christianity, the messiah was sometimes seen as semi-divine, even someone who would atone for the sins of Israel. Because Jewish law is largely silent on matters of belief, all of these views have held sway at one time or another.

As is well known, messianic fervor has continued unabated to this day. Many nondual Hasidim today believe that the last Lubavitcher Rebbe will somehow return from "apparent" death to unite all the world. Many Christians believe that the rapture will take place within the century. And many others believe that the year 2012 will usher in a new era for humanity.[8]

In contrast to such supernatural accounts of messianism, there has been a longstanding Jewish tradition to regard the messianic age as one of evolving consciousness rather than revolutionary history. Like the doctrines of nonduality, this view is most closely associated with the Hasidic movement, which, in Gershom Scholem's words, "neutralized" the Jewish messianic element (which had risen to a fever pitch in the Sabbatean heresy, during which one-third of European Jews believed the Messiah had arrived) by claiming that the messianic "world to come" could be experienced here and now, in moments of spiritual ecstasy. That is to say, "There is no Messiah, and You're It," in the words of the contemporary writer Rabbi Robert Levine.[9]

This redefinition of messianism, which has its roots in older Kabbalistic sources, largely de-historicizes our concepts of a messianic age: messianism becomes more a state of mind than anything else. But not entirely. There is also the view, expressed in the eighteenth-century Kabbalah of Rabbi Moshe Chaim Luzzatto (Ramchal), reflected in that of the Baal Shem Tov, and refined in the work of the twentieth-century Rabbi Abraham Isaac Kook, that brings ahistorical and historical messianisms together. The messianic age, these sources suggest, is a time at which the consciousness that all is God will fill the earth. And it is a time which will come gradually, as more and more people begin to transcend the illusions of the separate self and realize the truth of their natures. The contemporary Kabbalist Rabbi David Friedman writes, "According to Luzzatto, the messianic era (the 'days of Messiah') is the culmination of one huge evolutionary learning process which was conceived with the Universe, born with the emergence of

Life, and becomes mature when Humanity easily achieves Divine Inspiration, Ruach Hakodesh."[10]

At its apogee, such a change in consciousness becomes an apotheosis, not through transfiguration but by an understanding of the divine state we inhabit already. This is how a nondualist rereads the prophet Joel: "And it shall come to pass afterwards, that I will pour out my Spirit upon all flesh; and your sons and your daughters shall prophesy. Your old men shall dream dreams, your young men shall see visions"[11] And it is how one may understand the epistle of the Baal Shem Tov, in which the Besht is told that the messiah will come "when your teachings become publicized and revealed to the world, and your wellsprings have overflowed to the outside . . . so that others, too, will be able to perform mystical unifications and ascents of the soul like you."[12]

Notice too the language of "the wellsprings of your teachings are spread out" around the world. Naturally, the eighteenth-century rabbi despaired at this news: how distant it must have seemed to him! Yet from a nondual, pluralistic perspective, we may understand it somewhat differently. The "wellsprings" of the Besht's teachings—that would be their source, not their final expression. And that source? That *alzt is Gott*, all is God, all is One, separation is illusion. And this source is indeed found throughout the world.

The messianic age being one of nonduality is also the message of the late Lubavitcher Rebbe in his discourse *On the Essence of Chassidus*. There, he says that

> The Essence of Messiah is Yechidah ("Oneness"), which is the essence of the soul that is above differentiation, as its name implies . . . Just as Yechidah is the essential nature of every soul, so too of the soul of all of the Chain of Being, in which Yechidah (the aspect of Messiah) is the essence of the core of the life force beyond any formal definition . . . [W]hen the aspect of Yechidah will flow through all the worlds, they will live in essence, and totally perfect and complete.[13]

The essence of messianism, then, is not a transformation of manifestation but a realization of essence. Yechidah of the world, of the messianic age, is when Oneness is manifest.[14] The messiah (*moshiach*) enables us to see that all is extension (*nimshach*) of the Ein Sof, not separation.

Imagine a world in which everyone understood that all of us were God. Not one in which each person thought he or she was God alone—that would be disaster. But one in which the nonduality of Being was understood, in some form or fashion, by all human beings. This would be an entirely different world from the one we now inhabit, free of the conflicts and crises, petty and grotesque, which fill our moment. And imagine what it would be like, right now, to believe that, as Ramana Maharshi has said, "civilization . . . will finally resolve itself—as all others—in the Realization of the Self."[15]

Such a time is, of course, far off. But this conception of the historical evolution of consciousness helps contextualize, explain, and enliven the development of religious consciousness from its most primitive to its most refined stages. Religious consciousness evolves, as Spirit comes to know itself in history (Hegel). We move through different stages of individual and communal religious consciousness, each at our own rates, according to a myriad of circumstances. But we move toward one nonsupernatural Omega point (Teilhard de Chardin): the knowledge—the intimate knowledge—that all is One.

Now, in our postmodern information age, the noosphere (Teilhard de Chardin again) is indeed upon us. Already, thanks to global information technology, the hidden mystical teachings of the world's religious traditions are accessible to everyone, as are the great wealth of scientific, cultural, philosophical, and artistic works from the better part of humanity. As Ken Wilber has written, we can now, for the first time in history, "put it all on the table"—the "sum total of human knowledge . . . the knowledge, experience, wisdom, and reflections of all major human civilizations."[16] But even this is just the beginning. The internet, nanotechnology, and wearable computers are but the initial stages of a noetic revolution in which nonmaterial information may displace material matter as the ultimate future of the body. Most probably, we are only a few decades away from being able to upload our minds onto renewable data media. Is this the "immortality of the soul" of which some religions once spoke? What is the meaning of humanity if we are able to transcend the limits of matter? And more proximately, what is the significance of this new knowledge, accessible all over the world—including, for our purposes, the highest truth (singular!) of so many spiritual traditions, that there is really no one either reading or writing these words?

The messianic age is already unfolding, in this interpretation, and the gradual emergence and dissemination of nonduality is among its signal phenomena. The wellsprings of the Baal Shem Tov's teachings have indeed spread out throughout the world; they are already flowing on every continent and in every city with unrestricted access to the internet.

As Wilber has found, the realization of nonduality is both the beginning and the end of the dance of multiplicity, as well as the "omega point," of diverse spiritual and religious traditions. More than that: as readers of Wilber know well, the growth of religious consciousness from archaic to magic to mythic to rational, pluralistic, and integral parallels the development of human psychology, self-identity, faith, values, and consciousness itself. These congruities appear in numerous developmental models, including those of Jean Piaget;[17] Robert Kegan, who proposes five stages or "orders" in cognitive development;[18] Susanne Cook-Greuter, who traces the development of ego;[19] James Fowler, who identifies "stages of faith" in the religious life;[20] and Lawrence Kohlberg;[21] as well as human development systems such as "Spiral Dynamics"[22] and others. Based on these models and associated cross-cultural research, Wilber maintains that the general progression from stages of conventional consciousness to successive realms of unconventional consciousness (gross/nature mysticism to subtle/deity mysticism to causal/formless mysticism to nondual/both emptiness and form) mirrors the progressions of cultural systems, social structures, even physical structures. For Wilber, this progression can be represented as mineral > vegetable > animal > impersonal > personal > spiritual; for the Hasidim, it is *domem > tzomeach > chai > medaber*—inanimate, vegetable, animal, speech.

In other words, what Luzzatto and the Baal Shem Tov understood to be the messianic age is, for Wilber, the integral age at which emptiness and form, the vast manifestation of sociocultural phenomena and the emptiness that fills them all, are understood to be nondual in nature— and on all the different lines and levels of human development. To put things in perspective, Wilber optimistically projects that only about one half of one percent of people currently alive today hold this sort of view. But understood as a *telos*, the slow expansion of this view tells us something important about the arising of emptiness and then, later, nondual consciousness within Jewish and other cultural histories. Nonduality is a stage along the path—perhaps, as it seems logically to be, the fully inclusive, terminal one. As with other developmental projects, such as Hegel's, who knows if Wilber's system truly embraces all. But it does at least endeavor to embrace all that we know right now.

Wilber's methodology also helps shed light on how nondual Judaism relates to other Judaisms. For Wilber, as for most contemporary academic scholars of mysticism and religious experience, there is no experience apart from interpretation. This is so not merely because mystics must interpret their experiences according to the language and culture they know, but because those linguistic and cultural structures condition the nature of the experience itself. Perhaps "I" will "have" a "vision" of "angels," but all of the quoted terms are cultural constructions. The "myth of the given" (as discussed in chapter 1) is indeed just that—a myth, a kind of simplistic false consciousness. Indeed, one refutation of the myth is the nondual truth itself, which denies that "you" are "having" an "experience" at all.

But the structural/historical conditioning of experience is unavoidable, so much so that it makes little sense to speak of "experience" or "God" or "mysticism" apart from the stages in which such experience is interpreted. Put simply, God looks different depending on where you stand. From what Wilber (following the philosopher Jean Gebser) calls the magical stage, God looks like the provider who answers all of your needs. From the mythic stage, God—as understood in your faith tradition exclusively—is the sole source of salvation, and everyone who doesn't believe in Him is doomed. From the mental-rational stage, God is a moral principle and the Bible a useful, though flawed, teacher of ethical truths. From the pluralistic stage, God is love, expressed in a thousand ways by a thousand religions, all deserving of respect. And from the various integral stages, God is variously Nothing, and all of the above.

Experiences of all types are available to all kinds of people. But the same experience will be immediately contextualized and interpreted according not only to one's religious/spiritual/scientific tradition but also one's "stage" of religious development. Perhaps an experience of light is a spirit, or an angel, or the Agent Intellect, or an opening to the Ein Sof—all interpretations of luminous internal light found within Jewish mystical sources. Perhaps it is merely an experience, which opens the soul but which, in and of itself, is no closer to the Ein Sof than waiting in line at the post office. The point is not that there is a True God perceived in these partial ways; rather, these partial ways define what is meant by "God." A nondual rereading of a text from the mythic stage of human development is important homiletically, but the fact that the mythic-stage text has a different idea of God is really no big deal. Expecting it to be otherwise would be like expecting that same text to talk about germ theory or poststructuralism. Thought evolves.

The nondual embrace can be seen in this light as a fulfillment of the dear hopes of the mystics and the speculations of the philosophers. This is especially so because, unlike many messianisms, nondualism is not triumphalistic. It does not exclude other traditions and does not depict "earlier" stage religious experiences as variously imperfect approximations of this one true one. No patronizing allegorization of myth and narrative. No reductive confusion of the prerational with the transrational. Neither the offensively naive privileging of mythic-stage gender roles, nor the erasure of mythic power in the attempt at egalitarianism. Utopian ideal? Exactly—and that is exactly the function of the messianic urge, here reconfigured away from nationalism, triumphalism, and supernaturalism, and toward the dawning of realization on earth. Will everyone be Jewish in the messianic age? Will a magical chariot descend from the sky? Obviously not—not in this picture anyway. Rather, the nondual wellsprings of the Baal Shem Tov's teachings will water a thousand plants in Eden, a biodiversity of spirit which, as in ecology, nourishes the whole by supporting difference. Consciousness will shift until such a point at which even the lion may lie down with the lamb.

Of course, spiritual consciousness is not the only movement of human thought that is arising in our times. Sometimes it seems as though we are in a race between the forces of growing awareness of interdependence on the one hand, and an ever more sophisticated technology of destruction, suffering, and death on the other. All times in human history have given rise to apocalyptic speculation, but only in our own has the possibility of global environmental devastation, or warfare, been a real one.

In this light, perhaps the evolution toward nondual messianic consciousness is of more immediate import than would first appear. For it is the *yetzer hara*, the selfish inclination, the ego that attempts furiously to defend the nonexistent, which is the cause of so much of this opposing movement in human evolution. The need for more, for dominance, for hierarchy and control—all of these stem from the ego's desperate attempt to make the self whole. The task is impossible, for the self does not exist at all. But the ego—particularly the male ego—tries nonetheless, subjugating others, steeling itself to suffering, and striving for dominance. Of course, the ego is natural; we share these drives with other animals, and without the *yetzer hara*, says the Talmud, no houses would be built and no roads paved. Fair enough; but today we have too many houses and too many roads. Now is a time for less ego, less sense of separation, and less of the resultant need to consume and oppress. Our species has only had a few thousand years in which to transcend the most basic of our animal natures—a blink of an eye, in biological time. But if we are to survive beyond that short span of years, the theoretical evolution which Wilber and others describe, and which fulfill so elegantly the prophecies of the Jewish sages, must be translated into reality.

This is the vision with which we conclude the "theoretical" part of this book: an integral Judaism that "transcends and includes" (Wilber again) as much as possible: the different stages of Judaism, reflected in the Jewish community today, with no triumphalist narrative or patronizing claim that one form is intrinsically superior to others; the different religions of the world, again without a triumphalist hierarchy; and different modes of understanding, psychological/spiritual, cognitive/scientific, social/economic and cultural/artistic. And it is one which contributes to the arising of more compassion, and more peace, throughout the world.

Imagine the great *shabbos* that could unfold if we really believed that all concepts are masks. Our certainties and pronouncements would be interrupted by little notes of uncertainty, of unknowing, of remembering that the mystery lies beyond our grasp and that even sacred totems are only best efforts. Nonduality sits as one perspective among many, a bit more aware of itself than some others, but ultimately as powerless as all of them to comprehend what cannot be spoken. We return, perhaps unexpectedly, to a state of wonder—wonder both at the One and at the Many. As Heschel wrote, "The greatest hindrance to knowledge is our adjustment to conventional notions, to mental clichés. Wonder or radical amazement, the state of maladjustment to words and notions, is therefore a prerequisite for an authentic awareness of what is."[23]

Speedily, in our days . . .

Part Two

ARETZ: PRACTICE

6

MIND: SEEKING AND STOPPING SEEKING

Religious truths need verification by everyone. To see God is the one goal.
—VIVEKANANDA[1]

I came to realize clearly that mind is no other than mountains, rivers, and the great wide earth, the sun and the moon and the stars.
—DOGEN[2]

When one contemplates things, everything is revealed as one.
—ZOHAR[3]

The essential facts of nonduality, and of the nondual Jewish God, Torah, and Israel, are, in a sense, the map. The coming chapters are the territory.

It is difficult to write about spiritual practice without sounding like the author of a cookbook, but there is no alternative; a religion of dogmas may be fulfilled entirely secondhand, but mysticism requires the experiential. "Without feeling, the thought of unity is just imagination," says R. Aharon of Staroselye.[4] Imagine, to suggest a different metaphor, if one only viewed maps of the world, and never left home; such would be the incompleteness of *nishmah*, "we will understand" without *na'aseh*, "we will do." Indeed, as the verse from Exodus suggests, experience may generate theology, rather than flow from it; Scholem called Hasidic panentheism "not the product of some theory or other, not even of a Kabbalistic doctrine, but of direct, spontaneous religious experience."[5]

As we turn, then, to practice, it is worth remembering a certain paradoxical aspect of nondual spirituality. There is great truth to the maxim that the only thing preventing enlightenment is searching for it. If it is the case that all is one, or in Jewish language that all is God, then surely the only "obstacle" to realization is the erroneous belief that it's not already here, now. It's not that we aren't enlightened; it's that we think we aren't. Really, since God is reading these words right now, enlightenment is more about losing knowledge—specifically, that of self and other, and of the "God" out there in the world—than gaining it. For this reason, many nondualists, especially in the contemporary period, shy away from any notion of spiritual practice or progress.[6] The very notion implies a fallacy: that at some later date, under the right circumstances, you'll be more a part of the Infinite than you are right now. For these teachers, surrender is the only true practice. This is it, and that is that.

R. Aharon of Staroselye, like most Jewish nondualists, has a different view. Yes, from God's point of view, everything is God, the world doesn't truly exist, and there is nothing wrong with anything, including our own limited and confused points of view. But from those limited points of view, a great deal seems to be wrong. We suffer, we cause harm to others, and our hearts are subject to the vicissitudes of life as a human being. Of course, we also rejoice, and love, and build; it's not that human life is *purely* suffering. (Even the Buddha never said that; he said only that suffering exists, not that life "is" suffering.) But, no matter how often some nondualists repeat the assertion that there is nowhere to go and nothing to change—a principle to which we will return at the end of this chapter—our human minds experience separation, and thus alienation, all the time.

For that reason, practice, *avodah*, spiritual work, remains necessary, even though it is, in a sense, a conscious descent into delusion: *Avodah* involves the relative world in order to shake the mind free of it. As the Taoist philosopher Wei Wu Wei said, "Teaching can only be given via a series of untruths diminishing in inveracity in ratio to the pupil's apprehension of the falsity of what he is being taught."[7] This is also the meaning of R. Nachman's parable of the tainted grain. In that story, all the subjects of the king, save one, eat tainted grain and go mad. Since there is no way to communicate with them, the king and his sane subject eat the grain as well, but place a mark upon themselves, to remember they once were sane. That way, they can enter into the world of the deluded in order to liberate them.[8] So too does spirituality immerse us in dualism—in order to pull us free of it.

The next three chapters are the practical reflections of the previous three: mind, heart, and body—or thought, feeling, and action—are interiorizations of God, Torah, and Israel; creation, revelation, and redemption; *briyah*, *yetzirah*, and *asiyah*. For the mind, R. Aharon prescribes contemplation of God's unity, immanence, and omnipresence. For the heart, R. Aharon emphasizes ecstatic prayer, which provides the experience of what contemplation shows to be true. And for the body, R. Aharon teaches the path of the *mitzvot*, which makes the reality of God manifest precisely in the material world that we tend to regard as most separate from it. In R. Aharon's terminology, these are called *hitbonnenut* (contemplation), *hitpa'alut halev* (ecstasy of the heart) and *poel mamash* (actions/Torah and *mitzvot*),[9] corresponding to *mochin* (mind), *middot* (attributes of heart), and *guf* (body),[10] *haskalah v'havanah* (enlightenment and understanding), *hitpa'alut hamiddot* (purification of attributes), and *kiyum hama'aseh* (actual fulfillment);[11] *bittul* of intellect, emotions, and substance;[12] and the three horizontal layers of the *sefirot*: *chochmah, binah, da'at* (mind); *hesed, gevurah, tiferet* (heart); and *netzach, hod, yesod* (body).[13] Homiletically, these three facets of practice are mapped onto Deuteronomy 4:39: "Know this day, and lay it upon your heart, that YHVH is God in heaven above and upon the earth beneath; there is nothing else." Contemplation is the knowing, love and ecstasy are the laying upon the heart, and actions are the extension of God from heaven above to earth beneath.

Here it is all on one chart:

	MIND	HEART	BODY
ASPECT	God	Torah	Israel
GOD	Ein Sof	YHVH	*Shechinah*
STAGE	Creation	Revelation	Redemption
RELATION	I-I	I-You	I-It
WORLD	Briyah	Yetzirah	Asiyah
IN NONDUAL JUDAISM	Nonduality	Jewish religion	Community, history
IN THE SELF	Mind (*mochin*)	Heart (*middot*)	Body (*guf*)
IN THE *SEFIROT*	Chochmah, Binah, Da'at/Keter	Hesed, Gevurah, Tiferet	Netzach, Hod, Yesod
DEUT. 4:39	Know this day	Lay it on your heart	There is nothing else
ACTIVITIES (HEB.)	*Hitbonnenut*	*Hitpa'alut Halev*	*Po'vel Mamash*
ACTIVITIES (ENG.)	Contemplation	Ecstatic prayer	Actions/*mitzvot*
RESULTS/PRACTICAL	Knowledge	Experience	Manifestation
RESULTS/PERSONAL	Enlightenment	Purification of heart	Action in world
VEDANTA	Wisdom/*jnana*	Devotion/*bhakti*	Action/*karma*
THERAVADA BUDDHISM	Wisdom/*pañña*	Concentration/ *samadhi*	Virtue/*sila*

MAHAYANA BUDDHISM	Wisdom	Compassion	Action
WESTERN LIBERALISM	Philosophy	Religion	Politics/activism

The next three chapters provide a contemporary rendition of these three elements. The present chapter discusses meditation: contemplation, mindfulness, and the nondual practice of "just this," or nondistracted, non-meditation. The next, chapter 7, focuses on ecstatic prayer and other Jewish heart practices. And chapter 8 discusses the embodied *mitzvot* of kashrut and Shabbat construed as nondual spiritual practices. Of course, all three are interrelated.[14] Doing *mitzvot* in the world leads to *bittul ha-yesh*. Contemplation leads to an upwelling of love and a mystical experience of its own. And purification of the heart leads to a mandate for action in the world.

If religion consists of outward forms of piety, and spirituality inward experience, then nondual spiritual practice transcends and includes them both. We are not here searching for new and novel ways to get high; those are easy to find. Nor are we trying to rationalize a system of dogma and code. Rather, the purpose of practice is to bring wisdom and love to every moment, be it profound or profane. Of necessity, its motion will be of *ratzo v'shov*, running and returning between expanded mind and contracted mind, God's point of view and our own. Indeed, the hallmark of this practice will be an inclusion of both perspectives as aspects of the Divine. It will not make every moment a happy one, but it can bring about a clarity, an acceptance, and an intimacy which, for me, has long been the penumbra of God.

MEDITATION: FOUR WAYS OF NOT LOOKING AT A BLACKBIRD
Contemplation

The primary form of traditional nondual Jewish meditation is *hitbonnenut*, contemplation: the focusing of the mind on a single idea or teaching. This meditative technique differs from methods more commonly practiced today (discussed in the next section) in that it uses cognitive content to "fill" the mind, rather than using an object of attention to "empty" the mind. The net result is the same: distracting thoughts are quieted, and the "static" is turned down. But contemplation is quite different from mindfulness. Whereas mindfulness yields direct observation of experiential facts, contemplation has an image or idea as its focus. This process tends to condition a certain result. If you visualize the Virgin Mary, for example, you're likely to have a mental experience of the Virgin Mary. For this reason, many meditators prefer "transparent" mindfulness to contemplation.

Yet contemplation has its place in all the world's inner traditions, not just Judaism. Theravadan Buddhists contemplate aspects of the dharma. Christian mystics contemplate the mystery of the Trinity, or the Passion of Christ. Mahayana and Vajrayana Buddhists visualize bodhisattvas and deities. Some Islamic mystics contemplate the unity of God. In these and other traditions, contemplation deepens wisdom by allowing the mind truly to investigate the meaning of core religious ideas. Contemplation, after all, is not just thinking about something. It requires preparation: seclusion, solitude, quiet, and intention. The eyes are generally closed, and the body relaxed for some period of time. Distracting thoughts are dropped, rather than followed. Once some degree of inner quiet is attained, the subject of contemplation is introduced—perhaps *ein od milvado* or *memaleh kol almin*, to choose two Hasidic favorites. Over a period of minutes or hours, the experience will deepen, as the implications of these phrases are realized on an intuitive level and insights fly like sparks. Sometimes, rational or logical thought will emerge, which is fine, so long as the mind is disciplined and not flying off in multiple directions. Sometimes it may seem like a deep well of creativity has just been tapped and is overflowing with intellectual, emotional, artistic, and spiritual waters.

Eventually, as the mind becomes one with the object of contemplation, there may be a sense of dissociation from the world; as the founder of Chabad Hasidism, the Rabbi Schneur Zalman of Liadi, describes:

> The whole corporeal world and all the corporeal things in it are complete nullity and nothing at all . . . The true *avodah* is to divest one's mind, one's heart from all corporeality.[15]

This is especially likely when a nondual source such as *ein od milvado* has been utilized. As a bumper sticker, this phrase is simply an idea. But when the idea truly penetrates the mind, the mind is not the same.

Rabbi DovBer Pinson, a contemporary Chabad rabbi based in Brooklyn, teaches contemplation in the traditional Hasidic mode. In his book *Toward the Infinite*, he describes a three-stage process of contemplation of *bittul ha-yesh*, or "how all the physical pleasures pursued are in reality imaginary, void, and devoid of any genuine content, and all that truly exists is Oneness."[16] According to Pinson,

> the first stage involves thinking through the subject until it becomes illuminated within the mind. After this stage you will begin to feel the energy of the thought that you have been contemplating; this is the inner energy of the subject. Finally you will feel the transcendent quality of the subject.[17]

Eventually, Pinson writes, "through continued meditation over a period of time a person's everyday rational, mundane consciousness is transformed into thinking, experiencing, and feeling the energy of the infinite that sustains and imbues all existence."[18] In the words of the Tanya:

> When the intellect of the rational soul contemplates and immerses deeply in the greatness of God—how God fills all worlds and surrounds all worlds, in whose presence everything is considered as nothing—there is born and awakened in the mind a feeling of awe for the transcendent. And his thought is to fear, and be humble before, this blessed greatness, which has no end or limit, and fear of God in his heart. Then his heart will be afire with an intense love, like burning coals, with desire, longing, and a passionate soul, for the greatness of the blessed *Ein Sof*. This is yearning of the soul.[19]

The eighteenth-century philosopher Solomon Maimon described Hasidic meditation (disapprovingly) this way:

> Their worship consisted in a voluntary elevation above the body, that is, in abstracting their thoughts from all things except God, even from the individual self, and in union with God . . . they became so absorbed in the idea of the divine perfection, that they

lost the idea of everything else, even of their own body, which became in this state wholly devoid of feeling.[20]

With these basic instructions, it is not difficult to take up contemplation as a spiritual practice. Simply select a phrase to contemplate, perhaps reflecting on a particular aspect—and stay focused. The exact words may yield fruit. For example, in contemplating the Shema, one might consider Rabbi Shmuel Schneersohn's observation that the Shema uses the word *echad* rather than *yachid* "to bring closer to the intellect how the world and all that fills it are null in relation to the light of the Ein Sof, may he be blessed."[21] Or the phrase in general may mysteriously sink into one's consciousness in a union of the Knower, the Knowing, and the Known.

It is possible to adapt contemplation to our hectic age by contemplating a phrase right in the midst of our daily activities. Of course, this is not as deep a practice as formal contemplation, but, if you lead a busy life of *ratzo v'shov*, contemplating short "reminders" can break the circuits of *yesh* and allow a brief recollection of *ayin*. Here's how you can do it. First, notice that you're caught in egoic thinking, or holding on to something. Second, pause; take a breath; relax; don't judge, or evaluate; most important, don't decide whether or not you want to do the practice—if you wanted to do it, you wouldn't be stuck. Then, from that place of stillness, bring to mind one of the short phrases from the list below and let it sink in—you may have to say it a few times (slowly!). Try to do this without any expectation of any particular result. Don't try to re-create some past state or experience; just let go anew of absolutely everything that comes and goes—that's *bittul ha'yesh*, the nullification of the sense of there being something solid to hold on to. What's left over? Well, that I leave to you to find out. Here are some of the phrases that I have found work well in this practice, although of course, you should also use your own:

Everything happens as it must, not as it should.
God does not exist; God is existence itself.
The spiritual journey is the strangest one. Each step is the destination.

Stop looking somewhere else for God.

Love and let go.

Ein od Milvado.

(For these two, insert whatever you're seeing, or thinking about,
     or having trouble with:)

_____ is not a flaw in the system.

_____ is a flavor of God.

The true light lies within.

God's name is "Is."

 If there's no self, what is there?

Shiviti Adonai L'Negdi Tamid.

This moment's not so bad, is it? ("Yoga for pessimists.")

What you really want is already here.

Well, it all comes down to this.

Duality and nonduality are the ultimate nonduality.

Arranging conditions so that we will be happy, is not the way to
     happiness.

Prioritize the holy.

Memaleh kol Almin: God fills all the worlds.

Cultivate stillness.

Everything is changing.

Science calls it "It." Religion calls it "You." Mysticism calls it "I."

Every time I think I've "got it!" I'm getting the same thing.

The present never ends.

There is nothing under your control—least of all the part that
     thinks it's doing the controlling.

Look at what's in front of you the way you look into someone's eyes.

The best part is when we get beyond reasons for loving.

Love is truth as seen by the heart.

I am always here.

Is it now? Is it "is"?

The only thing better than an open mind is an empty one.

These miniature contemplations work by reminding us precisely
what we aren't interested in hearing. Spiritual practice is easy and un-
necessary when you're already at peace with the world. It's precisely

when you don't want to do it that *avodah* is necessary. It's not that any of these pithy phrases are The Answer that will end all striving. Rather, they're short reminders of what you may once have known, but have since forgotten, and subsequently forgot that you have forgotten. "What matters most," Goethe said, "should never be at the mercy of what matters least." And yet, this is how we live our lives: miracles incarnate, we fret over mortgages and missed trains. These contemporary contemplations are not exactly what the Chabad elders prescribed, but then again, the way we live would astonish them.

A final form of contemplation, similarly accessible in the midst of worldly life, is to contemplate an external object with focused attention on its "empty," or wholly dependent, nature—what Thich Nhat Hanh calls "interbeing." In one famous passage from *Peace Is Every Step*, he describes it this way:

> If you are a poet, you will see clearly that there is a cloud floating in this sheet of paper. Without a cloud, there will be no rain; without rain, the trees cannot grow; and without trees, we cannot make paper . . . If we look into this sheet of paper even more deeply, we can see the sunshine in it. Without sunshine, the forest cannot grow . . . And if we continue to look, we can see the logger who cut the tree and brought it to the mill to be transformed into paper . . . We cannot point out one thing that is not here—time, space, the earth, the rain, the minerals in the soil, the sunshine, the cloud, the river, the heat . . . As thin as this sheet of paper is, it contains everything in the universe in it.[22]

Contemplation of a text, image, or a piece of paper may seem more intellectual, more cognitive, than most meditation practiced today, but perhaps that is a good thing. These days, many spiritual communities are deeply anti-intellectual, no doubt motivated by the hyper-intellectualism of the professional world and the academy, and, in the Jewish case, the text-fetishism, rationalism, and fear of mysticism found in many religious establishments. Frequently, however, spiritual communities move too far in the opposite direction. Contemplation can be a welcome integration, utilizing as it does the powers of the intellect and the inspiration of the heart.

Insight Meditation: Seeing Mind as a Phenomenon

If contemplation, which fills the mind with focused thought, is the main traditional nondual Jewish meditation practice, then various forms of "emptying" meditation, largely derived from Buddhist and Hindu sources, are the main contemporary ones. Some of these forms of meditation have become so universal, and so extrapolated from their initial contexts, that one hesitates to ascribe them to any particular tradition at all, and indeed, many Jewish meditation teachers omit this lineage, afraid that it might alienate potential students. However, as a personal matter, I prefer to be clear about sources, for reasons of intellectual honesty and out of respect for a tradition which, unlike the Jewish one, has had meditation at its center for over 2,500 years. Judaism is greatly enriched by its contact with such traditions; they have made a science of mind, and, in some traditions, regard the realization of non-self and nonduality as the paramount goal. For these reasons, I see no reason to hide the lineages of these meditation practices, and, on the contrary, have spent many months on *vipassana* (insight) meditation retreats as a primary part of my own spiritual path.

Having said that, because many handbooks on these forms of meditation have already been written (some are listed in the bibliography), my objective in this book will be to identify how they relate to nonduality and how they may be situated into a nondual Jewish framework specifically. We will look at three such practices: insight meditation from the Theravada Buddhist tradition, nondual inquiry from Vedanta, and "non-distracted, non-meditation" from the Tibetan tradition.

The first of these is insight meditation, or *vipassana*, widely taught in America in Buddhist centers, Jewish centers, community centers, hospitals, schools, and prisons. Insight meditation produces at least two significant consequences for the nondual Jewish path. First, I sometimes think of insight meditation as a form of "upgrading the mind." Normally, our minds are tugged out of themselves by all sorts of stimuli, which we either want to hold on to, or try to push away. As we saw earlier, this is surely the result of evolution: if we didn't feel a sense of insufficiency with what is, we wouldn't eat or reproduce, and if we didn't cringe from the unpleasant, we wouldn't run away from predators. But it is possible to transcend this aspect of our natures. By coming to see the impermanence, unreliability, and essential unreality of all phenomena, a contrary movement arises, a warm detachment from conditioned formations, and a relinquishment of the forces of greed, hatred, and delusion. Desire arises, but it's just not as urgent as it was.

From the nondual perspective, R. Aharon might call this transformation one from "our point of view," one of smallness of mind, to "God's point of view"—not because any new information is imparted, but because the clouding filters of the ego have been lessened somewhat. "God's point of view" does not depend on content; it's not that the view is always of flowers and birds. Nor is it the result of a particular state of mind. Rather, it is subtractive in nature; God's point of view is that from which the selfish perspective is removed. According to the Buddhist doctrine of dependent origination, clinging—*tanha*, the origin of suffering—ultimately results from ignorance of the truth. If we know the truth, intuitively and through our own experience, clinging doesn't arise. And conversely, without clinging, the truth shines through.

Second, there is the content of that truth. One of the three characteristics of all conditioned phenomena is that of *anatta*, or non-self. As we explored in chapter 1, while ordinarily it seems that "I am doing something," it is possible to slow down enough to see clearly, and directly, that this isn't actually true. It's a useful label to say that "I am writing these words," but actually, what's happening is an uncountable multitude of causes and conditions, coming together: what I learned from others, my genetic predispositions, my upbringing, the setting in which I find myself, various desires—whatever the causes are, they are leading to effects, and the result is this paragraph.

Insight meditation yields a direct experience of this truth. Through very attentive mindfulness and concentration, it enables the clear seeing of these causes in operation. As with contemplation, some preparation, solitude, and intentionality is required. Then, after building up sufficient concentration (a process which really takes several days, but which can be approximated in fifteen to twenty minutes), attention is turned to the moment-by-moment perceptions and sensations that constitute our experience. Discursive thought, emotions, stories, and ideas are not pursued; like sport fishing, the point is to catch and release. Eventually, it is possible to directly perceive the non-self-hood of every percept—and the reflexive grasping on to pleasant things, and pushing away of unpleasant ones, loosens.

At the earlier stages of the path of insight meditation (the fifth-century text known as the *Visuddhimagga*, or Path of Purification, describes the progress along this path in intricate detail), such moments, whether of release or of non-self, may be fleeting, and merely pleasant interludes of relaxation. Nothing wrong with that, of course. At the later stages of the path, however, radical reorientations take place. The egoic processes are seen as part of the show, not the audience of it. The experiences of contentment and equanimity are so pronounced that the mind finally learns that relinquishing desire is preferable to fulfillment of it. Indeed, the relinquishment becomes so pronounced that the mind begins to let go of consciousness itself, experiencing a peace beyond manifestation.

As William Blake wrote in *The Marriage of Heaven and Hell*, "If the doors of perception were cleansed every thing would appear to man as it is: infinite." For our purposes, *anatta* is the key: seeing the egoic mind as a phenomenon, not a real separate self. Our egos try to assert control of things, but actually nothing is under control—least of all the controller. So if there's no self, what is there?

For a traditional nondual Jew, what is left over when the self is taken away is Ein Sof, or God. For a nontheist, such as the American-born Thai Buddhist master Ajahn Sumedho, what is left over is simply *dhamma*, or "the way it is." Ajahn Sumedho writes, "If you have the insight that all conditions are impermanent, all dhamma is not-self then there's knowing . . . the Dhamma, the truth of the way it is . . . There's no distortion: consciousness and the five aggregates and the sense world are seen as Dhamma rather than as self."[23]

To bring these lofty concepts a bit closer to earth, I'll explain with a story about a dog.

On a retreat I sat a few years ago in Israel, I had been struggling with one of those petty irritations that meditators work with all the time: restless yogis making noise. So I went to go sit outside, on a bench overlooking a beautiful valley. Inspired by the wind and the quiet, and re-lieved to be away from people shifting in their seats, I quickly fell into a groove of watching my breath, and noting sensations. Not ten minutes after I sat down, however, a dog appeared and, panting heavily in the heat, invited me to play by dropping a stick in my lap. I tried to ignore her, but she was persistent. Okay, I thought: this is what is happening; I surrender. So I threw the stick, and the dog retrieved it. I threw it again, and she brought it back again. After a few minutes, the game had worn thin (for me) and I decided to return to more formal practice. I decided to sit still, no matter what.

The dog was having none of it. She wanted to keep playing, and was not interested in my being a good meditator. She picked the stick up with her mouth and dropped it on my lap—over and over again. Maybe I didn't understand how to play; maybe I needed a hint.

In an instant, the frustration I had been experiencing inside the meditation hall subsided, because "non-self" was suddenly, utterly clear. I wasn't angry at the dog for doing what its conditioning caused it to do—so why be angry at my fellow yogis for what their conditioning caused them to do? And, perhaps even more important, why be angry at myself for being frustrated? My conditioning, the world in which I had been living—all these causes and conditions were giving rise to their inevitable result, just like the dog and the yogis.

Sure, the dog had personality—but "personality" is just a label for an amalgamation of behaviors and preferences, each of which is wholly caused by other things. The learned behavior of playing, the desire for companionship, the physical act of chasing the stick—the dog was do-ing just what it had to do. In Rabbi David Cooper's terminology, it was "dogging."

And me too, and the other yogis, and the teachers, and everyone else I knew, too. The conditions caused the dog to play; other conditions caused me to be variously charmed, impatient, insistent, and indulgent. We were all just acting out our infinitude of conditions. For humans, there are more conditions, and far more complicated motives and fac-tors in play—but the principle is the same. There is simply, as Sartre said, a great emptiness where we expect to find agency.

A simple story—but a real opening with real consequences for me.

I don't like rules, morals, and oughts. I never have. I can't will myself to be compassionate or patient. But when I saw that all that was happening, in the meditation hall and on the bench outside, was the vast matrix of causes and conditions, compassion arose naturally—for the dog, the restless yogis, and me. There was no one there to be angry with. There is only Being—only the vast net of causes and conditions. *Ein od milvado*—there is nothing else beside. Coming to see this reality—that only God exists and that everything that seems to exist is actually empty—is *bittul ha-yesh*, annihilation of the sense of self, not in the negative sense, as in societally conditioned stories of unworthiness or invisibility, but in the positive sense of seeing right through all the facets of the self, seeing them as luminous, beautiful, and not mine.

That there is no one to be angry with, and no one who grows angry, is akin to the Hasidic teaching that anger is a form of idolatry. When I am angry, it's as if I'm saying "God is this way, but I reject It." This statement actually contains two mistakes. First, there is the idolatry of creating a God out of preference: God has manifested as a traffic jam or an inconsiderate person, but I have a better idea about how God should look, and I'll worship that instead. Whereas the true God is YHVH: That Which Is. And second, there is the idolatry of separation: God is this way, but *I* reject it, or feel angry about it. I, separate from God. Whereas, there is no separation. God is the arising of anger, and the feeling of it. The knower, the knowing, and the known. And also, thank God, the passing away. In that "thank God," I think, is the beautiful conundrum of religion.

Of course, in a world we share with other people, it's not always possible simply to accept and surrender to all of one's challenging emotions. But reflecting on one's own habits can lead to, at least, a brief reprieve from the tyranny of the ego. Ultimately, as with contemplation, the practice of insight is best pursued in the context of quiet and concentration, and its most valuable fruits can only be obtained on retreats of seven days or more. But it can be of value in daily life as well. Find yourself a place and time to meditate. It can be a half hour in the morning, twenty minutes on the subway, or five minutes in the bathroom (my book *God in Your Body* has plenty of instructions, including the bathroom part). Let the mind slow down, turn down the static of life so you can hear the real Radio Station more clearly. Just by subtracting the noise and listening to what's left, you'll be halfway Home.

Inquiry

A classic nondual contemplative practice begins where the last one left off: given that it's possible to watch the personality develop in the mind, who are you, if you are not that personality?

Pursuing this line of self-inquiry is the chief practice advocated by Ramana Maharshi, the great Indian nondualist whose teachings we have already encountered. Of course, when we first ask ourselves this question, we come up with all kinds of attributes: names, backgrounds, occupations, self-definitions. Conventionally speaking, we are all of these and more. But Ramana is not speaking conventionally. His question is deeper: who is the "you" who is asking the question "who am I"?

In a sense, the practice of self-inquiry relates back to some of the introspection described back in chapter 1. I like Genpo Roshi's voice dialogue method, which invites us to embody the many different voices inside of ourselves. As a therapeutic practice, it is deeply healing. As a nondual practice, it makes abundantly clear the fact that "we" are always one or another of these voices. Here I speak as the writer, but other times I am the lover; now I am a child craving attention, now I am a caregiver. But who is the "I" who sees all of this, even the property of seeing and witnessing itself? Simply keep asking yourself this question; keep trying to find the "I" that is the subject, rather than the object, of thought. Even distraction can be grist for the mill. As Ramana suggests, "If the mind is distracted, ask the question promptly, 'To whom do these distracting thoughts arise?' That takes you back to the 'I'-point immediately."[24] Eventually, self-inquiry leads to a kind of void which Sartre understood as nothingness; it is an ineffable *ayin* that is at the core of each of us. For Sartre, it is a deeply uncomfortable place to be. But for Ramana, "stillness is the sole requisite for the realization of the Self as God."[25]

Self-inquiry of this type is not an indigenous Hasidic form, but it is a valuable method of *bittul ha-yesh*. As each of the illusions of self drops away, the ordinary self, the personality we're used to inhabiting, disappears into the Self. Eventually, the great "I don't know" of self-inquiry yields almost imperceptibly to the great "I know," once the egoic garments are sloughed off at last. Inquire after the seeker long enough, and the Asker is the Answer.

Nondual, Non-Distracted, Non-Meditation

Finally, there are many contemplative practices in the Tibetan and Zen traditions which are so devoid of content as to even reject the term "meditation." One such practice, taught by Tibetan Buddhist teachers including Lama Surya Das, Tsoknyi Rinpoche, and others, is sometimes called "non-distracted, non-meditation." It has no focus, no sense of a meditator meditating; just awareness of awareness itself. On one retreat I sat with Surya Das, the instructions included "beach chair meditation": to sit, eyes open, just relax into awareness, with nothing to do and nowhere to go, as if you're lying in a beach chair, not thinking, not meditating, just being.[26] That's all: just, for a moment, dropping the mind, and becoming aware of awareness itself; inhabiting it, so to speak.

The difference between "beach chair meditation" and actually lying in a beach chair is that in the former, there is enough concentration present to stay focused on awareness itself, rather than drifting off into thought. This is why basic mindfulness and concentration are essential prerequisites for meditation of any kind.[27] But with some practice, it's possible, in daily life, to "drop in" to simple, ever-present, already-perfect awareness (*rigpa*), over and over, as many times a day as you can. It just takes a moment; I find it helpful to relax the body as I relax the mind; it helps me drop the "me." But even this is not necessary for more advanced practitioners.

Sometimes, simple "pointers" can be helpful. These are not subjects of contemplation, as in the Hasidic model, or even phrases in the adapted contemplation practices discussed earlier in this chapter. Rather, they launch the boat, so to speak, and then are released. For example, you might begin with a word or two, such as "open to effortlessness," or "nonjudgmental, mirrorlike awareness." Or, you're not trying to get anywhere or do anything. Enjoy the view. Non-seeking, non-desiring mind. Surya Das is famous for these pithy instructions: "Done is what needs to be done." "Relax and enjoy the view."

"You do not need to iron out the ocean." The triad of "Stay in the view, Lou," "Keep your head, Fred," and "Go with the flow, Jo." And one favorite: "Having a great time—Wish I was here." Or, with a bit more detail, "Simply relax and watch the rolling waves of sea or river, or the clouds pass by while the mind unfurls, as the soul unfolds and the infinite sky opens up revealing the joy of meditation."[28] All these are *kavvanot* in the original sense: directions in which to travel. If you like, you can set a *kavvanah* from the Jewish tradition, such as those discussed in chapter 2; *shiviti adonai l'negdi tamid*, I have set YHVH before me always, is the most widely used, artfully inscribed on synagogue walls around the world. Or, simply naming what is before you at any moment as YHVH, What Is. Remember, YHVH is as present when you are restless as when you are calm.

So is awareness, ever-present, spacious, open, and clear—surrounding even the arising of a nervous ego. Of course, the "you" does not disappear: your mind, personality, habits, desires continue to pop up. But something may be different; you may see that "you" are a phenomenon which arises, in much the same way as the song of a bird, or the sound of a car driving past me here in Jerusalem as I write. "You" are more tenacious than these other perceptions, of course, but the real You is not made up of thought; it's not this "you" ego-phenomenon at all. What is it, then?

In the Jewish context, we might understand *rigpa* not only as primordial awareness but as Divine awareness, as the ineffable *keter* reflected in our own consciousness as *da'at*, knowledge. Again, the practice is subtractive; Genpo Roshi's voice dialogue method, which we just described, often culminates in a negative instruction to embody the "non-seeking, non-desiring mind." Try this now, if you like. Take a breath, and, as if you are an actor playing a part, rest, right now, in your non-seeking, non-desiring mind. No goal, no agenda, no wish for anything to be different. No hope (of enlightenment, joy, satisfaction), no fear. Let things be perfect exactly as they are. Sounds arise, thoughts arise, but You are just witnessing those phenomena—including the phenomena of "you" and your mind. With some sustained effort, nonduality begins to dawn in consciousness. As Pinson puts it, in the context of Jewish meditation, "the meditator loses his sense of self and becomes entirely absorbed in the Infinite. There is no thing-ness to focus on, and paradoxically, there is no thing-ness contemplat-ing . . . it is nothingness meditating on itself."[29]

If these forms of practice are too airy for you, it will be better to an-chor yourself in contemplation, concentration, or mindfulness, all of which give the mind a little more to do. Just don't forget, in the Zohar's use of the words, Who You really are or What You really want. Nondual "meditation" helps You remember.

STOP SEEKING

In order to arrive at having pleasure in everything, desire to have pleasure in nothing.
In order to arrive at having pleasure at possessing everything, desire to possess nothing.
In order to arrive at having pleasure at being everything, desire to be nothing.
In order to arrive at having pleasure at knowing everything, desire to know nothing.
—JOHN OF THE CROSS[30]

In this chapter on practices of mind, I have had several occasions to de-scribe meditation as the cessation of something: discursive thought, emotional dramas, sensations of self, even the activity of "meditation" itself. Funny, since spiritual folk are often called "seekers," that what we're really trying to do is stop seeking, that the spiritual path is the search for the non-search, the path toward no path.

But stopping seeking takes effort, because human beings are geneti-cally and environmentally conditioned to seek all the time. Every mo-ment, most of us are wanting something pleasant (food, entertainment, love, distraction), thinking about the future or the past, or trying to avoid something unpleasant. Sometimes we're just clueless. Once in a blue moon, we're *sameach b'chelko*, happy with what we've got. But usu-ally, in ways so subtle that they escape attention, we're seeking some-thing. This is how we're genetically predisposed to be; if we didn't seek, we wouldn't eat, or make love. But seeking necessarily involves a little bit of suffering. See what happens if you seek distraction but can't find it. Or what happens when you can't sleep. And, for me, even when I do get what I want, I want to make sure I don't lose it, or I want to taste it again. This is what seeking is: an endless procession of thoughts and desires which reinforces the sense of separateness.

Seeking also necessarily privileges that which is being sought over YHVH, that which Is. God may be right here—but I want the good stuff over there. How many times have we all eaten a meal and barely tasted the food? Let alone had sex while worrying about how it's going. Of course, searching, wanting, and righteously arguing all have their place, but awakening is about giving all of them a break to drink more deeply from the well of life, slowing down the mind's relentless, evolutionarily designed efforts to search for that "something else" that is going to bring happiness. To "stop seeking" is thus to start living.

Once in a while, seeking stops on its own: at peak experiences of delight or danger, holding a baby, relaxing after sex, eating a gourmet meal. But most of the time, to stop seeking requires, paradoxically, a search for the ways in which seeking is still going on, and the ways it can be, if not stopped, at least slowed down. Thus the spiritual path, the "search for non-search" begins.

As many spiritual seekers know, however, seeking ways to stop seeking can become, itself, a narcotically addictive search. Comparing this meditation technique against that one. Searching for ever-more-transcendent peak experiences. Or cultivating what Chögyam Trungpa Rinpoche called "spiritual materialism," in which the path to non-self becomes instead a path of gratifying the self with more power, more identity, more trinkets, more attainments, more pride. It can even devolve into a cosmic treasure hunt, in which the goal is to know as much esoteric nonsense as possible, or a trinket-laden consumer lifestyle to enhance, relax, and generally please Me. And because spiritual practices bring about highly pleasant mind states, among the most beautiful sensations humans can experience, they can spoil precisely what they are meant to enhance: the everyday. Compared with the mind-blowing contentment, bliss, and sensations of unity I feel on meditation retreat, regular pleasures sometimes aren't enough. Like a connoisseur of wine no longer being able to enjoy ordinary merlot, I only want the extraordinary stuff.

The worst, though, is the search for justification. Naturally, since spiritual practice takes a lot of time and effort, and since it gets sneered at by many smart people, those of us who do it spend a lot of time explaining why it's so important. Not just something we want to do, and not just something which helps life be a little juicier, a little more meaningful—but really Important. Thus one hears all the time that "the purpose of our being here is to awaken to who we are," or that people who aren't "awake" aren't truly happy. Nonsense. That's just the New Age version of Jews thinking they're the only Chosen People, or Christians thinking that only Christ can save you.

Spiritual practice is all about letting go, and that includes forgoing justification, specialness, pleasure, power, particularism, ego. At some point, it might be better to just admit that we are doing what we want to do, because any holding on to a sense of purpose is going to be counterproductive. As Alan Watts once asked rhetorically,

> Why not sit back and let things take their course? Simply that it is part of "things taking their course" that I write. As a human being it is just my nature to enjoy and share philosophy. I do this in the same way that some birds are eagles and some doves, some flowers lilies and some roses.[31]

Let go of any sense of searching, of purpose, or goal. Rest in what is. You've been home all along.

And remember, this doesn't just mean "do what you want," because doing what you want is going to mean more seeking. It takes a lot of effort to do nothing, to let the *yetzer hara* be, without following or judging its whims. To really believe that this is all there is, this moment, with all its neuroses and problems and perceived flaws, this really is it, this awareness, which never leaves, which is colorless and odorless and is often quite banal—to know that is going to take work. Just don't think it's going to get you anywhere special.

When the giving up becomes total, liberation is present. Everything must be held lightly, including spiritual advice. "All the rules one makes for himself in the service of God are no rules, and this rule itself is no rule," said Rabbi Simcha Bunim of Przysucha.[32] But there is one final challenge, one final goal, one final *thing* that religious people often find it hard to let go of: God.

THE PART ABOUT GOD—OR, WHAT IF IT'S ALL DELUSION?

On meditation retreats, I have been able to slow down the mind so much that literally watching paint dry is fascinating, beautiful, and interesting—even if the paint is already dry. It is possible to let go of thinking so that a sense of unity arises, or that the emptiness of things becomes a directly apprehended reality. Even the self unravels, and the "non-seeking, non-desiring mind" appears sufficient in itself, blissful, ever-present.

There is a sense of presence in these experiences that is more than a sensation of having one's mind altered. A great love arises, and a certainty that the love is not just arising within the self. Rather than the self containing the feeling of love, the love seems to contain the "self" and everything else within it. Do the practices, I have found, and what the texts say happens, happens—and often with sense of deep certainty, of knowing, of coming home.

But all these are but sensations, experiences. Am I, at such moments, really in touch with Brahman, God, or whatever? It makes sense on paper: if the self is an illusion, a phenomenon that only exists when seen from a certain perspective, then who is doing all this knowing, if it's not "Jay"? And it does *feel* that way; I feel a closeness, an intimacy, even a communication—and through it all, a certainty. Then again, we feel certain about a lot of things that turn out not to be true. Which is it— cosmic consciousness, or a nice bit of relaxation? What if all of it—the experiences, the sophistries of theology, the inspiring quotations—is just delusion? What if it's all *just not true*?

This can be a corrosive question to ask—but also a very useful one, with at least four equally useful responses.

The first response is to learn from the presence of desire. As discussed in the last section, the claim to cosmic consciousness is itself a form of seeking. As if it's not enough that meditation makes me happy and opens my eyes to pleasure and pain—it also has to take me to God (whatever that is), which is somehow more present when I'm relaxed than when I'm stressed out (even though nondualists insist that it's present all the time). From the nondual Jewish perspective, this indicates a certain idolatry, an imputing of fixed beliefs onto the ineffable. From the perspective of mindfulness, it indicates the presence of greed; I want this experience to mean something, to be something more than just an experience. So, the first response to doubt is an admission, if only to observe the grasping of the *mochin d'katnut*, the small, desiring mind.

Second, and continuing in the refusal to engage with the question itself, there is the quality of *safek*, doubt, itself. Doubt can often be quite useful; if we didn't doubt the value of the Western, consumerist-materialist world into which most of us were born, we might never begin the spiritual path in the first place, might never ask whether our pleasant lifestyle entails suffering for others. But doubt can also be corrosive, undermining everything, not out of a noble search for truth but purely for the sake of undermining. Over the years, I've worried that I am too sensitive, or not sensitive enough; that I'm too materialistic, or not materialistic enough; that I'm too wild or too tame, too serious or too playful—the self-doubt never ends, and it perpetuates itself even after the merits of any particular debate have long been exhausted. So when doubt arises regarding my own peak experiences, enduring truths, and core commitments, I try to be aware of doubt itself.

But I do not end there, because, as Locke observed, religion is precisely the arena in which doubt is most called for. So there is a third response to the skepticism of contemplative practice, which is to evaluate the evidence as clearly as possible. For Ken Wilber, following Pascal, contemplative evidence should be regarded in the same way as scientific testimony, with no more or less respect: if you doubt it, repeat the procedure, and see if the data is consistent. As Wilber puts it:

> When someone asks 'Where is your empirical proof for transcendence?' we need not panic. We explain the instrumental methods of our knowledge and invite him or her to check it out personally. Should that person accept and complete the injunctive strand [i.e., repeat the contemplative procedure] then that person is capable of becoming part of the community of those whose eye

is adequate to the transcendent realm. Prior to that time, that person is inadequate to form an opinion about transcendental concerns. We are then no more obliged to account to that person than is a physicist to one who refuses to learn mathematics.[33]

Repeat the procedure, and see what happens.

Fourth, though, is to take this auditing of mystical experience as a welcome refinement of theology. Admit it all, and say so what. Let Being simply be what it is, whatever it is, without label or ascription, without looking for God, labeling an experience as God, or in any way claiming something is or isn't God. And then, what might you notice? Perhaps a tone of relaxation, a quieting in the mind. The sound of the breeze, the feel of the air, ordinary sights of trees and sky. In other words—whether God is delusion or not, your experience would be the same. Recall that nonduality is where monism and atheism shake hands. Nothing is added or taken away from the universe as it appears. So, when the foundations are kicked away, the house remains exactly as it was.

So admit it all. The mystics' sense of certainty—just a sense. Their sense of love and communion—a mere feeling, perhaps a projection. Still, there is the sound of the breeze, the feel of the air—nothing has changed. Remember, "God" is but the naming of Being as God, and as Arthur Green notes, "to ask whether 'being exists' is itself a redundancy."[34] What is really being asked is not whether Being exists, but whether it merits being named as God. It makes no ontological difference. Admit it all, and see that Nothing has changed.

This final relinquishment of seeking is a blessing, not a curse. What do I really know about the experience of union? I certainly don't know that it's with an omnipotent Deity who gave His only begotten son to redeem the sins of mankind, or who liberated the Israelites from Egypt. If we suppose that mysticism can prove the mythic assertions of the Bible, we are mistaken (and dangerously so—nothing is more volatile than mythic religion plus powerful spiritual experience). But careful mystical theology is also better nondual theology. If we strip "God" of associations and concepts, we are being more faithful not only to our experience, and not only to our ethics, but to God as well. Any concept we have of God is not God; it is a finite concept, tied to the finite mind,

MIND   171 conceptualized in terms of finite substances and ideas which, in their limitation, are not God-in-godself (a concept which itself is inaccurate, because it is a concept). If you have an idea of God, God negates your idea.

Any idea or concept imposed upon the ineffable mystical experience actually takes us further from the Divine. Every term is a diminution. Think of something you'd like to say about a mystical experience—that it was truly of God, for example—and you'll see that it is actually about a concept. It is wrongly finitizing the Infinite. *Samadhi, devekut*—these are mind states. The only time we get into the question of "Is this real or am I deluded?" is when we are claiming an experience of something— some *thing*. And that is error. From a negative-theological perspective, the claim is always going to be false, because it is a claim about some-*thing*. And from a nondual perspective, the claim is false because it is a claim of something outside the self. Either way, the less said, the better. Delusion, in a nondual perspective, has nothing to do with God. It only has to do with mistaken utterances about the world of appearance.

And really, as long as you know that your ego isn't your self, then whether you're nothing or God is of little consequence. Which words you use to describe your ultimate nature are up to you—as long as it isn't "someone." That is, as long as we know there isn't someone doing all that knowing, that there's just the epiphenomenon of knowing itself, then the difference between God and nothingness is primarily seman- tic. After all, God doesn't have a self either. We tend to say "Being" as if a gerund were really a noun, but it isn't; there is not a "Knower" sepa- rate from the known. God is not something in addition to the universe, because a "something" is not unsayable, unknowable, and unthinkable. The notion of some tangible God-consciousness that stands apart from all the strands of reality, and that either does or doesn't exist, is bad the- ology. It is yet again to make an error of selfhood, this time on a huge theological scale. God, also, is Empty—indeed, God is the Emptiness itself.

A Buddhist might report, after a mystical experience: "I feel love." A Jew might report: "I love you, God." The more we can efface the difference between those statements, the closer we are to heaven.

7

HEART: PRAYER
AND ACTS OF LOVE

Love is not restricted by limitations. For love does not have any bounds, being an aspect of the Infinite Love. If one has love for something physical, then this physical thing becomes a vessel for love. But when one has love for the Infinite Being, then his love is clothed in the Infinite. Both the love and its vessel are then boundless.
 —IMREI TZADDIKIM[1]

Religion begins not with doctrine, not with tradition, but with the need to pray.
 —ARTHUR GREEN[2]

Since nonduality often appears as a philosophical position, and since it is often most readily known with the mind, it has been my intention throughout this book to emphasize the ways in which, for me and many others, it has been a path of the heart as well. I sometimes say to my students (on retreats and in synagogues, not necessarily at law school) that I only teach what I have tried, and what has transformed my life. Nonduality is no exception.

And so we turn to practices of the heart, to devotion and lovingkindness and prayer and repentance, for any deep transformation requires the engagement of the heart. In this turn there are at least two aspects. First, there is the natural continuity between wisdom and compassion; from the knowledge of our true Self comes a caring for human beings and other living things, as if by a miraculous outflowing of often hidden love. From a relaxation of the boundaries of the conventional self comes more patience, more resilience, more openness. In this way, insight leads to love.

But there is also the second movement, one more complementary than consequential. Here the heart speaks its own language, often foreign to that of the mind. Over the years, I have studied some of the most abstruse doctrines of the Kabbalah and the thickest of postmodern perplexities. And yet, I have noticed that the principles which have truly transformed me are often the most banal; the deepest truths of my life, I am ashamed, as a writer, to admit, often could fit on a bumper sticker. Even more: many of the practices of Judaism, as we saw in chapter 4, rest on untenable, even absurd, philosophical foundations. Here sentiment departs from intellect, but if we are willing to follow its course, love leads to wisdom.

As we have already had occasion to remark, it is in the emotive, devotional realm that nondual Judaism becomes the most *Jewish*. Cosmologically, philosophically, and even in terms of contemplative practice, there are only limited differences between elite, nondual Judaism and elite, nondual Hinduism, Christianity, and Buddhism. Ultimately, our different languages converge in the One beyond words. But most of us do not live our lives in the aeries of contemplative thought. We are embodied, en-souled, en-hearted creatures, and as a consequence, we live in our particularity. So, while I meditate with Buddhists, I *daven* with Jews. I know the Sanskrit terminologies of mind, but I sing in Hebrew and Yiddish.

Following R. Aharon, I will take the practice of ecstatic prayer as my primary focus here, though I will also shed light on other Jewish practices of the heart. On their face, these practices are challenged by nonduality. If everything is God, to whom or what are we praying? What is the value of the *tshuvah*, the introspection and "return," that Judaism so forcefully extols? Our answer is the same as before: while at the endpoint of realization, all is one; in the manifest world, the one becomes many. And in that world, we speak from our relative positions, from the beautiful conundrum of being human.

Recall from chapter 4 the maxim that even when the mind knows one, the heart knows two. It yearns, it burns, and it feels joy and sadness and love. On the Jewish path, these are not merely feelings to be noted and investigated; they are also gifts, God-given, that allow us both to be fully human and to strive for the just. There's a Sufi teaching that the yearning for God is the last tool to be set down before total union takes place; it carries us all the way to the door, and is laid aside only at the end. Yet perhaps even this is insufficient; perhaps the embracing heart which cares for the world is less a vehicle than a destination in itself. This love is accessible, and real.

ECSTATIC AND CONTEMPLATIVE PRAYER: THE GLUE OF TRANSCENDENCE

Prayer as a spiritual practice has a long lineage in Jewish tradition—beginning with the very word for "pray," *l'hitpallel*, a reflexive verb which indicates that prayer is something one does to oneself. The oft-repeated notion that prayer is "the service of the heart" is actually a poor translation of *avodah sh'balev*, which really means "the service that is *in* the heart"—it happens in the heart, not somewhere else. And its rewards are there as well: ecstasy (*hitpa'alut* and *hitlahavut*), union (*achdut*), and cleaving to the Divine (*devekut*). The heart's need for prayer endures notwithstanding the truth of nonduality. As one Hasidic text, rendered here by Rabbi Arthur Green, says:

How many walls there are between man and God.
Even though God fills all the world, He is so very hidden!
Yet a single word of prayer can topple all the walls and bring you
     close to God.[3]

This type of prayer is quite different from conventional forms. If traditional prayer is petitionary in nature—asking God to fill one's needs or wants—prayer as a spiritual practice is about forgetting the self entirely. According to R. Dov Ber of Mezrich, the successor to the Baal Shem Tov:

A person must think of himself as nothing [*ayin*], and forget himself utterly, and ask in his prayers only for the Shechinah. In this way, he will be able to transcend time, to the World of Thought, where everything is equal: life and death, sea and dry land . . . He cannot do this if he is attached [*davuk*] to materiality and this world, because he will be attached to distinctions between good and evil . . . Moreover, if he thinks of himself as something [*yesh*] and asks for his needs, the Holy One cannot be clothed in him, because the Blessed One is infinite [Ein Sof], and there is no vessel that can contain Him, except when one thinks of himself as nothing.[4]

Notice how for R. Dov Ber true prayer is equanimous, or at least transcendent of the distinctions of this world. It takes one to a realm beyond multiplicity, space, and time, even beyond goodness, spirituality, holiness, or peace. Only by thinking of oneself as nothing is it possible to make negative space for the infinite.

How is this task accomplished? There are two main models of Hasidic prayer: contemplative and ecstatic. In the contemplative model, prayer acts to replace egoic thoughts with holy ones. Pre-prayer, I am thinking of my mortgage payments and to-do list, but post-prayer, when it works right, I am thinking of the omnipresence of God, or the daily wonders of human life. Contemplative prayer is essentially a variation on contemplative meditation, except here the concepts of prayer provide the subject matter for focused reflection and consideration.

In the ecstatic model, concepts drop away entirely. Instead, the letters and words of prayer, perhaps aided by song, vigorous movement, visualization, and heartrending devotion, become a technology for personal transformation. Here, the change is less from ignorant to grateful, than from ignorant of unity to knowing it—a "knowing" that is less an intellectual concept than an Adam-knew-Eve, in-your-*kishkes* kind of knowing, the way you know the deepest truths, and the most obvious ones, such as the fact that you're seeing right now. If in contemplative prayer, the mind shifted subjects, now it drops subject and object entirely. The "you" is burned away, and God is what is left over. According to one Hasidic source:

> Before he begins to pray, a person should cast aside that which limits him and enter the endless world of Ayin. In prayer he should turn to God alone and have no thoughts of himself at all. Nothing but God exists for him; he himself has ceased to be.[5]

Hasidim split on which model was preferable. For R. Aharon, ecstasy is a necessary prerequisite to enlightenment; it is like a refinery for the heart, purifying it from its sense of separation. Precisely by involving itself with the attributes and the heart, ecstasy is able to burn the separation away and provide an actual experience of union—a view which resonates with many contemporary enthusiasts and spiritual seekers.[6] But R. Aharon's rival, R. Dov Ber of Lubavitch (not to be confused with R. Dov Ber of Mezrich, quoted above), believed that the risks of egoic, spurious ecstasy outweighed the costs—a concern which surely resonates in our own time of zealous, fundamentalist enthusiasm.[7] Who is right? History initially favored R. Dov Ber; he ascended to leadership of Chabad. But today, most Hasidic sects favor the ecstatic mode. Their prayer is heartful, heartrending, noisy, and chaotic. It is like lighting a fire within one's heart, yearning to taste the sweetness of union with the Holy One or the *Shechinah*; engaging all aspects of the self; throwing caution to the wind. Individually, this may mean rhythmic swaying (*shuckling*), or praying in one's own words, crying out before God in the manner of R. Nachman of Bratzlav's *hitbodedut* until—and this is the critical point—the sense of self seems to melt away in tears or laughter or both. The energies that are cultivated in this practice are powerful, and erotic—not sexual, but erotic. As the Baal Shem Tov is reported to have said:

> Prayer is coupling with the Shechinah. Just as there is movement at the beginning of coupling, so too one must move at the beginning of prayer. Afterwards one can stand still, without motion, attached to the Shechinah with great *devekut*. As a result of your swaying, you can attain great bestirment. For you think to yourself: Why do I move myself? Because the Shechinah is standing before me. This will cause a state of great rapture [*hitlahavut*].[8]

To be sure, making love to the immanent Divine Feminine may seem too radical for some—and the Hasidim were alternately ridiculed and condemned for their wild and boisterous prayer gatherings, with shouting and singing and banging on the walls. The neighbors of New York's Carlebach Shul make similar complaints today. But particularly for those either uninspired or affirmatively turned off by traditional prayer language, Hasidic ecstatic prayer can be a powerful alternative, whether in its traditional forms, or in new ones, accompanied by drums, instruments, and chants taken from multiple traditions. Like any ecstatic practice, ecstatic prayer lowers the barriers of self and puts the mind into an altered state which, because the egoic self is quieted, often has a quality of union. While the ecstatic prayer state is not as otherworldly or dissociative as those associated with entheogens and shamanic practices, it is nonetheless a going-beyond, an *ec-stasis* of the soul. Perhaps one day, neurologists will be able to explain such experiences as neurochemical phenomena. Perhaps they will do so for love as well. But even if they do, would such experiences be any less delightful, any less intimate?

ORDINARY PRAYER: THE RETURN OF THE CONVENTIONAL GOD

At first appearance, conventional prayer is problematic for nondual Judaism. Petitionary prayer is perhaps the most problematic, for it asks God to take certain actions, and thus assumes that God may or may not choose to respond. This is psychologically, as well as theologically, dubious; if everything happens as it must, rather than as it should, then what is the point of wishing really hard for it to be otherwise? Indeed, to do so is to push away What Is, and erect an idol of our preferences; it cultivates the mental clinging that leads to suffering and separation. Yet even nonpetitionary prayer—thanksgiving and praise being the two other major Jewish types—seems to assume a dualistic gap between human and Divine, which prayer seeks to bridge through communication. The language of prayer implies, and sometimes actually states, that "I" am here and you, God, are there.

If prayer is an ecstatic or contemplative practice, as described in the last section, then the theological contradiction of a nondual Godhead and dualistic prayer does not arise. Likewise if prayer is but a reflection on one's life, or a way of circumscribing the selfish inclination—that is, if we do not take its language seriously—or if, as in the Kabbalistic model, it is a theurgical act based upon the potency of the Hebrew letters. All of these answers, and more, have been proposed by Jewish mystics and philosophers. (Indeed, what's surprising is how few of them actually have the conventional notions that prayer pleases God, or warms Him up to fulfill our requests.) In much of my own work, I've tended to follow a similar line of thinking. In my book *God in Your Body*, for example, I spoke at length about the modalities of kneeling (*barchu*), listening (*shema*), and standing (*amidah*), the three embodied "movements" of traditional Jewish prayer, as voluntarily subjugating selfish desires to something which is greater than them, listening to the truth, and taking a stand for what we believe. This makes prayer function as a form of spiritual practice without theological puppet-strings.

But these answers miss why we pray in the first place, which is not in spite of the dualistic language of prayer, but because of it. It takes only a moment's review of the Psalms, still the urtext of Jewish prayer, to see that Jewish prayer is, at its core, devotionalistic in nature. Even Maimonides, the great rationalist, understood prayer as a time for the heart to open. Yes, devotion implies a devoted-to. It implies duality. But as the saying goes, in the trenches, or in the hospitals—at such times theology and atheism go out the window, and the heart cries in a language the mind may neither approve nor understand.

Devotion can be embarrassing for thoughtful people. We are trained, those of us who read long books and have a stake in culture and art, to develop our minds, and we are rewarded, with money and degrees and approbation, for displaying the mental dexterities which show us to be successful and advanced human beings. Yes, there is talk these days of emotional intelligence, and elite culture is itself a notion increasingly under attack. But in our academies, and in the worlds of business and the professions, the important skills are those of the mind—not the heart. Indeed, some of the most devoted religionists (fundamentalists, "mystics") are either weak-minded, or brutish, or both. So who wants to admit that we remain, on a primal level, in some need of prayer and supplication?

Ironically, the nondual view, which at first seemed so hostile to traditional prayer, here comes to its rescue. When the truth of nonduality actually penetrates through the veils of ego and delusion, dualistic prayer language suddenly flows much more freely than it did previously. In those precious moments at which nonduality is the truth and ego is the delusion, not just the illusion of separation, but also inhibition, and the pretensions of knowledge, drop away. A great "I don't know" replaces arrogant (and ridiculous) claims to metaphysical certainty. This "I don't know" is the negative theology of the "cloud of unknowing," the limits of reason according to Kant, the limits of language according to Wittgenstein, the mystery of Being according to Hegel and Heidegger. It is the absurdity of Zen, the transrational of Ken Wilber, the transcendent *keter* of Kabbalah, the impossible unity of emptiness and form. It is that toward which art gestures, the mystery that is rendered banal by explaining, the poetry lost in translation. Who knows?

From this unknowing springs a kind of permission given to the heart. Of course, prayer is absurd. Its language is primitive, outmoded, and ridiculous—nearly as ridiculous as love itself. But to those of us who seek to know the intimations and stirrings of our souls, to go without the self-abnegation of prayer is like forgoing music or wine. Of course, life goes on. But without the heart allowed to cry in the modality of prayer, some of its flavors are drained out, like the industrial foods that pass for produce today. The essence of prayer is its heartfelt intention, because in that intention is the reason we pray in the first place.[9]

And so prayer flows from surrender—chiefly the surrender of "I." As we have already seen, one often hears in the Jewish world a language of wrestling: with problematic texts, with ideas, with that in which we don't believe but struggle. But in the nondual view, the wrestling of Jacob with the angel is the wrestling of the One with the One. It is not a contest; it is an embrace, an act of love in which God is the only lover. It is a Divine role-play, one moment taking on the submissive role, allowing, begging, being pressed to the ground, and the next assuming the dominant role, insisting, demanding, expressing the will. It is none other than the drama of prayer itself, once the demands of the intellect bend to the dance of the imagination.

This is nondual prayer, set loose from the shames of the self and the fantasies of theology. It is the heart dancing, imagining, and, of course, projecting. It imagines a God, asks this God for favor. It senses energies and knows how the heart awakens. And it dares to use language, traditional or new, in its approach to the unsayable. Unlike naive prayer, it does not assume the existence of a separate Deity who will answer the petitions of the sufficiently pious. Unlike rationalized prayer, it does not masquerade as meditation or magic. And unlike the hesitations of the overly uptight, nondual prayer does not submit the needs of the heart to the auditing of the intellect or the embarrassment of the ego.

What appears to the mind as Being, appears to the heart as God. And while non-self is glimpsed in meditation, the self stretches forth in prayer—right until it breaks. This is a prayer unashamed of its nakedness, pleading and demanding, *shuckling* and clapping, or, at times at which the soul is in constriction, going through the motions in the hope that something, somewhere, will loosen. Is prayer preposterous, susceptible to fanaticism and delusion? Yes, but so are all the stirrings of the heart, and the heart has eyes through which the mind cannot see.

I thirst for such prayer, even if it is not answered. Real love is not about serving my own needs; it is not a fair-weather romance pursued only when convenient. Sometimes it goes unrewarded, even unrequited. Sometimes the lover is distant, sometimes he does not answer me when I call. And yet, it feels better to call out than to remain silent. Likewise, there are times when prayer yields no apparent spiritual reward. Yet when I offer it as a service, I feel the holiness of yearning for holiness. Perhaps God remains obscured, but the wanting fills the vacuum with sacredness. Said one Hasidic master, "When a person knows that God is hidden, God is not really hidden."[10] Sometimes I need to pray even for that.

LOVE AS A NONDUAL SPIRITUAL PRACTICE

God
ripened me.
So I see it is true:
all objects in existence are
wildly in
love.
—MEISTER ECKHART, rendered by DANIEL LADINSKY[11]

In chapter 4, I suggested that the Jewish path, insofar as it is specifically Jewish, ought essentially to be a path of love. Nonduality is universal, it is conceptual, and it does not vary according to our individual circumstances. But love is particular; in fact we may say that it is all particulars. As Franz

Rosenzweig wrote, we love one another not as instantiations of some universal traits, but precisely as particular individuals. The Other interrupts the universal, and in that alterity is revelation. In love there is an uncovering of the unexpected, and thus the ineffable.

Some today would consign love to other religions, leaving only the law for Judaism—as if the Psalms and the Song of Songs were somehow alien to Jewish tradition. But in the Kabbalah, the entire universe is the act of cosmic lovemaking, and in the Hasidic tradition, earthly and heavenly love are the foundations of the mystical life. Love is a spiritual practice, and spiritual practice leads to love. Truly to yield, to give without expectation, to love without hope of reciprocity, lowers the boundaries of self as powerfully as any meditation or prayer. It may be expressed *bein adam l'makom*, in the luscious rapture for the Beloved characteristic of Sufi mysticism, or *bein adam l'havero*, in the Hasidic and neo-Hasidic recognition that God is most readily found in the souls of our fellow men and women, especially those who are suffering.

To begin with the first mode, Judaism provides ample guidance: in dualistic, anthropomorphic God-language, Jewish religionists have declared this love for millennia. "You shall love the Lord your God with all your heart, with all your soul and with all your might," commands Deuteronomy 6:5, immortalized as the first paragraph of the Shema. Deuteronomy 10:12–13 asks, "And now, O Israel, what does YHVH your God ask of you but to stand in awe of YHVH your God, to walk in all God's ways, to love God, to serve YHVH your God with all your heart and with all your soul, and to observe YHVH's commands and decrees that I am giving you today for your own good?" "Love God, all God's righteous ones!"[12] and "With all my heart I have sought you!" shouts the Psalmist.[13] "The compassionate One wants the heart," says the Talmud.[14] This kind of relationship with God, like any relationship, takes work. It won't just happen, or even if it does, it won't simply remain forever. Thus meditation, ritual practice, prayer, study, nourishing the body, *hakarat hatov* (appreciating that which is good), arranging life so there is time for reflection, not always rushing—all of these, and of course many more, become practices of love. Not always easy—but if love were easy, it wouldn't be love at all.

From a reductive, materialist perspective, such love must perforce be sublimation. No one would deny that religious people have an experience of love; a reductionist simply insists that it is an experience only, that there is no external referent to this love, and that it is a diversion of repressed earthly desires. Interestingly, from a nondual perspective, such critiques become almost irrelevant. To paraphrase the words which closed the last chapter, the more we can efface the difference between "I love you, God" and simply "I love," the closer we are to understanding the truth of the Beloved. If the Divine is the Everything and the Nothing, then of what "object" of love are we speaking here? Is there even a hairsbreadth between the materialist who says that the religionist is simply drunk with love, and the nondual mystic who says she is drunk with love for the One? Except perhaps that the latter is more apt to be happy.

For Rabbi Meshullam Feibush Heller, the greatest love is experienced not by the mystic but by God:

> When we recognize that we are really as nothing and apprehend that there is nothing in the world besides God, just as before creation, then God, as it were, experiences the true delight that He hopes for from us. Just as a father and mother hope to give birth to a child and to bear it in their arms, so God, as it were, experiences delight from His children who come to His arms for kisses and embraces.[15]

Notice the oscillations in this narrative. On the one hand, God is the father and mother, loving their child—a straightforward dualistic image. On the other hand, the delight takes place when the child realizes she no longer exists as a separate entity—in other words, when God-as-child recognizes Herself. This is why the poet Daniel Ladinsky titled his anthology of mystical poetry *Love Poems from God*, rather than "to God": because when mystical love is consummated, it is the love in which there is only one Lover.

From this love spring all the forms of religious life described in chapter 4. Whether construed traditionally or not, the life of religious love becomes a life of religious devotional practice: traditionally, through the *mitzvot*, but also in the everyday attitude of gentleness and love for Being itself. In this way, love is less a particular spiritual practice than a constant spiritual orientation toward the practice of life itself. It encompasses everything, for everything, even the terrible, is susceptible to love.

Naturally, such love leads toward its second, human aspect. How might we approach strangers on the street, if we were convinced that we and they were God? Perhaps, as I like to remind myself in a crowd, as different flowers of the same plant. Surely we would be a bit kinder, a bit more forgiving—not because it is the right thing to do, but because what we have seen in contemplative practice makes it obvious. Just as the contemplative observes in meditation that her own personality is really an amalgam of transitory, conditioned, and selfless thoughts, feelings, and actions, so too when someone else acts or speaks unkindly, she can see the same processes operating within them. Who is really saying the unkind words? And, if you feel angry or hurt as a result, who is reacting that way? No one. The conditions are present—they are who is speaking and reacting. Cause and effect, nothing more. And it's hard to get angry at conditions, especially if you know the conditions are God. As the Baal Shem Tov said, "When speaking to people, first attach yourself mentally to the Creator, Blessed be He. The soul of the other, too, is bound up with the Creator. For every person lives but by virtue of the Divine emanation infused into all creatures."[16]

In such a love—what the contemporary teacher Yitzhak Buxbaum has called "the mystical path of loving people"—there is at once a melting of individuality into unity, and a reappreciation of diversity and surprise. This is not God as God, but God as you, and me, and she, wearing a thousand disguises all the more colorful for being seen as they are. Then *hesed*, lovingkindness, flows freely—not as abnegation of the self, but as nourishment. It can be as simple as nonjudgment, politeness, or refusing to instrumentalize the people we encounter in our daily activities. Or it can take the form of generosity, patience, and authentic care. I love to remember the voice of Louis Armstrong interpreting our daily how-do-you-do's as synonyms for "I love you." What else are we saying, really, as we make conversation?

Applied to those who are suffering, love turns quickly to justice. This was the crux between nondual theology and social justice for Abraham Joshua Heschel: that, as in liberation theology, God is seen in the suffering of the poor and the destitute. It is God's face that seeks to be seen by us, and God's suffering that our *tikkun olam* repairs. Vivekananda used to insist that his disciples know that suffering anywhere is "my suffering," because the Consciousness that sees suffering is the same Consciousness that suffers. In the words of St. Francis of Assisi (as rendered by Daniel Ladinsky):

> God came to my house and asked for charity.
> And I fell on my knees and cried,
> "Beloved, what may I give?"
> "Just love," He said. "Just love."[17]

In the Jewish tradition, as is well known, our greatest this-worldly imperatives are phrased somewhat differently: not only to love but to pursue justice,[18] to support those in need,[19] and not to do to others what we would not wish done to ourselves.[20] Among the Hasidic masters, there was concern that the heights of mystical ecstasy not be so high that the *tzaddik* neglects to provide for his community and its this-worldly needs. These traditions emphasize that the recognition of nonduality leads to an upwelling of love and compassion which leads directly to the prophetic demand for justice. The nondual Ein Sof may transcend all knowledge, but our God is the Compassionate One, not the impassionate.

In its most extreme form, the act of submitting to love asks us to love even that which is terrible to bear: to see light in everything, including places of darkness. Sadness, grief, anger, loneliness, loss; these, too, are modalities of the One, and the religious question becomes not how they may be averted but how they may be accepted, even loved. I remember, on a forty-day meditation retreat, discovering how much homophobia and self-hatred I still carried within myself, years after coming out and coming to terms with myself. Nothing could dislodge this awful self-hatred: not watching it, not trying to heal it, not my desperate attempts to uproot it. It just sat there, and hated, and I hated the hatred. Eventually, I simply had to give up. Like the Tibetan sage Milarepa, I surrendered myself to the demon, placed my head in its mouth, and let it devour me. And, as in the story, once the surrender was complete, the demon disappeared. I found I could embrace even the hatred, love even that which seeks to annihilate me. Only then did its power begin to subside.

To admit everything, to have a heart as wide as the earth to meet a mind as spacious as the sky: this is the invitation. "Develop a heart so full of love, it resembles space," Sharon Salzberg once taught me on retreat. Gather in the exiles of shadow and doubt, invite them in like strangers to a Passover seder. Sadness, anger, loneliness—these may be unwelcome visitors. But all must be admitted for our hospitality to be like Abraham's.

Love is how God appears from the perspective of the heart. When the heart expands, it contains multitudes, and the aspect of the self that is separate from all else recedes. Perhaps nonduality is but sublimated love; perhaps the reductionists are right. Or perhaps love is a reflection of the infinite. Either way, its fruits are sweet.

TSHUVAH

To put it mildly, the Jewish conception of God is often a troubling one. Ours is not only a God who loves, but also a God who demands, even judges. But what is the meaning of sin and repentance, if everything is God?

As before, it is not hard to come up with a convenient mystical answer. All of us live with the delusions of the ego, the *yetzer hara*, which sees the world not as it is, but as divided into many different, separate objects, some of which we want and others of which we don't. Delusion is as ordinary as "have a nice day"—"nice" being a term that means "pleasing to the self." It is conditioned by aeons of evolution and natural selection—pure nonduality doesn't do well at crosswalks—but it is still delusory. "Seems" is not "is." There may seem to be a separate self living between your ears, but in fact, every thought you are having, at this moment as at every other one, is wholly conditioned by an uncountable number of causes, which are themselves wholly conditioned by other causes, ad infinitum—ad Ein Sof. So *tshuvah*, translated as "repentance" but literally meaning "return," is simply a return to a way of seeing clearly, the return to Who we really are, and the mending that comes from it.

Fine—but this is not the tenor of *tshuvah* as expressed on the Days of Awe. The traditional Jewish path to return is not through emptiness, but through *kapparah*: atonement, catharsis. It's not meditation—it's breaking the self. If nondual meditation is Chabad-style contemplation, Jewish *tshuvah* is R. Nachman's *hitbodedut*, a searing self-examination which, far from leaving the self behind, puts the self through the metaphorical ringer. Beating the chest, reviewing one's transgressions, fasting to break through the resistances of the ego—the mainstream Jewish path of Yom Kippur is one not of nondual Right View but of dualistic wrestling with the small self, asking a dualistic God for forgiveness, and feeling the gaps between the ideal and the real. Does this have any place within nondual Judaism, or must its guilts and "oughts" be set aside at last? Where, after all, does such pietism end—with self-mortification? Denial? Repression?

I want to propose an emphasis not on the repentance aspect of *tshuvah*, but on the aspect of forgiveness. In the Jewish tradition, real *tshuvah* requires that we ask forgiveness of those we've wronged—and grant it to those who've wronged us. That is work that can't be done alone, even if the only one to forgive is yourself.

Richard Smoley, the author of *Inner Christianity*, is a nondualist Christian and centrally interested in the notion of forgiveness. For Smoley, forgiveness is an exercise in enlightenment. He invites us to ask just who we think is really wronging us. Why did that person make the choice, say the words, do the deed that she or he "chose" to do? Well, obviously, because of a thousand causes and conditions—and not a hairsbreadth of soul more.[21] Being angry at someone for an offense they have caused is like when we get angry at traffic, or a computer, or a crying baby. Everyone is doing the best they can—if they could do better, they would. If wisdom were stronger, they'd make better choices. If patience were stronger, they'd be less angry. But these factors are not "me" or "you." Really, the only one you're not forgiving is God.

Forgiveness is seeing clearly. And as such, it is not something we do for other people; it's something we do for ourselves. Every Yom Kippur, I think of the people who really angered me or hurt me in the previous year. I'm certainly not virtuous enough to smile and move on; I inhabit the wrong anew. But what gets me through the heart-wrenching process of *tshuvah* is, ironically, self-concern. The more I hold on to the idea that the driver who cut me off, the lover who betrayed me, the coworker who irritated me are each separate people out there, the angrier I get. And then I get angry at myself for getting angry. But as the Gospel of John says, the truth will set you free.[22] In this case, the truth is that being a jerk arises, in me and in others. It's the result of many causes and conditions. It's not that it's justified; it's just that it's a phenomenon that isn't "owned" by the jerk himself. From the perspective of *mochin d'gadlut*, causes lead to effects. That is all.

Likewise my own sense of indignation; it too is simply an effect of many causes. So, seeing clearly in the light of dependent origination (in Hebrew, *seder hishtalshelut*), I can act more skillfully, out of love for myself. I got hurt. Is the anger helping, or hurting me more? Likewise, too, if I remain in denial about the harm I have caused: is this refusal to accept responsibility leading toward truth or away from it? With the ego seen for what it is, *cheshbon ha-nefresh*—the accounting of the soul— can proceed more honestly.

Nondual *tshuvah* is where mind and heart meet in healing. It is not a breast-beating shame, but an all-allowing forgiveness. And I find this perspective opens my heart. Yes, relationships and joys and hurts continue as before. But this is nonduality from personal, rather than theological language: that what we take to be a world of people who please or displease, whom we regard or disregard, is really a great play of life, filled with actors who don't know they are acting. Including me. This is the real return to Who You are: knowing clearly that there is only God, pretending to be wronged, pretending to be evil, pretending to forgive, pretending to be you.

And where there is suffering—on the planetary scale, or in the political world, or in your own life—there the work begins.

8

BODY: THE DWELLING PLACE
OF THE INFINITE

I do not know which to prefer,
The beauty of inflections
Or the beauty of innuendoes,
The blackbird whistling
Or just after.
—WALLACE STEVENS, "THIRTEEN WAYS OF LOOKING AT A BLACKBIRD"

The meaning of Y-H-W-H is One is not that He is the only God, negat-
ing other gods, but . . . there is no being other than Him, even though
it seems otherwise to most people . . . Everything that exists in the
world, spiritual and physical, is God Himself . . . Because of this, ev-
ery person can attach himself [to God] wherever he is, through the
holiness that exists within every single thing, even corporeal things.
—SFAT EMET[1]

There is a spectrum of nondual thought regarding the importance of the body, and the material world as a whole, to spiritual development. We may divide this spectrum into three basic approaches.

The first consists of disregard. Some nondual sages care little for the physical body, regarding it as just another part of the dream of materiality; it is no more nor no less important, or real, than anything else. The body aches; the sun shines. The body ages; the tree is green. It's all just another part of the program. Indeed, some see the body as at best a distraction, at worst a trap of desires and separateness. If enlightenment consists of the cessation of mistaking yourself with your ego, the body locates the "me" in this place, rather than that—as a cloud, speaking metaphorically, rather than the sky. And, of course, the energies, desires, and demands of the body are so great that they can pull the mind into selfishness, separateness, and confusion. So, many nondual Jewish traditions exhort followers to keep their thoughts only "above," negating the physical world.[2] We will not explore these texts here, but we should acknowledge that they form an important part of the Jewish wisdom of the body.

The second approach to the body is to regard it as an important tool, a skillful means toward waking up. The body, and materiality as a whole, may be a site of *avodah b'gashmiut*, spiritual practice in corporeality, whether in the traditional form of the fulfillment of the *mitzvot*, ascetic forms such as fasting, or other forms such as yoga, energy work, and body-based mindfulness. The body may also be a site for *hitpashtut hagashmiut*, the divestment of corporeality, as it is seen through, felt through, and understood to be nonseparate from the rest of the world. In a sense, this second type of nondual body practice moves us from *yesh* to *ayin*, from contracted mind to expanded mind, from a sense of separateness to a sense of union. These are the familiar patterns of spiritual practice in general.

But there is a third way we might regard the body, a way that is more esoteric and perhaps more revolutionary. This is to regard the body not as the place where we wake up to God, but where God wakes up to us. Here we move from *ayin* to *yesh*, leaving behind even the notion of spiritual practice to regard ourselves as the dance of God in corporeality; what the Chabad sages call *dirah b'tachtonim*, God's dwelling place "below." This corresponds to the "lower unity" of the Shema, which as we have already seen is actually the higher unity, as it embraces the One as the many. It is an extremely subtle form of practice, but contains the aroma of Eden within it.

A MEANS TO AN END: THE BODY AS THE SITE OF NONDUAL SPIRITUALITY

Acknowledge God in all your ways.
—PROVERBS 3:6

The Blessed Creator is endless and surrounds the worlds . . . We are ever walking about in God, Blessed be He, and we could not make a single movement without God's influx and life-flow.
—LIKKUTIM YEKARIM[3]

By now, it is familiar to most Westerners that the body can be a useful place to start awakening from the delusion that God is somewhere other than here. It can enable mind states wherein nonduality, and a host of other spiritual truths, may be realized. It can enable the flow of energies which yield a sense of connectedness, rather than separateness. And, precisely because we often cannot control the body, understanding phenomena we regularly arrogate to the self—emotions, for example—as things which happen to the body can help dislodge the sense that "I am happy" or "I am angry," and replace it with a more self-less sense of happiness or anger arising.

There is, of course, a wide spectrum of body practices designed to aid realization, some of which may seem more palatable to us today than others. To take one unpopular example, for ascetics, the body is useful to the extent that it can be placed under duress. By undoing our innate sense of self-preservation, the ascetic transcends bodily conventions and liberates the mind from ordinary thinking. Asceticism quiets the passions, lowers the physical energies, and enables liberation. In addition, in the Jewish world, as in the Christian and Muslim ones, intense fasting and self-denial are also practices of the penitent. They open the heart and enable the experience of grace. They are not popular today, but they have always been powerful. Note, too, that ascetic practices are not necessarily the same as mere disregard or disdain for the body. They affirm that the body is powerful—but they use that power in practices of self-denial.

More affirmatively, for many spiritual practitioners, the soul is activated in the body, or even present within the body, and is awakened by the skillful interaction with it. Thus the Hindu tradition has given birth to yoga, which activates the flow of bodily energies, enables enlightened consciousness to arise, and prepares the body for meditation. And, in the Jewish tradition, as I have written about in my book *God in Your Body*, there are countless practices which utilize the body as a means to spiritual understanding. Ecstatic, embodied prayer; blessings over eating and excreting; the sanctification of sexuality; the *mikva*; all of these practices, and many more, honor the body as the most skillful means to expanded consciousness. The Hasidim, building on the biblical maxim that "in all your ways shall you know God"[4]—and the *Shnei*

Luchot HaBrit's daring statement that one may serve God even with the *yetzer hara*, in eating, drinking, sexuality, and so on[5]—saw every physical act as an opportunity for God-consciousness. As the *Keter Shem Tov* directs: "Let one consider that in 'all your ways shall you know God.' This is a marvelous thing, for one must consider every material thing and raise it and link it and join it to God, to be one."[6]

In the traditional model, this practice consists of the *mitzvot*, which (especially as elaborated upon by customs and folklore) govern all aspects of life, from which foot one puts on the ground in the morning to what time one goes to sleep at night.[7] In nontraditional models, embodied spiritual practice encompasses everything from observing the changes to the body during eating or exercising and during sanctifying physical acts such as sexuality or even going to the bathroom, to becoming more attuned to the energies that comprise our daily experience and how they are connected to the world around us. In both cases, this is *avodah b'gashmiut*, the service of God in corporeality. Sometimes, in Kabbalistic and Hasidic texts, it is symbolized as "raising the sparks" of the Divine that reside in every material thing.

It is sometimes said that practices of the body, because they involve the "lowest," or most separate-seeming aspects of existence, are the "highest" forms of spirituality. It is relatively easy, R. Aharon says, to apprehend unity in intellectual contemplation and to feel it in emotional ecstasy. But because the material world most insistently presents us with duality and shadow, to see the light there is a further step along the path.

Here, too, there is a spectrum of practice. At one end are energetic practices which cause a lowering of the boundary between self and other: ecstatic dancing, energy work, or something as simple as being in a natural place and observing the changes in the body caused by the changes in environment. Such practices teach, experientially, that we are not so separate from the cycles of the earth (and the sun and moon) as we suppose; by interrupting the dominion of the ego, they give a taste of both transcendence (of the separate self) and immanence (of the Divine). Though sometimes mocked as pagan, or indulgent, or in some way ethically inferior, such practices embrace a greater embrace of human experience than those which shirk from the Dionysian. They do not celebrate only the pleasant; they invite in light and shadow together. Their dance is in the difference—the joys and sorrows, seasons and sexes—and they celebrate the many energies of our embodied lives.

At the other end of the spectrum, *avodah b'gashmiut* gives way to *hitpashtut hagashmiut*, the divestment of corporeality. These are practices which focus not on the differences but the unity of nature: not the waves but the ocean. The result, according to one Hasidic master, is not a negation of the world but an enlivening of it:

> We perceive our world as material and coarse only because we chase after empty goals and physical desires. However, if we are discerning and adhere to the pleasantness and sweetness of the light of God and the constant performance of the *mitzvot*, this world is proven to be good and valuable. For then, in every place, one sees nothing but the sweetness and the pleasantness of the vital energies of the Creator [*hiyyut haborei*], his Name be praised. As it is written "You give life to all"[8]; "You fill and surround all worlds."[9] In every place one can commune with the Creator of the world, "for there is no place free of him." Thus the entire world is nothing but a portal and gate to perceiving and communing with God.[10]

Or, as Spinoza said, "the mind can bring it about, that all bodily modifications or images of things may be referred to the idea of God."[11] Contemplating the myriad of "programs" executing in a forest—seeds becoming trees, crickets and their din—I see that I, too, am a program executing in the mind of God, no different in kind from the birds. All around me, inside me, there is but the dance of the Goddess, in which everything She touches, changes; the immanence of the *Shechinah*.

Here, too, the purpose of spiritual practice is not to cultivate some special "spiritual" states and deify them with appellations, but rather to see God in all feelings, times, and states of mind or body. If we suppose that God is only present in the pleasant—on a summer's day but not in a cancer ward, when we feel relaxed but not when we are tense—then we are still making the same dualist error: God is here, but not there. As

Meister Eckhart wrote, "whoever seeks God in some special way, will gain the Way and lose God . . . But whoever seeks God without any special Way, finds Him as He really is . . . and He is life itself."[12]

In this form, nondual spiritual practice provides neither the allure of the pleasant nor the expiation of the difficult—but, rather, a devotion which is utterly transparent and thus always available. Drinking a cup of tea is not holy because it is special tea, or a special cup, or a special time of the week. It is holy because it is an ordinary cup of tea, poured by God into God.

Yet even this is not the ultimate form of embodied nondual practices. For even when extended into every aspect of our lives, using the body as a site for spiritual practice is only half of *ratzo v'shov*, running and returning: the *ratzo*, moving from facticity to Godliness. But for nondualists, whether they be yogis, Jews, Tantrikas, or devotees of any other tradition, there is also the *shov*, the returning, in which the body is valued for its own sake, as a manifestation of the Divine play. Here the movement is not from the body to God, but from God to the body. As we will now see, the body is, precisely because it seems to be the furthest from the One, the greatest extension of its unity.

AN END IN ITSELF: NONDUALITY, KASHRUT, AND THE TRANSPARENCY OF GOD

All souls are playing, some consciously, some unconsciously.
Religion is learning to play consciously.
—VIVEKANANDA[13]

Kabbalah consists of opposing, balancing motions. Being and nothingness, running and returning, light and dark, expansion and contraction, higher and lower, Absolute and Relative. The path of nonduality, as it reconciles opposites in what Rachel Elior calls "the paradoxical ascent to God," necessarily involves itself in the resolution and integration of supposed binarisms and dimorphisms, much as Jewish mysticism seeks the inclusion of the left within the right, the lower within the upper. Here, just as we may use the body to move from *yesh* to *ayin*, so too does the performance of *mitzvot* draw the *ayin* into the *yesh*, the light of the

Divine into materiality.[14] This movement is expressed by Rabbi Schneur Zalman of Liadi in terms of the unification of *kudsha brich hu* and *shechintei*, the formula we explored in chapter 2:

> The essence of the unification is to draw down the influx of the blessed Light of the Infinite by study of Torah and performance of the commandments for it is for the unification of the Blessed Holy One and His Divine Presence . . . that is to draw down the influx through the Torah and the Commandments so that divinity will be revealed *in this world.*[15]

This unification is also what is referred to in Chabad philosophy as *dirah b'tachtonim*, the lower indwelling of the Infinite. God is not merely experienced in the physical—God is *expressed* in the physical. As we have seen already, for the last Lubavitcher Rebbe, "the essence of Hasidism is the extension of the *Ein Sof*"[16] into all worlds, all realms, all places. And it is precisely in the *alma diperuda*, the world of separateness, where God can do Her dance as us. Again and again, Hasidic sources state that God created the world so that the king could have subjects. This metaphor may have lost its meaning for many of us—perhaps R. Nachman's statement is better, that "God created the world through God's love. God wanted to reveal God's love, and if the world were not created, to whom could God express it?"[17] But the point is the same: God and the world "inter-are"; and the infinite is made manifest precisely in the finite.

We are not, each of us, mere parts or sparks of God. We are the whole of God, looking through different eyes. And it would seem that God delights in the hide-and-seek game of our embodied lives. Says the Maggid of Mezrich, "The world would not have been created if not for the delight of the Holy One and the pleasure in performance of the mitzvot."[18] Notice the radicalism of the Maggid's dance which God has chosen to do, and God derives pleasure from it—through us. Or, moving from an eighteenth-century Hasidic master to a twenty-first-century best-selling author, Elizabeth Gilbert:

> A spontaneous handstand . . . isn't something a disembodied cool blue soul can do, but a human being can do it. We have hands; we

can stand on them if we want to. That's our privilege. That's the joy of a mortal body. And that's why God needs us. Because God loves to feel things through our hands.[19]

In other words, as Gilbert quotes her guru as saying, "God dwells within you, as you."[20] "God is the Speaker and we are the speaking," says David Aaron.[21] "What we truly are is God manifest in time and place," says Rami Shapiro.[22] Precisely in our bodies, in our world, we are the dance that God is dancing, and nondual "spiritual practice" is simply learning to dance consciously.

All this has been somewhat abstract, so let's now turn to a single example, that of kashrut, the Jewish dietary laws and practices. Along with the Sabbath and prayer, kashrut is perhaps the most demanding of Jewish ritual observances; it is a discipline that requires daily attention and can seem quite overbearing at times. However, kashrut is a prime example of nondual spiritual practice, precisely because it can be so devoid of traditional spiritual meaning.

Most of us know the basic rules—and actually, there are only three of them. First, only some animals may be eaten. Second, those animals must be killed in a certain way. Third, their flesh cannot be mixed with milk. That's about 90 percent of it—but as anyone who keeps kosher knows, things quickly get complicated. For example, we would all agree that if a strip of bacon were fried in a pan, and then an egg were fried right in the leftover bacon grease, that the egg is not kosher, even though there's nothing intrinsically nonkosher about the egg. Well, what if a single drop of nonkosher gravy is dropped into a huge vat of kosher chicken soup? Generations of rabbis have busied themselves with such questions and have created a huge, ornate body of rules and regulations as a result. Doubtless this is all too familiar to many observant Jews.

As with most Jewish practices, the traditional importance of kashrut is in its physical performance, not in the reasons for it. Neither the Torah nor the Talmud explains why the rules even exist. Thus, one hears countless explanations and rationales: God commanded it, it imbues mundane acts with holiness, it connects one to the Jewish people (and separates Jews from everyone else), it teaches discipline, it respects animal rights, it's healthy, it is an ancient system of order and taboo, it yields insights into interbeing and non-self—or perhaps it makes no sense at all but is a purely devotional practice that inspires, somehow, love.

All of these, from the sublime to the ridiculous, are essentially explanations of why kashrut works as a spiritual practice. (You might notice the last one is essentially the theory put forth in chapter 4, and the next-to-last that of the previous section.) But only the first—"God commanded it"—is actually present in the original texts. And I want to suggest that a nondual reading of "God commanded it" is "God becomes it." Rather than search for a "spiritual meaning" to the rules of kashrut, a nondual approach to it might prefer to see the practice as purely a matter of materiality. Kashrut is a body practice, and recognizes the value of the body, of the material world, on its own. The pointlessness is the point: this is how the ineffable is extended into the worldly.

Of course, the particulars of the practice likely have some historical reason: Mary Douglas's analysis in her classic anthropological study *Purity and Danger*—that these are ancient systems of order and taboo, reflecting the notion of an ordered creation—seems the most likely. And one of the strengths of Jewish practice is that it accommodates so many philosophies within it. But if we choose to set aside all explanations, we recenter spiritual practice from that which affects the individual to that which gives nonsensical form to the sensible. It simply *is*, which might be the point.

This approach also takes us a step beyond regarding the body as a tool for the spirit. We are conditioned to believe that the body is merely a tool to affect some non-embodied "spirit" or soul or heart because of body/spirit dualism, chiefly exemplified by Greek dualism as filtered through the apostle Paul, who saw the body as flawed, fallen, and mortal but regarded the soul as pure, capable of salvation, and immortal. To use Paul's chief example, how could mere circumcision of the flesh have any meaning compared with circumcision of the heart? By now, such dualism has so won the day that I think most of us take for granted that religion is a matter of heart and soul.

But the Talmudic sages disagreed. They argued, in their version of the "New Testament," the Mishna (literally, "second"), that the significant sphere of religious life was the body, not the disembodied soul. This is why "pointless" embodied commandments such as kashrut are discussed in such intimate, endless detail: because the body is the point.

Here the nondualism of nineteenth-century Hasidim and the legalism of sixth-century *tannaim* somehow come together. If we try to make each detail of legalistic Judaism conform to some higher "spiritual" purpose, most of us will get very frustrated. On the other hand, if we approach the minutiae of kashrut as configuring the physical universe in a holy way—not because of how it makes us feel, but because of how it physically is, in itself—then we are liberated from the yoke of spiritually and we find ourselves in a place of honoring the physical bodies we inhabit. Your body is of importance, whether the ego feels it or not. *Halacha*, the Jewish "path," exists trans-subjectively—that is, beyond the sensations it brings about.

All of this rather traditionalist conversation accords quite neatly with the nondual revolution in the realm of the spirit. In such a view, the soul is not a feeling, not a faculty in addition to the body, mind, and heart; it is the point of connection between those aspects of the self and the reality of the One. Feelings are part of the picture, but the true "goal" of spiritual practice is to embrace all of the parts, on their own terms. To be sure, nondual practice is "advanced" practice, because a colorless, feeling-less truth is only attractive for those who have first tasted the ecstasies and joys of contemplative life. First, taste the energies, know them, and know that several thousand years of hidden wisdom are not nonsense after all. And, by all means, apply spiritual sentiment to a spiritually starved life; it can sustain us in times of darkness. But as you come to know the delights of form, complement *yesh* (form) with *ayin* (emptiness): come to see that all feelings and energies, not just the pleasant ones, are all manifestations of God. Enter the nondual view, in which your awareness is larger than your body, and thus, paradoxically, at home with it.

If we only perform those rituals that give us a certain feeling, then we are mistaking a certain feeling for God. But the Infinite is truly infinite, not just in the places we enjoy. God is in the fire, in the wind, in the still, small voices which nurture us at night—and in the physical body as well. In this light, kashrut, as with circumcision, technical Sabbath observance, and hundreds of other Jewish rituals, extends the infinite into the realm of the finite; it is the aspect of *shov*, and its subject is God, not the ego. It refuses to say that the material world is fallen, or irrelevant, or only important because of its effect on the "soul," whatever that is. It sanctifies the ordinary not by creating a special feeling, but simply by being.

And then, in my experience, feelings do arise. What I have experienced, when I am able to practice this way, is a different sort of love from the one I read about in books. It is an egoless, transparent love which inheres in the actual food I put in my mouth, in the actual stomach which digests it, and in the actual nutrients absorbed by my bloodstream. And it is an embrace that holds me even when I do not feel it, even when I do not want to be held. It is as inescapable as an Infinite Being should be: always with me, always touching every atom of my being, just waiting for me to wake up.

The nonduality of the embodied self leads to an enlightenment far deeper than the dualistic flight from the body. Holding on to a separation between the body and the soul, it's easy to imagine a soul independent from the rest of the world, like a puppetmaster pulling the strings of our body. But this whole picture is simply not true. What we call "the soul" is a net of causes and conditions determined by genetic information, environment, culture, society, and the myriad "accidents of living" we encounter. Consciousness is a trick played by a well-functioning brain, the result of decades of data and millennia of genetic evolution. Everything has its conditions, including your reading, my writing, and the sounds around you right now. In fact, since everything is fully dependent upon those conditions, you might ask: who really is reading, who really is writing, and what really is going on?

Some people worry that, without immortal, immaterial souls, we are merely machines, with no accountability and no humanity. But as we will see in the next chapter, neither consequence is true. Actually, seeing oneself as a "machine," that is, as a body governed by the laws of the universe, is not a diminishment; it is a release from the delusion that who you are is this small self, this ego, separate from the rest of the universe, a soul trapped in a body. Precisely the scientific materialism so derided by many religious and spiritual people is the key to enlightenment itself. You are not a "soul" unfortunately trapped in a body. You are not your ego—the ego is just a computer program. You are "starstuff" (in Carl Sagan's words), and your mind is a temporary repository of the dreams of the universe.

As I have written about before, the great spiritual achievement is not transcending the body, but joining body and spirit together. Only then can form be dissolved in emptiness, and emptiness manifest as form. To return to a favorite image of mine, the six-pointed Jewish star has two triangles, one pointing upward—toward heaven, transcendence, the upper unity, *ayin*, the emptiness of the Infinite—and another pointing downward—toward the earth, Immanence, the lower union, and the endless varieties of experience. The goal is not to privilege one triangle over the other—to flee the material world in favor of the spiritual one, or vice versa. It is the sacred marriage of the two. This union of unions has many iterations: body and spirit, earth and sky, experience and theory, the Presence and the Holy One, feminine and masculine, immanence and transcendence, substance and form, the many manifest energies of the world and their ultimate, essential unity. On the plane of *ayin*, the entire cosmos really is all in your head—only, it isn't your head. On the plane of *yesh*, the physical is as real as the "spiritual." And both planes are true.

As long as the individual self still believes that its own dispositions are the barometers of the Infinite, the idolatry of the *yesh*, of form, endures. Liberation cannot happen if spiritual practice is about feeling good, or mystical, or special. Yet it's the simplest, most obvious thing in the world when the desires for those feelings are released, and the world is sufficient as it is: perfect, and up to you to make it better. Then the ego drops, the body is real (as real as anything, that is), and the real work at last can begin.

This form of nondual "spirituality" is really an overturning of conventional spirituality. Where spirituality prefers ecstasy and loving-kindness to boredom and doubt, nondual spirituality has no preference at all. Since God is everywhere, nondual practice is about cultivating an inner space large enough to accommodate even the most difficult of emotions and circumstances. To say "yes, this too," *shiviti adonai l'negdi tamid*, to our greatest pains, betrayals, and fears; to include all of it, the beauty and the terror; allowing them, feeling them, and letting Being be—bringing the light of the Ein Sof into the world.

Paradoxically, the nondual view is both that conditioned things do not really exist—"the worlds do not maintain any substance at all from the perspective of God's truth, insofar as there is nothing beside him"[23]—and yet the world is pervaded by God: "The whole earth is full of his glory and there is no place devoid of him . . . God is everywhere."[24] On the one hand, appearances are to be seen through: "Do not see anything in the world as it appears, but raise your eyes to the heights, by means of contemplation and study, to see only the divinity clothed in all things in the world."[25] On the other, the nondual embrace is a re-awakening of the body, a re-delighting of sex, a re-appreciation of art and culture and politics and ethics and food and beauty. On the one hand, when all is seen as it is, all is seen through, as in this Sufi poem:

> In the market, in the cloister—only God I saw
> In the valley and on the mountain—only God I saw . . .
> In favor and in fortune—only God I saw . . .
> Myself with my own eyes I saw most clearly,
> But when I looked with God's eyes—only God I saw.
> I passed away into nothingness, I vanished,
> And lo, I was the All-living—only God I saw.[26]

And yet on the other hand, markets, cloisters, mountains, and valleys are all newly miraculous, newly alive. As David Loy put it, "to shrink to nothing is to become everything, and to experience everything as One is again equivalent to nothing—although a different sense of nothing."[27]

In this dialectic, in the inversions and recombinations, is the life of the nondual: good and evil, being and nothingness, *yesh* and *ayin*, upper unity and lower unity, God in Godself and God in the world. As R. Aharon says, "All is one, unified power alone, and it is by means of God's wondrous power to combine to opposites in one thing."[28] In Elior's elaboration:

> Each of these two aspects conditions the other, for at their root, the phenomena visible to man, the Yesh, or corporeality, are

dependent on the divine Ayin, from which they draw their vitality and substance. In contrast, the divine Ayin is dependent on the modification that limits the corporeal Yesh for its discerned manifestation.[29]

This view is not unlike the Taoist notion of interdependence, represented by yin and yang and by utterances like

> It is because there is "is" that there is "is not"; it is because there is "is not" that there is "is." Thereupon, the self is also the other; the other is the self . . . But really are there such distinctions as self and other, or are there no such distinctions? When self and other lose their contrarity, there we have the very essence of the Tao.[30]

And it is not unlike the negative-theological deconstruction of implicit and explicit dichotomies, most important those of sense and sound, presence and absence, that has marked much postmodern philosophical thought.[31] As Nicholas of Cusa wrote, "God is to be found beyond the 'coincidence of contradictories.'"[32] The ultimate transcendence is immanence; as Rabbi DovBer Pinson puts it, "To see beyond the *ayin* and realize that the Infinite is within the physical as it is beyond it."[33]

Beyond the *ayin*! This is the process of *hashva'ah*, of equalization: to transcend even the notion of transcendence, to return to the world in a state of utter equipoise. *Hashva'ah* "define[s] the absolute divine presence throughout all of existence, which is the unity of opposites, and the essential equality of the divine unity in all worlds,"[34] says Elior. For the Divine, this *hashva'ah*, this equivalence and coincidence of opposites, is already the case: As R. Aharon says, "Before Him, blessed be He, Who is all powerful, *Yesh* and *Ayin* are 'equal,' for before him, blessed be He, heaven and earth are called the same, since *Yesh* and *Ayin* are in absolute equality."[35] But for us, the task is to imitate the Divine precisely in this embrace:

> Now the whole essence of the intention is to reveal his blessed equanimity (*hashva'ah*) in actual activity: that is, so that all of reality and the levels in actual activity (*poel mamash*), in their details

will be revealed and unified and connected in their essence—separated and yet united.[36]

In a final irony, this embrace of opposites means a return back to the utterly ordinary, away even from the buzz of nonduality; but back with a knowing, an irony, perhaps, an almost camp playfulness with respect to what so many take so seriously. There is a touch of the trickster to non-duality; on good days, it's as if God laughs and cries simultaneously.

9

ETHICS: THE PROBLEM OF
EVIL AND IMPROVING ON GOD

Everything is foreseen; yet free will is given.
—PIRKEI AVOT 3:15

As long as you believe yourself to be in control, believe yourself to be responsible.
—NISARGADATTA

It would be impossible to write a book on nondual Judaism without at some point taking special notice of the problems nonduality raises for ethics. First, there is the issue of quietism: in principle, the notion that "all is one" can lead to a certain disregard for the reality of suffering, or complacency about injustice, which after all is just as God-filled as justice. Second, there is the problem of nihilism: if everything is God, then what is the meaning of the dualisms of good and evil, justice and injustice? And third, there is the problem of responsibility: if "I" am just a program, a result of causes and conditions that are not "me," can this "I" ever be said to be responsible for his actions? Is nonduality the "abuse excuse" writ large?

As we have had several occasions already to remark, these concerns are based to some degree on historical antecedent, but largely on the erroneous supposition that nonduality is merely the erasure of boundaries and barriers. Unity is exactly half of the matter. Nonduality is both-and, not either-or: both one and many, both illusion and reality. And to the extent that any of us continues to identify with our illusory selves, then obviously we must still subscribe to the other "illusions" of the relative world, distinction-based morality included. As the nondualist sage Nisargadatta said in the passage quoted above, "As long as you believe yourself to be in control, believe yourself to be responsible."

This is the kernel of the matter: few of us are enlightened enough to set aside the imperatives of ethics, and if we were, the imperatives would arise on their own anyway. As it is, not only the general norms but the noble, relative work of parsing and debating the specific content of ethical obligations remain with us. And from that germ is reborn the quintessential Jewish pursuit of equality and social justice—today often associated with the Kabbalistic term *tikkun olam*, or completion/repair of the world—because in the world of the relative, suffering exists and it is our job to transform it. As one of my teachers used to say, the world may be perfect, but it's up to you to make it better. Or as Rabbi Michael Lerner has put it, "The revolutionary impact of Judaism has been its willingness to bear witness to the aspect of God that allows for the possibility of transformation from that which is to that which ought to be."[1] As Lerner notes, this is a "relative truth" only, not an absolute one, since God is What Is as well as What Ought. But Judaism, as a householder religion, is concerned with the relative, with society, and with justice. All of this remains untouched by encounters with the absolute.

Yet there are some important changes wrought by nonduality, or more particularly, its application to the (non-)self. What we mean by "free will" shifts. And how we understand the arising of compassion does as well. For all its paradoxes and esotericisms, perhaps the greatest mystery of nonduality is also the most banal: that we are good at heart after all.

INTEGRAL NONDUAL ETHICS: BEYOND QUIETISM AND NIHILISM

One often hears, in some circles, a criticism that contemporary spirituality is narcissistic; it soothes us too much, turns us from pressing concerns of the day to endless self-absorption. Is this true? Does spiritual practice lessen our political motivation or sense of ethical responsibility—and if so, should it?

This is essentially the critique that spirituality is quietistic, raised most articulately with respect to nondual Judaism by the scholar Rivka Schatz Uffenheimer in her study of Hasidism. Historically, there surely was what Schatz Uffenheimer calls "indifference toward the world, society and the self"[2] in the elite theological literature of Hasidism. Yet as other scholars have shown,[3] many Hasidic leaders were quite activist in orientation—including the founder of Chabad, who commented on the Napoleonic wars, intervened with Russian authorities on behalf of his community, and spent time in jail.

In practice, it seems clear that outlooks varied. In principle, however, quietism is a categorical mistake. The world is both unitive and multiplicitous, both one and many, and thus requires different modes of consciousness depending on context. Spiritual technologies point toward the absolute, and are useful for cultivating the heart, expanding consciousness, and freeing the mind from habitual patterns of greed and delusion. Political technologies are relative; they help us to alleviate the suffering of others and to understand our (relative) world. These are different technologies, used for different purposes, and while spiritual practice may tend toward radical acceptance, responsible political practice may incline toward action and change. Of course, there may be interaction: yoga and meditation can make you more compassionate and gentle, which then informs your political activism. But they won't tell you which presidential candidate (if any) to support; only careful research, reflection, and knowledge will do that. Likewise, all the post-Marxist theory in the world won't give you a taste of the *ayin*: you've got to sit on the cushion and find out for yourself. Different forms of knowledge, different technologies— and complementary, not contradictory. Nonduality has no political program, other than the side effects of love. Ramesh Balsekar is helpful here:

> I define enlightenment as permanently eliminating the basic perceptions that either duality or unity is the answer, and thus attaining to permanent non-dual realizations that are unshakable. It has nothing whatsoever to do with how things manifest and everything to do with some basic understanding of those things."[4]

Of course, if you're involved in spiritual practice but have no political consciousness, you're missing a big part of the nondual point. Quietism as to the absolute, yes, but in a time of global ecological collapse, quietism as to the relative is suicide.[5] But the converse, one might argue, is equally imbalanced. Confusion results when one zone's criteria are used to evaluate another zone's activity. Enlightenment, if it is defined as knowledge of the absolute, does not imply any relative merits. One may be spiritually advanced and politically, physically, financially, intellectually, or emotionally backward. They are different lines of human development.

That said, there is certainly debate as to the necessary ethical consequences of the nondual view. In contemporary Vedanta circles, the gap is wider than in Judaism: there are radical determinists who understand everything, including one's neuroses and ethical missteps, to be part of a mechanistic playing out of Being, and more moderate voices who maintain some notion of individual ethical responsibility. Ramesh Balsekar is a famous exponent of the more radical view. He told one student, "Do you want to know how to live life? Let it be! Let it happen. Everything that everyone is *doing*—let it happen! Be still, *do* whatever *you* want, and don't bother about the world!"[6] And his teachings include statements such as "Whatever happens to anyone is the will of the Source or God" and "All action is a divine happening through human object—it is not something done by someone."[7] This makes a great deal of sense: if "*Ein Sof* completely fills the whole earth temporally and spatially,"[8] then by definition, everything we do is Divine. It is not some sort of subterfuge, an excuse to do what one wants; it flows directly from the understanding of causation and Ein Sof. But it does have the troubling consequence that "individual responsibility" is an error.

There are other voices, however. For example, Sri Siddharameshvar said, "Realize the Self and behave accordingly!"[9] implying that there are some forms of behavior that accord with realization, and others that do not. And many Vedantists distinguish "between the level of Absolute truth (*paramarthika-satya*) [and] conventional, pragmatic truth (*vyavaharika-satya* or *samvriti-satya*), that in this world of relationships and activities there is a meaningful distinction between true-false, right-wrong, appropriate-inappropriate, skillful-unskillful, helpful-harmful, kind-cruel, and so forth."[10] Many also maintain that moral virtue is a precondition for awakening.[11] Both sides continue the debate, often rancorously: the radicals are said to act egoically and unskillfully, the moderates to be stuck in dualism.

In the Jewish context, a similar debate occurred in the eighteenth century. Then, the Jewish radicals were the heretical Sabbateans and

Frankists, who believed that the messianic age had begun in secret and that the manifest world was essentially a lie. Thus not only had many of the restrictions of Jewish law been lifted, but in some sects, the best way to prove one's faith was deliberately to transgress legal norms and prove the insignificance of the apparent world. The Hasidim, on the other hand, were clearly in the "moderate" camp. They insist that the apparent world does exist in some way, and that our actions within it still have significance. They never advocated antinomianism, quietism, or abrogation of ethical norms; on the contrary, the paradigm of the *tzaddik* is one who acts as a vessel or a pipe, bringing the Divine outflowing to a community deeply in need of it.[12] The Hasidim clearly "won" the debate; they survived, and the Sabbateans did not. Thus few Jews today openly espouse a religiously-derived antinomianism, anomianism, or quietism. Ethics, justice, politics, activism—these all remain on the mainstream Jewish agenda. Perhaps a nondualist sees them from a slightly different perspective, and with perhaps a little less zeal. But social, spiritual, material, and cultural truths are all faces of the nondual as reflected in the relative.

The "you" reading these words may indeed be a phenomenon of the brain, a computer replicating the social and cultural memes of late capitalism, of art and literature and language. And, reading these words, "You" are the awareness that gives birth to the cosmos, radiant in emptiness, at one with God. Yet for all that, you also remain a nexus of ethical responsibility, and are empowered to transform that which is cruel and unjust into that which is ever more capable to receive and reflect the light.

FREE WILL: THE LAST GASP OF THE UNENLIGHTENED MIND

So, the ethical imperative, and its elaborations, remain mostly unchanged. Yet at least one notion does not: that of "free will," the principle that each of us is free to choose and thus bears responsibility for whatever choice we make. As an ontological principle, free will is the last gasp of the unenlightened mind, the last, desperate attempt to maintain the illusion of self. But, as we will see, the notion retains its usefulness as a description of moral decision making—that is, as a relative concept—and the moral anarchy predicted by some of its most zealous defenders simply does not occur.

Naive notions of free will persist today notwithstanding the withering attack on the concept by scores of philosophers, neuroscientists, and biologists.[13] John Locke and David Hume called it nonsensical. Schopenhauer argued that it is only an a priori perception, not an actual description of events. Hobbes said it has only apparent reality; in Nietzschean terms, it has conventional truth only. In Spinoza's words, "men believe themselves to be free, because they are conscious of their own actions and are ignorant of the causes by which they are determined."[14] If we knew all of the numerous causes of our actions, we would no longer "believe in" free will.

The scientific community, too, long ago rejected the Cartesian dualism of an immaterial soul interacting with a material brain, or some ego watching the percepts of consciousness go by like a movie.[15] Consciousness—in particular our consciousness of "self" or ego—is made up of thousands of memes, culturally written software that runs on the hardware of the brain.[16] Scientifically, there just isn't a self, a homunculus hunched inside the brain. It's just not there.

Really, the question of free will is essentially a subset of the classic philosophical distinction between determinism and indeterminism. Normally, of course, most of us live our lives according to determinism. We expect that when we are ill, there is a cause of the illness, and we are quite clear that rain does not materialize out of nothing in the sky. All phenomena have causes; they do not blip in and out of existence on their own (bogus adaptations of quantum mechanics notwithstanding). Yet most of us live our ethical lives according to indeterminism, believing that we make choices and that those choices are "ours," rather than caused by other things. The buck stops here. At this moment, you could continue reading or turn to another page—and of course it seems that the choice is yours.

Seems, but not is. Setting aside neuroscience for a moment, this seeming choice does not even comport with what is directly observed in meditation. As we have seen earlier, every mental decision is wholly caused by the sum total of causes and conditions which have brought you to the moment of choice. Where else would it come from? Some of these causes may be proximate—how interesting this chapter is, how restless you are, what you have to do in five minutes—and others may be quite distant: how you respond to philosophy; your gender, race, and class; and so on. It is beyond our ken to identify all these different causes and conditions, but surely they exist. Yet even if a choice seems totally impulsive, even random, it is caused by something, is it not? And whatever that something is—or rather, whatever the uncountable myriad of somethings are—already exists as the product of other causes and conditions.

As we saw in chapter 6, this process is observable through meditation, which is as close to the scientific method as the introspective mind can get: decisions are phenomena caused by other phenomena. If you want to repeat the experiment, get trained, sit down, and slow down the rapid-fire flow of thought to an extent that the mechanism of causation and choice can be seen more clearly. You will see how involuntary actions which ordinarily pass unnoticed are actually detailed sequences of desire and repulsion; how just brushing away a mosquito can seem like a choreographed ballet. This is observed—not merely felt. The smooth clockwork of discursive thought is deliberately interrupted in such contexts, and its mechanistic nature can be observed. There is no self driving the gears—just more gears. What seems to be "free will" is actually an emergent phenomenon of uncountable mental factors, causes, and conditions. This is what can be observed empirically, on the phenomenal level of the mind.

Of course, it is possible that some weird, nonmaterial, nonprovable, nondisprovable, nonobservable self is actually calling the shots, but the principle known as Ockham's Razor suggests that the best solution tends to be the simplest one—not least because, after three hundred years, no one has been able to show how material and nonmaterial forms interact.[17] And no, quantum theory doesn't work either.[18] As minute as neurons are, they are gargantuan in size compared to subatomic particles blinking in and out of existence. Suggesting that quantum flux influences the brain is like saying that an ant crawling across my floor suddenly built my home.

No—our brains obey the basic laws of cause and effect. Somewhere, deep within the recesses of the brain, there are memories, learned behaviors, memes, cultural artifacts, genetic predispositions and preferences, that are combined, in a fraction of a moment, to form decisions. As I ponder the next words to write, thirty-seven years of experience and millions of years of genetic engineering are determining the choices that I make. Of course, the way these factors are combined will be different for each of us, thus giving rise to unique personalities and creativity; the materialistic view certainly does not deny the wondrous powers of the human mind to innovate, invent, and create new "combinations" that have never existed in the world before. Indeed, our sense of agency is also part of "what nature intended," just as much as our instincts are.[19] We really are in the image of God. But not because we somehow stand outside the material universe.

So is there no free will?

Yes and no. "Free will" is a convention. It is useful for describing our perception of, and responsibility for, decisions. As a phenomenon of consciousness, it evolved over time, and it in turn has helped human beings and human culture evolve.[20] In the classic compatibilist perspective, it is coherent as a mental phenomenon, even if it makes no sense absolutely—but morally, ethically, this is all that is needed. It is only important that the causes of one's decisions be traced, as Daniel Dennett says, "not to infinity, but far enough back to give my *self* enough spread in space and time so that there is a *me* for my decisions to be up to."[21] This is sufficient, ethically speaking, and entirely coherent nondualistically. It allows for the ultimate nonexistence of the self, the total determinism of all phenomena, and yet also the relative truth of the self and ethical responsibility for one's actions. As a lived, perceptual phenomenon—a phenomenon, not more—obviously free will exists. And that is sufficient for all the ethical and jurisprudential consequences of free will to fall into place.

This is how we might explain Rabbi Akiva's statement that "everything is foreseen; yet free will is given."[22] In actual reality, everything is "foreseen," if by "foreseen" we mean seen by an omniscient God who, like Laplace's demon, can actually know the billions of causes and conditions influencing each of us at every moment. But our small selves are not that God, and so freedom seems to happen—and that is enough. In the Buddha's words, "There is free action, there is retribution, but I see no agent that passes out from one set of momentary elements into another one, except the elements [themselves]."[23]

Some believe that without free will, we are mere biological instruments, with no spark of the Divine and no human soul. But from a nondual perspective, this argument is backward. The autonomous soul isn't the gateway to God; it's the gateway to delusion. This is precisely the *yetzer hara*, the selfish, separating, and, occasionally evil inclination that sees the self as the center of the universe. Whereas, when I'm able to see, just a little bit, that my choices and feelings are the results not of my autonomous "free will" but of a vast Indra's Net of causes and conditions, the overwhelming majority of which I cannot know—not only a sense of perspective, but also a sense of peace, can arise. It is what it is, and it will be what it will be—*ehyeh asher ehyeh*—and my choice is simply what to do about it.

This kind of letting go is not a detachment from the imperative of *tikkun olam*, but a revitalization of it. Which perspective is more likely to lead to pursuing justice: one centered on my self and my needs, or one which sees the arising of "my needs" as just one more strand within a web of causes and conditions, a web often given the name of God? Personally, I'm a lot less selfish when I'm not self-centered; it seems almost a tautology. Nondual action is the same as dualistic action, except without the notion of a "doer," or the hindrances that come with it.[24] It is a clear-seeing that actions are the results of mental factors, not agents. There is simply no one there to blame.

Nor is the erasure of the self an erasure of individuality. Letting go of the delusion of free will doesn't mean that, beforehand, I'm a creative, idiosyncratic, sensual person and afterward I'm a null set. Everything still arises; it's just seen for what It is, rather than what it isn't. This is why some of the most enlightened teachers around today are still very much Brooklyn Jews, or British contrarians, or whatever their histories have shaped them into being. They may not even seem nice at first, and I'm sure that sadness and anger still arise for them; only phonies always smile. But they see the ego for what it is: a program determined by causes and conditions, just part of the web.

Free will is an illusion of the well-functioning brain, a trick of the mind, and oftentimes the joke's on you. Let go of it; you've got nothing to lose, and Nothing to gain. And there's a big difference between nothing and Nothing, even though I can't quite tell you what it is.

ONE LAST MIRACLE

There is one peculiar miracle left: that compassion is natural after all.

Somehow, the surrender into Being, into God, does make us kinder, even without the heteronomies of law. Just silence, just stillness, just seeing things as they are, and compassion, lovingkindness, and wisdom appear on their own, without any oughts from us. You just feel it. As Rami Shapiro has said, "To be holy, then, is to live the unity of Yesh and Ayin. Living this unity, we know what is right is so powerful a way that we feel commanded to do it. There is no real choice. The knowing is too strong."[25]

It's heartbreakingly banal: when the mind is concentrated enough so that you really get to who you are, underneath all the neurosis, alongside the deep wounds from childhood, you find yourself to be a compassionate person who, just like all the rest of us, simply wants to love and be loved, and to live life right. At least, that's what I've found. And it's what, in near-unanimity, generations of other contemplatives have also found.

This is not necessarily "goodness" in any particular moral sense. I love the stories of Ikkyu, the Zen monk who, after his enlightenment, would carouse with prostitutes and get drunk, much to the chagrin of the traditional authorities. But a natural goodness does tend to arise, when one no longer needs to defend the boundaries of self. In a seemingly paradoxical way, when the spiritual work is being done, the good heart emerges on its own.

This is quite different from the view that you must repress your deepest instincts because they are evil or animalistic. Of course, animal instincts do exist, and it is not reasonable to expect everybody to go off on extended retreats; doing so is a privilege, conditioned by economic ability as well as by taste, luck, and circumstance. So the usual ethical rules and regulations remain. But when the path is allowed to unfold, the contemplative practice of seeing clearly—not superimposing moral thinking atop some rotten foundation, but just seeing what is—leads effortlessly to more justice and more peace. For example, by allowing the ego to melt, even if only in part, the realization of nonduality counters our historical moment's seemingly unstoppable urge to convert nature into property, earth into wealth. The more ego, the more need; the more need, the more consumerism, objectification, property, and waste. In short, the more self, the more stuff.

To repeat, this is not to deny our basic survival instincts, which we share with animals, and which seek to aggrandize the self so it can survive and reproduce. But humans also have countervailing instincts, which we also share with some animals, to nurture and share and care for one another. The Tanya called these two sets of instincts the animal soul and the human soul, and the essential religious impulse is to cultivate the latter, and rest (or, for some, sublimate, channel, or repress) the former. And all who have experienced the natural lessening of the "animal soul" in peak experiences, spiritual practice, or the everyday love of others know that when the selfish instincts are lessened, compassion and love immediately arise. We are good at heart after all, at least partly so.

Nonduality says nothing about how this fundamental ethical impulse is to be translated into specific norms and responsibilities. It does not demand pacifism, or vegetarianism, or any particular ideology. All that is the province of the relative, and of ethical and legal thinking. But the awareness of nonduality does set the ethical wheels into motion. It makes obvious the folly of defending the self when there is actually nothing there to defend. It does call our attention to when acts of violence are truly necessary, and when they are simply desired by the ego (again, usually the male ego) seeking to establish dominance and hierarchy, or by simple selfishness and greed. The wiser we become, the easier it is to discern when we act unwisely. And we discover that beneath the need, or perhaps alongside it, there is indeed goodness.

I can't convey to you how transformative it was for me to see not merely that "all people are good at heart," as Anne Frank said, but that I am, in particular. Me! Clumsy, fumbling, needy me; ironic, cynical me; underneath, or rather alongside, all those pieces and strategies is really a very simple loving person who is—gasp—good at heart. This can be very embarrassing to realize, let alone express. But knowing that goodness is within, rather than superimposed from without, has nonetheless been deeply empowering as I go about the business of trying to live gently and justly.

Anne Frank was not naive. Imagine her knowing, even as she was victimized and brutalized beyond our capacity to conceive, that what was happening was not the evil essence of humanity, but a mistake. Imagine a surrender not to despair, but to the unfolding of Being itself. Imagine the slightest loving smile, held even amidst tears.

10

ENLIGHTENMENT: KNOWING AND NOT KNOWING

You live in illusion and the appearance of things.
There is a Reality. You are that Reality.
When you understand this, you will see that you are nothing
And being nothing, you are everything. That is all.
—KALU RINPOCHE[1]

God does not proclaim Himself; He is everybody's secret.
—KATHA UPANISHAD

The glory of God is to conceal a thing.
—PROVERBS 25:2

KNOWING: WHAT THE WORLD IS, AND WHAT TO DO ABOUT IT

If you have read these words, and your mind has occasionally rested in what might be called the View of What Is, perhaps you have noticed that a sense of knowing may arise which transcends words and simply *knows*. And yet, it is a knowing that does not know anything: it knows only mystery, only the ineffable—as if it knows that it knows, but also that it does not know what it knows. All this must sound like paradox if you have not experienced it. But I do not mean to be obscure; it is the description of the dearest knowledge of all.

Suppose we said it a different way. Suppose we said that the universe is a vast field of matter/energy, sometimes referred to in scientific discourse as space-time. Sometimes space-time appears as matter (substance) and sometimes as energy, although we have recently learned that these two are ultimately the same. This single, incomprehensibly large and ancient field of matter/energy—call it "Being"—is singular, but not uniform: matter has coalesced in some places, and in other places it is relatively absent, all according to certain rules and principles, which govern everything from galaxy clusters to subatomic particles. But it is one field of Being.

In our solar system, matter coalesced around a certain star and formed planets, one of which became the site for a manifestation of Being called "life," an organization of matter/energy governed by the relationships among certain molecules (DNA, proteins, and so forth), and between such molecules and a very large number of environmental factors. Life evolves as some molecular/genetic patterns lead to traits or behaviors that in turn lead to more replication than other patterns do. Humans evolved in this way.

Suppose we continued this scientific way of speaking, broad and general as it is, and observed that, apparently alone among life forms, humans have evolved the ability to think conceptually, and have created enormously complex cultures, artifacts, and even explanations for how the universe came into being. One such explanation is that God created the universe with Wisdom. Although the term "God" has frequently meant a sort of superhuman personality, for which evidence is lacking, if the term is applied to Being itself, then this explanation has the same meaning as the narrative two paragraphs ago.

Enlightenment is the complete knowledge of what has just been said. Although in one sense this knowledge is quite simple to attain (after all, you have just read it), this knowledge is not "complete," and because it is only an intellectual understanding, it is quickly forgotten. "Map is not territory." Moreover, human beings have evolved the tendency to see themselves as individuals, distinct from Being, rather than as appearances or epiphenomena of it, and this tendency is necessary for human genetic patterns to be preserved and reproduced. Thus, to really possess the "knowledge" we have spoken of requires unlearning a basic conception about the nature of the self. This unlearning is what we have meant by "spiritual practice," and it takes many forms.

Is this simpler? That enlightenment is simply knowing how things are, but knowing them in a way that is territory, not map?

Of course, there are other goals beside enlightenment: family, activism, career, love. The contemplative path may interfere with some of these. But awakening to one's true nature does lessen suffering, increase the capacity for love, and bring about many senses of the holy. The truth will set you free—and help you to love. Who knows, maybe it is true that Being in general has tended to evolve across time toward the direction of greater knowledge of Itself.

It is a very simple matter to know intellectually that all of space-time is one field of matter/energy, that the individual self does not have any existence independent from the One, and that all creatures, matter, and energy are but fleeting manifestations of Being. However, truly to know it—that is, to live according to this truth—is to know one's real nature, to end the selfish desires which cause one's own and others' suffering, and to experience a peaceful yet indescribably, achingly beautiful sense of spaciousness in the One that Is, here, now, everywhere, and always. The factors which hold one back from this path vary from individual to individual, according to the values and fears residing in each mind. Yet the end of the path is the same: an end to desire and suffering, an experience of unbounded love and peace, the merging with the One.

NOT KNOWING: IS LIFE BUT A DREAM? IS MYSTICISM BUT A FEELING?

God is true. The universe is a dream.
—VIVEKANANDA[2]

Row, row, row your boat
Gently down the stream.
Merrily, merrily, merrily, merrily
Life is but a dream.
—ANONYMOUS

Then again, who knows?

I do not want to end the book with a pretension of certainty or closure. I want to admit in all the doubt and the uncertainty as well—but all of it, not just some. Because only when the defeat is utter can the surrender be complete.

Suppose the "knowing" in the previous section is just a *feeling*. Yes, for many of us, there is a resonance inside—but maybe that's all there is: a neurosis, not a stirring of truth. I've felt it since the first moment I heard, twenty years ago, sitting in a class in college, that *tat tvam asi*, You are That. I felt it then, I feel it now. But maybe it's just a sensation, merely a neuron firing inside the mechanistic brain. We are still just a few generations descended from monkeys in the trees. What do we know about anything?

Perhaps it doesn't matter: the sages do not suffer and that is what is important. And, even if they are deluded, they are not in asylums. Perhaps, then, this is a desirable delusion.

Yet if the seal of God is truth, living according to a lie cannot be reckoned as holy. So, let us suppose that the whole of nonduality is a delusion—a sham of the mind. Really admit it, and relinquish the pretention of opinion. Look what happens: a release of destination, aggrandizement, or any conceit of being right or being enlightened or being anything at all. And toward nothing. Don't know, got no idea, have no business talking about it, writing about it, teaching, who would know anyway, just the knowing which isn't knowing. Isn't that progress? As Chögyam Trungpa Rinpoche is reported to have said, "Disappointment will become your greatest ally."

But don't stop there. If nonduality is delusion, so must be the word "holy," the projections of "God," and, for that matter, love, and the rest of the values we intuit from the movements of the soul. If we doubt one foundation, we must doubt them all. For that matter, why doubt the nondual experience, but not every other experience? After all, Ramana and Nisargadatta and Wei Wu Wei insist that life is but a dream. Maybe, as I wrote earlier, it really is all in your head—only it isn't your head. When does that end?

To be clear, this is not the traditional nondual Jewish way. The Hasidim are more normative, more world-maintaining, than the Vedantists. They speak of *ratzo v'shov*, of oscillation. From God's point of view, there is absolutely no difference between pre-creation and post-, and so the world is indeed but a vapor—*hevel* in the words of Ecclesiastes, air, emptiness. Yet from the ego's point of view, we are here and we are doing our best, and somehow that seems to matter.

But who knows—maybe our understanding of the Jewish sources is incomplete. There are stories about sages up in the mountains, or in caves; the ones who don't write books. Or the Kotzker Rebbe, who suddenly shut himself in his room and never emerged again. Maybe for every world-affirming Jewish nondualist, there have been a dozen renouncing ones. We'd never know; they wouldn't tell. Perhaps those who say "both-and," both absolute and relative, are simply hiding from the annihilation of the ego. Perhaps integration is really a failure of courage.

From this shore, it may seem impossible to distinguish between the enlightened and the mad, as if "ego-death" is a kind of psychotic event. Yet from the other shore, the erasure of self is the simplest of relinquishments. Once during a shamanic ceremony, I had a near-death experience: moving toward the light, being drawn to it. At that time, I felt pulled back by my love for my partner, my youth, and my desire to create in the world. "Not yet," I thought, recoiling in fear. And yet, less than two years later, when the hoped-for dissolution arose in the context of an extended meditation retreat, it was the most obvious thing in the world. It was the divestment of nothing, the setting down only of an illusion. And life went on exactly as before, exactly as the nondualists said it would.

Eventually, it becomes impossible even to distinguish enlightenment from the everyday, the Divine from the ordinary, and the only response is the compassionate smile of the Buddha, the minor-key dance of the Hasidim. For who, then, can distinguish between the delusion of self, from which liberation seems to be a mirage, and a liberation from a mistake, a concept which, upon its dissolution, is revealed never to have existed at all?

If you doubt, doubt everything. Look into the eyes of the Dalai Lama, and doubt that he is any wiser than the silliest of pop stars. Look into the eyes of generations of enlightened beings—sages, rabbis—and find their gazes, and suppose that they are all deluded. You must doubt rigorously, and reduce all the experiences themselves to neurological events. But you must be consistent, and doubt it all: God, no God, Big Mind, existence, love, money, self, non-self, everything. Do not retain anything: not comparing oneself to others, not the hope that life is worthwhile, not the merest iota of value. And in this doubting, in this rigorous, thoroughgoing rejection of every possible meaning, in this burning away of significance, lies the ultimate defeat of the self, the ultimate victory of what transcends it, the ultimate triumph of surrender. I don't know; I don't know; I don't know. And when the failure is utter, what's left is the real.

Who knows? Yes, Who knows.

KNOWING

let me commence
the knowing
of knowing
the peeling back
of the garments
the gentlest undressing
of this

let me arouse
the quality
of being
and fall into
the embrace
the immersion
into the knowing
of knowing itself

like swimming
in a warmth
that has every synonym
and none
or discovering
one is water
melting into a pond

like disappearing
in the sweetest dissolution
in the consummation

that is
now
like a delightful surrender
to yourself
only to discover
it isn't yours

it is only knowing
it is only is

the thinnest meridian of an instant
this most transparent love

an arena
of sky
with everything within it

we have so few words
for kisses
so few concepts
for embrace
for surrounding
for dissolving into
for the
simultaneous
merging
and emerging
or for the yearning, the coming to know
the song
the holy playfulness
of being itself
the secret seduction
of seducing itself

we have so few words
and every one of them

points in the wrong direction
so, beloved,
let me put an end to language
let me commence
this undressing
of reality
this unwording
of simplicity

let me know
the nakedness
of experience

coming near

nearer

that is none other
than

ACKNOWLEDGMENTS

The author would like to thank Rabbis Zalman Schachter-Shalomi, Arthur Green, David Ingber, David Cooper, Jacob Staub, Ohad Ezrachi, Rami Shapiro, Arthur Waskow, Phyllis Berman, Jill Hammer, Michael Paley; teachers Shoshana Cooper, Javier Regueiro, Rachel Elior, Elliot Wolfson, David Brodsky, John Makransky, Christopher Titmuss, Sylvia Boorstein, Ven. U Vivekananda, Ven. U Jagara, Leigh Brasington, Eliezer Sobel, Avraham Leader, David Friedman; editors Beth Frankl and Chloe Foster; Leonard Jacobs; plus all at *Reality Sandwich*, *Zeek*, *Forward*; invaluable assistants Josh Ring, Avi Shmidman, Joshua Spiro, Chani Getter, Margaret Vetare, Andrew Novak; communities and retreat centers Nehirim, Elat Chayyim, Insight Meditation Society, Dzogchen Center, Short Mountain, Easton Mountain, Burning Man, Body Electric, Spirit Rock. This book was written during a time of great spiritual opening and deep personal pain. My heartfelt thanks go to Jacob Staub, Michael Cohen, Andrew Ramer, Kenji Yoshino, Stephen Cassidy, Adam Ring, Rachel Dobkin, Joel Stanley, Beth Resnick, Kenneth Folk, Andrew Shugerman, Bara Sapir, Bob Pileggi, Amichai Lau-Lavie, Corey Friedlander, Gabriel Blau, Dylan Stein, Jonathan Vatner, David Berger, John Stasio, Michael Grohall, Zvi Bellin, Eric Cohen, David Schildkret, Dan Friedman, Roman Palitsky, Daniel Max, Danny Arguetty, David Ingber, Alana Newhouse, Nehama Benmosche, Tamuz Shiran, Rebecca Jupiter, Jennifer Goldstein, Beverly Pincus, Sarah Chandler, Yocheved Amrami, Julia Appel, Shayna Korb, Sarah Lefton, Amelie Davidson, Joe Wielgosz, Daniel Sieradski, Shir Feinstein-Feit, Ari Weller, and Shoshana Jedwab; to my family, Lorna, Maia, Nancy, and Henry Michaelson; and to many others whose names I should not have forgotten, for their help in seeing me through both. In your light, I see Light.

This book is dedicated to you who reads and writes these words, recognizing Yourself in the dance.

NOTES

INTRODUCTION

1. Daniel 12:3.
2. Zohar II:2a.
3. Arthur Green, *Seek My Face, Speak My Name: A Contemporary Jewish Theology* (Lanham, Md.: Jason Aronson, 1994), p. xxiv.
4. Daniel Matt, *God and the Big Bang: Discovering Harmony between Science and Spirituality* (Woodstock, Vt.: Jewish Lights, 1998), p. 36.
5. Genesis Rabba 68:9. The Midrash asks "Why is God called a 'dwelling place?' (Psalms 90:1) Because God is the dwelling place of the world and the world is not God's dwelling place." The term panentheism was coined by German philosopher Karl C. F. Krause (a disciple of Schelling) in 1828.
6. Psalms 65:2.
7. David Aaron, *The Secret Life of God: Discovering the Divine within You* (Boston: Shambhala, 2005), p. 161.
8. David A. Cooper, "The Godding Process," *Parabola*, http://parabola. org/content/view/137/.
9. David Loy, *Nonduality: A Study in Comparative Philosophy* (New Haven, Conn.: Yale University Press, 1988), p. 17.
10. See Rachel Elior, *The Paradoxical Ascent to God: The Kabbalistic Theosophy of Habad Hasidism*, trans. Jeffrey Green (Albany: State University of New York Press, 1992), pp. 25–26.
11. "Running and returning," Ezekiel 1:14. See R. Yakov Yosef of Polonnoye, *Toldot Yakov Yosef*, Yitro 54b: "This is the mystery of *ratzo v'shov*: that there are two levels, Gadlut [expanded mind] and Katnut [contracted mind]."
12. *Yeridah* and *aliyah* are often associated with the angels on the ladder in Jacob's dream, Genesis 28:12.
13. Nisargadatta, *I Am That: Talks with Sri Nisargadatta Maharaj*, trans. Maurice Frydman (Durham, N.C.: Acorn Press, 1973), p. 269.

CHAPTER ONE

1. Christopher Isherwood and Swami Prabhavananda, trans. and eds. *How to Know God: The Yoga Aphorisms of Patanjali* (Los Angeles, Calif.: Vedanta Press, 2007), p. 130. The wording I have freely translated here as "God" refers to "the Atman," which can also be translated as "Self." However, since in Vedanta, Self is the All, it corresponds to the nondual "God beyond God" discussed here.

2. See Loy, *Nonduality*, pp. 1–35.

3. R. Shmuel Schneersohn, *Mi Chamocha*, trans. in a bilingual edition by Yosef Marcus as *True Existence* (New York: Kehot, 2002), pp. 67–69. The translation here is my own.

4. See Daniel Dennett, *Consciousness Explained* (London: Little, Brown & Co., 1991); Patricia Churchland and Terrence Sejnowski, *The Computational Brain* (Cambridge, Mass.: MIT Press, 1992); John H. Crook, *The Evolution of Human Consciousness* (Oxford: Clarendon Press, 1980).

5. Transcribed by Sadhu Arunachala, in the introduction to Ramana Maharshi, *Talks with Ramana Maharshi: On Realizing Abiding Peace and Happiness* (Carlsbad, Calif.: Inner Directions, 2000), p. xxiii.

6. Ramana Maharshi, *Talks with Ramana Maharshi*, p. 257.

7. Ken Wilber, "From You to Infinity in 3 Pages," http://inintegralinsti tute.org/talk_infinity.aspx.

8. The term "meme" was coined by the evolutionary biologist Richard Dawkins. See Richard Dawkins, *The Selfish Gene* (Oxford: Oxford University Press, 1976), p. 192.

9. Dennett, *Consciousness Explained*, p. 210. See also Daniel Dennett, *Freedom Evolves* (New York: Penguin, 2004), pp. 175–81.

10. Ibid., p. 219.

11. Susan Blackmore, "Waking from the Meme Dream," in *The Psychology of Awakening: Buddhism, Science, and Our Day-to-Day Lives*, eds. Gay Watson, Stephen Batchelor, and Guy Claxton (London: Rider, 2000), pp. 112–22; also available at www.susanblackmore.co.uk/Chapters/awaken.html.

12. Ibid., p. 112–22.

13. Ken Wilber, *Integral Spirituality: A Startling New Role for Religion in the Modern and Postmodern World* (Boston: Shambhala, 2006), p. 277.
14. Ibid.
15. See Dennis Genpo Merzel, *Big Mind, Big Heart: Finding Your Way* (McLean, Va.: Big Mind, 2007).
16. See Peter Schäfer and Joseph Dan, eds. *Gershom Scholem's Major Trends in Jewish Mysticism: 50 Years After* (Tübingen: Mohr Siebeck, 1993), pp. 166, 175; Gershom Scholem, *Origins of the Kabbalah*, trans. Allan Arkush (Princeton, N.J.: Princeton University Press, 1987), pp. 8–10, 221–28, 423–25.
17. See Plotinus, *The Enneads*, trans. Stephen Mackenna, (New York: Penguin, 1991), 5.2.1, 6.9.4, 6.9.6.
18. Ibid., 5.1.7.
19. Porphyry, "On the Life of Plotinus," in *The Enneads*, trans. Stephen Mackenna.
20. For a nondualist reading of Heidegger, phenomenology, and deconstruction see Loy, *Nonduality*, pp. 79–89, 248–60. For Heidegger, subject-object dualism is but one way of looking at the world, and in fact a derivative one. Our true sense of being, *Dasein,* is a form of caring for Being, a finding of significance in it. Only secondarily do we divide up the world into various objects, some of which we regard and others of which we do not. For Heidegger, each percept necessarily carries with it a concept, and an emotive investment; pseudoscientific detachment and objectification are but one attitude among many.
21. Baruch Spinoza, *Ethics and Selected Letters*, ed. Samuel Shirley (Indianapolis, Ind.: Hackett, 1982), part 1, props. 2–6, 8, pp. 32–34.
22. Ibid., part 1, def. 6, p. 31.
23. Ibid., prop. 14, p. 39.
24. Ibid., part 5, p. 36.
25. Meister Eckhart, "Sermon IV: 'True Hearing' on Ecclesiasticus 14:30." In *Meister Eckhart's Sermons*. Translated by Claud Field. Grand Rapids, Mich.: Christian Classics, 1909), p. 13, www.ccel.org/ccel/eckhart/sermons.html.
26. See F. C. Happold, *Mysticism: A Study and an Anthology* (New York: Penguin, 1991), pp. 45–55.

27. *Or Ha Emet* 2b, in Arthur Green and Barry Holtz, trans. and eds., *Your Word Is Fire: The Hasidic Masters on Contemplative Prayer* (Woodstock Vt.: Jewish Lights, 1993), p. 55.

28. William James, *The Varieties of Religious Experience* (Cambridge, Mass.: Harvard University Press, 1985), pp. 390–91.

29. Wilber, *Eye to Eye: The Quest for the New Paradigm*, (Boston: Shambhala Publications, 2000), pp. 55–57.

30. Blaise Pascal, *Pensées*, translated by A. J. Krailsheimer (New York: Penguin, 1995), p. 28.

31. See R. Aharon of Staroselye, *Shaarei HaYichud v'HaEmunah* 3b. Citations to R. Aharon's books are to the new 2004 Jerusalem edition. Translations are my own unless otherwise indicated.

32. Arthur Green and Barry W. Holtz, eds. and trans., *Your Word Is Fire*, p. 14. See also *Maggid Dvarav L'Yaakov* 154 (likening the *ayin* to the liminal time of *bein hashmashot*).

33. R. Aharon, *Shaarei HaAvodah* 13a.

34. R. Aharon, *Shaarei HaAvodah* 7a–b.

35. Ramakrishna, *The Gospel of Sri Ramakrishna*, recorded by Mahendranath Gupta, translated by Swami Nikhilananda (New York: Ramakrishna-Vivekananda Center, 1942), p. 217.

36. *The Cloud of Unknowing*, trans. Clifton Wolters (New York: Penguin, 1978), p. 68.

37. Merzel, *Big Mind, Big Heart*, p. 101.

38. *Keter Shem Tov* II: 2b.

39. Ralph Waldo Emerson, "Nature," in *Selected Writings of Ralph Waldo Emerson* (New York: Signet Classics, 1965), p. 184.

40. See Karen Warren, *Ecofeminist Philosophy* (Lanham, Md.: Rowman & Littlefield, 2000); Greta Gaard, ed., *Ecofeminism: Women, Animals, Nature* (Philadelphia: Temple University Press, 1993); Judith Plant, ed., *Healing the Wounds: The Power of Ecological Feminism* (Gabriola Island, B.C.: New Society, 1989).

41. Adyashanti, *My Secret Is Silence: Poetry and Sayings of Adyashanti* (Los Gatos, Calif.: Open Gate, 2003), p. 27.

42. Rami Shapiro, *Open Secrets: The Letters of Reb Yerachmiel ben Yisrael* (Rhinebeck, N.Y.: Monkfish, 2004), p. 18.

CHAPTER TWO

1. Meister Eckhart, rendered by Daniel Ladinsky as "Expands His Being," in his *Love Poems from God*. (New York: Penguin, 2002), p. 112.

2. *Adyashanti, My Secret is Silence*, p. 41.

3. On the many meanings of *devekut*, see Miles Krassen, *Uniter of Heaven and Earth: Rabbi Meshullam Feibush Heller of Zbarazh and the Rise of Hasidism in Eastern Galicia* (Albany: State University of New York Press, 1999), pp. 5–7, 50–54, 237–38, discussing, and differing from, Scholem.

4. On the appearance of pantheism and panentheism in medieval texts, see Gershom Scholem, *Kabbalah* (New York: Plume, 1978), pp. 144–45. As Scholem notes (at p. 148), no Kabbalistic sources say that God has no existence apart from created beings.

5. Quoted in Scholem, *Kabbalah*, 144.

6. R. Aharon, *Shaarei HaYichud v'HaEmunah* 20b.

7. See Moshe Idel, *Absorbing Perfections: Kabbalah and Interpretation* (New Haven, Conn.: Yale University Press, 2002), pp. 83–110.

8. See David Cooper, *God Is a Verb: Kabbalah and the Practice of Mystical Judaism* (New York: Riverhead, 1998), pp. 65–66.

9. Michael Lerner, *Jewish Renewal: A Path to Healing and Transformation* (New York: Harper Perennial, 1995), p. 413.

10. Green, *Seek My Face*, p. 19.

11. Cooper, *God Is a Verb*, pp. 69–72.

12. Green, *Seek My Face*, pp. 18–19; see also Arthur Green, *Ehyeh: A Kabbalah for Tomorrow* (Woodstock, Vt.: Jewish Lights, 2004), p. 2.

13. Deuteronomy 6:4.

14. Aryeh Kaplan, trans., *The Light Beyond: Adventures in Hassidic Thought* (New York: Moznaim, 1981), p. 37.

15. Sfat Emet, *Otzar Ma'amarim u'Michtavim*, 75f, in Green, *Ehyeh*, pp. 22–23.

16. R. Shmuel Schneersohn, *Mi Chamocha*, p. 29. Translation here is mine.

17. *Shenei Luchot HaBrit*, Shavuot 189b.

18. An alternate translation of Deuteronomy 4:35.

19. R. Schneur Zalman of Liadi, Tanya, 161 (*Shaar HaYichud* chap. 6). Citations to the Tanya are from the 1981 printing by Kehot, the Chabad publication society (New York.: Kehot, 1981). Translations are my own unless otherwise indicated. Page numbers are from the standard London edition.

20. Moshe Gordon, "Vayishlach 5763." www.yoy.org.il/article.php?id=97.

21. Likutim Yekarim 14d, trans. Kaplan, *The Light Beyond*, p. 37.

22. R. Aharon, *Shaarei HaAvodah* 1a.

23. See also R. Menachem Mendel Schneersohn (the Tzemach Tzedek), *Torah Or,* Ki Tisa, 172, in Rachel Elior, *The Paradoxical Ascent to God*, p. 51: "'I am the Lord, I have not changed,'" for He has no change, just as before the creation of the world so too is He truly now, for all the worlds are annihilated in total annihilation before him . . . and although the worlds seem like an entity to us, that is an utter lie."

24. Psalms 139:7–12.

25. *Ruach* alone, meaning "spirit" or "wind," is found commonly in the Bible, beginning with Genesis 1:2. *Ruach HaKodesh* appears only twice, in Psalms 51:11 and Isaiah 63:10, 11.

26. On the *Shechinah* as "face," see BT Berachot 64a, BT Sanhedrin 103a; Deuteronomy Rabba 7:8 (commenting on Moses seeing God/*Shechinah* "face to face"). In some cases, the *Shechinah* was used in translation to modify the problematic theology of biblical statements. For example, Onkelos renders "God in Zion" (Psalms 65:2) as "God whose Shechinah is in Zion," "I dwell among them" (Numbers 5:3) as "My Shechinah dwells among them," and "Is God among us?" (Exodus 57:7) as "Is the Shechinah of God among us or not?" See Joshua Abelson, *The Immanence of God in Rabbinical Literature* (New York: Hermon Press, 1969), pp. 78–79, 98–99.

27. See, for example, BT Sotah 5a; Lamentations Rabba 25 (describing ten journeys of the *Shechinah*), Song of Songs Rabba 2 (describing *Shechinah* as "compressed" between the fingers of the priests during the priestly blessing). See also Abelson, *Immanence of God*, pp. 104–8.

28. Exodus Rabba 2:5. The remark refers to the "choice" of God to manifest in the burning bush.

29. See BT Sanhedrin 39a; BT Baba Batra 25a.

30. Pesikta d'Rav Kahana 1:4.

31. Zohar III:225a (Raya Mehemna, Pinchas).

32. Ibid.

33. *Iggrot Baal haTanya u'Bnei Doro* 97–98 in Elior, *The Paradoxical Ascent to God,* p. 16.

34. See Louis Jacobs, *Seeker of Unity: The Life and Works of Aaron of Starosselje* (London: Vallentine Mitchell, 2006), p. 119.

35. See, for example, Zohar II:85b. Later strata of the Zohar are more traditionally theistic. See Scholem, *Kabbalah,* p. 148.

36. Quoted in Schäfer and Dan, *Major Trends in Jewish Mysticism,* p. 222.

37. *Sefer ha Rimmon,* quoted in Scholem, *Kabbalah,* p. 147

38. R. Azriel of Gerona, quoted in Scholem, *Origins of the Kabbalah,* p. 423. (I have substituted "nothingness" for Arkush's "Nought.")

39. R. Azriel of Gerona, "The Explanation of the Ten Sefirot," trans. Joseph Dan, *The Early Kabbalah* (New York: Paulist Press, 1986), p. 94.

40. Ibid., p. 90.

41. Scholem, *Major Trends,* p. 222.

42. Exodus 32:8.

43. As one later Hasidic master said, "God Himself needs the presence of the Shechinah in the lower world." R. Menachem Nahum of Chernobyl, *Meor Einayim,* Noah, trans. by Arthur Green, *The Light of the Eyes* (Mahwah N.J.: Paulist Press, 1982), p. 100.

44. Scholem, *Major Trends,* p. 252.

45. Scholem, *Kabbalah,* pp. 149–51.

46. R. Moses Cordovero, Perek Helek trans. of the *Shiur Komah,* Modena manuscript, 206b, quoted in Bracha Zack, "Moshe Cordovero's Doctrine of Tzimtzum," *Tarbiz* 58 (1989), pp. 213–14.

47. R. Moses Cordovero, Elimah Rabbati 24d–25a. (The first sentence is: *ha'eloha kol nimtza, v' ein kol nimtza ha'eloha.*) See Scholem, *Kabbalah,* p. 150.

48. *Sefer Baal Shem Tov,* Va'etchanan 13, trans. Aryeh Kaplan, *The Light Beyond,* p. 37.

49. *Sefer Baal Shem Tov,* Bereshit 15, *The Light Beyond,* p. 43.

50. *Tzavaat HaRivash* 76.

51. *Keter Shem Tov* 51b. My translation.

52. Rabbi Menachem M. Schneerson, *On the Essence of Chassidus* (New York: Kehot, 1986), p. 28.

53. Zohar I: 18b.

54. Tanya, 154 (*Shaar HaYichud*, chap. 2).

55. Tanya, 155 (*Shaar HaYichud*, chap. 3).

56. Ibid.

57. R. Aharon, *Shaarei HaYichud v'HaEmunah* 2b–3a. See Jacobs, *Seeker of Unity*, pp. 98–99.

58. R. Aharon, *Shaarei HaYichud v'HaEmunah* 2b.

59. See Scholem, *Major Trends*, pp. 260–64. Scholem notes that Hasidic rereadings of *tzimtzum* are often pantheistic rebellions against a fundamentally theistic doctrine.

60. Tanya, 156 (*Shaar HaYichud*, chap. 4).

61. Tanya, 159 (*Shaar HaYichud*, chap. 6).

62. Ibid. In the Zohar, Elohim is usually associated with Binah. Both, however, are the principle of the "left side," the feminine, and that which contains, encloses, and bounds.

63. This phrase is found in the Shacharit (morning) prayer service.

64. Tanya, 164 (*Shaar HaYichud*, chap. 7).

65. Ibid.

66. Ibid.

67. Elior, *The Paradoxical Ascent to God*, p. 28.

68. R. Meir ibn Gabbai, *Avodat Hakodesh* (1531).

69. Rabbi Shmuel Schneersohn, *Mi Chamocha*. Translation here is mine.

70. The literal meaning is "thought makes new [or 'is made anew'], but the Holy One is ancient/primordial." Kaplan renders it, "Thought is something that was created, while God is without beginning," in *The Light Beyond*, p. 45. My reading is that thought's content is based upon new sense data and perceptions, whereas God is antecedent to all of these. Another reading might be: thought is *a posteriori* but God is *a priori*.

71. R. Levi Yitzchak of Berdichev, *Kedushat Levi*, Mishpatim, 190, translation mine. In the rest of this section, Rabbi Levi Yitzchak speaks of distance and nearness, transcendence and immanence, fear and love, in the context of revelation. The quotation here comments on

the Children of Israel standing back from Sinai. As the elders move closer, they are able to see both immanence and transcendence, which Rabbi Levi Yitzchak analogizes to the two "legs" seen at Sinai.

72. R. Yakov Yosef of Polonnoye, *Ben Porat Yosef* 50b.

73. R. Dov Ber of Mezrich, *Likkutei Amarim* 26b, trans. Elior, *The Paradoxical Ascent to God*, p. 17.

74. R. Dov Ber of Mezrich, *Torat HaMagid* II, p. 162, *The Light Beyond*, p. 37.

75. R. Menachem Nahum of Chernobyl, *Meor Einayim*, Noah, trans. Green, *The Light of the Eyes*, p. 100.

76. Ibid., Vayetze, *The Light of the Eyes*, p. 224.

77. *Likkutim Yekarim* 115b, trans. Krassen, *Uniter of Heaven and Earth*, p. 86.

78. Ibid., 117b, p. 91.

79. Ibid., 115b, p. 89.

80. R. Nachman of Bratzlav, *Likkutei Moharan* 33:2 (translation mine).

81. Yerushalmi Taanit 1:1.

82. Isaiah 21:11. "Seir" is generally a euphemism for Rome, or Christianity.

83. Deuteronomy 30:11.

84. R. Nachman of Bratzlav, *Likkutei Moharan* 33:2 (translation mine).

85. Tanya, 54 (*Likkutei Amarim*, chap. 22).

86. Rabbi Zalman Schachter-Shalomi, "A Triumphalist Table of In/Compatibility of Other Religions with Judaism," *Zeek*, www.zeek .net/802zalman/, February 2008.

87. Rabbi Zalman Schachter-Shalomi, *Wrapped in a Holy Flame: Teachings and Tales of the Hasidic Masters* (San Francisco: Jossey-Bass, 2003), p. 20.

88. Green, *Ehyeh*, p. 19.

89. Green, *Seek My Face*, p. 6.

90. Ibid., p. 7.

91. Ibid., p. 109.

92. Ibid., pp. 133–34.

93. Rami Shapiro, *Open Secrets*, p. 19.

94. Swami Prabhavananda and Christopher Isherwood, introduction to Shankara, *Shankara's Crest-Jewel of Discrimination (Viveka-Chudamani): Timeless Teachings on Nonduality*, trans. and ed. by Prabhavananda and Isherwood (Los Angeles, Calif.: Vedanta, 1970), p. 7.

95. Aitareya Upanishad 3.3, Rig Veda.

96. Mandukya Upanishad 1.2, Atharva Veda.

97. Chandogya Upanishad 6.8.7, Sama Veda.

98. Brhadaranyaka Upanishad 1.4.10, Yahur Veda.

99. Shankara, *Crest-Jewel of Discrimination*, pp. 72–73. For detailed expositions of Vedanta philosophy, see Hans Torwesten, *Vedanta: Heart of Hinduism* (Jackson, Tenn.: Grove Press, 1994); Eliot Deutsch, *Advaita Vedanta: A Philosophical Reconstruction* (Honolulu: University of Hawaii Press, 1969).

100. Ibid., p. 104.

101. The best philosophical treatment of nonduality of which I am aware is Loy, *Nonduality*, which compares nondual systems and theories of reality and language, and works through problems in duality and nonduality in a philosophically rigorous way.

102. Ramakrishna, *The Gospel of Sri Ramakrishna*, p. 32.

103. Vivekananda, *Living at the Source: Yoga Teachings of Vivekananda* (Boston: Shambhala, 2001), p. 3. *Living at the Source* is a compilation of selections from *The Complete Works of Swami Vivekananda* (available online at www.ramakrishnavivekananda.info/vivekananda/com plete_works.htm) In the original source, see vol. 2, p. 461.

104. Ibid., p. 4 (in original, vol. 1, p. 403).

105. Ibid., p. 118 (in original, vol. 8, p. 429).

106. Ramana Maharshi, *Talks with Ramana Maharshi*, p. 3.

107. Ibid., p. xix.

108. Nisargadatta, *I Am That*, p. 30.

109. Ibid., p. 16.

110. Ramesh Balsekar, *Consciousness Speaks*, ed. Wayne Liquorman (Redondo Beach, Calif.: Advaita Press, 1992), p. 384. See also p. 193.

111. On the interrelationship of Buddhism and Vedanta, see Loy, *Nonduality*, p. 199.

112. See Loy, *Nonduality*, p. 192–94.

113. Edward Conze, trans., *Buddhist Wisdom: The Diamond Sutra and the Heart Sutra*, (New York: Vintage, 2003).

114. Loy, *Nonduality*, p. 30.

115. James Broughton, "This Is It," in *Special Deliveries: New and Selected Poems* (Seattle, Wash.: Broken Moon Press, 1990), p. 88.

116. Ramakrishna, *The Gospel of Sri Ramakrishna*, p. 842.

117. Jan Kersschot, *This Is It: The Nature of Oneness* (London: Watkins, 2006), p. 25.

118. Jean Klein, *Who Am I: The Sacred Quest*, compiled and edited by Emma Edwards (Salisbury, U.K.: Non-Duality Press, 2006).

CHAPTER THREE

1. Vivekananda, *Living at the Source*, p. 5. In the original source, see vol. 2, p. 471.

2. Quoted in Rabbi David Cooper, "The Godding Process."

3. Ralph Waldo Emerson, "Brahma," in *Selected Writings of Ralph Waldo Emerson*, p. 524.

4. Meister Eckhart, "Tractate II," quoted in F. C. Happold, *Mysticism*, p. 275.

5. Nisargadatta, *I Am That*, p. 16.

6. Bereshit Rabba 9:7.

7. Leon Festinger, Henry Riecken, and Stanley Schachter, *When Prophecy Fails: A Social and Psychological Study of a Modern Group That Predicted the Destruction of the World* (New York: Harper & Row, 1964).

8. Quoted in Jay Michaelson, "The Buddha from Brooklyn," *Forward*, November 26, 2004.

9. R. Menachem Nahum of Chernobyl, *Hanhagot Yesharot*, trans. Arthur Green, *The Light of the Eyes*, pp. 35–36.

10. Aaron, *The Secret Life of God*, p. 138.

11. See Matt, *God and the Big Bang*, pp. 47–57.

12. Ramakrishna, *The Gospel of Sri Ramakrishna*, p. 80.

13. See Maurice Friedman, *Martin Buber's Life and Work: The Early Years 1878–1923* (New York: E. P. Dutton, 1981), pp. 99–123.

14. See Loy, *Nonduality*, pp. 283–91.

15. They are also devotional pathways. To quote Ramakrishna again: "Suppose there is an error in worshipping the clay image; doesn't God know that through it He alone is being invoked? He will be pleased with that very worship. Why should you get a headache over it? You had better try for knowledge and devotion yourself." *Gospel of Sri Ramakrishna*, p. 80. Of course, for Jews the "head-

ache" is more severe than for Hindus. In my own practice, I have found that respecting the form of Judaism often compels me to turn aside from other forms in order for the Jewish one to remain stable. In such moments, however, the emphasis is ideally on the fidelity to one form rather than on aversion, judgments, or disrespect regarding another.

16. Vivekananda, *Living at the Source*, p. 39 (in the original, vol. 8, p. 256).

17. Adyashanti, "There You Go Again," in *My Secret Is Silence*, p. 98.

18. R. Aharon, *Shaarei HaYichud v'HaEmunah*, 2b; Rabbi Schneur Zalman of Liadi, *Likkutei Torah*, 20c.

19. Charles F. Keyes, "Buddhist Economics and Buddhist Fundamentalism," in *Fundamentalisms and the State*, eds. Martin E. Marty and R. Scott Appleby (Chicago: University of Chicago Press, 1993).

20. See Elliot Wolfson, "Oneiric Imagination and Mystical Annihilation in Habad Hasidism," *ARC: The Journal of the Faculty of Religious Studies* 35 (2007): pp. 131–57.

21. R. Shlomo of Lutsk, in Norman Lamm, ed., *Religious Thought of Hasidism: Text and Commentary*, (Jersey City, N.J.: Ktav, 1999), pp. 23–24.

22. Nagarjuna, *Mulamadhyamikakarika*, 25: 19–20, in Candrakirti, *Lucid Exposition of the Middle Way*, trans. Mervyn Sprung (Boulder, Colo.: Prajna Press, 1979).

23. See Green, *Seek My Face*, pp. 14–17.

24. Rabbi Menachem Mendel Schneerson, *Torat Menahem: Hitwwa'aduyyot 5743*, vol. 2 (New York: Lahak Hanochos, 1993), p. 1060, quoted in Wolfson, "Oneiric Imagination."

25. See R. Hayyim Vital, *Etz Hayyim* 1:1b–1d, 8:1; *Shaar HaHakdamot*, R. Dov Ber Schneerson, *Torat Hayyim: Bereshit*, 243c–d, quoted in Wolfson, "Oneiric Imagination." The symbolism of circle and line has been traced to Pre-Socratic philosophers Parmenides and Heraclitus.

26. In classical Kabbalah, these symbols are gendered: line masculine and circle feminine. However, because of the dangers of essentializing gender and gender dichotomies, I have not emphasized this aspect here.

27. Exodus 25:8.

CHAPTER FOUR

1. e.e. cummings, "i thank You God for this most amazing," in *100 Selected Poems* (New York: Grove Press, 1959), p. 114.

2. St. Augustine of Hippo, Sermon 88, 5, in *The Works of Saint Augustine: A Translation for the Twenty-First Century,* edited by John E. Rotelle (New York: New City Press, 1990), p. 422.

3. Jack Kerouac, *On the Road* (New York: Penguin Classics, 2002), p. 5.

4. Friedrich Schleiermacher, *On Religion: Speeches to Its Cultured Despisers* (Whitefish, Mont.: Kessinger, 2008), p. 105.

5. Ramakrishna, *The Gospel of Sri Ramakrishna,* p. 217.

6. Green, *Seek My Face*, p. 25.

7. Loy, *Nonduality*, p. 283.

8. Ramakrishna, *Gospel of Sri Ramakrishna*, p. 138.

9. Vivekananda, *Living at the Source*, p. 36. In the original source, see vol. 2, p. 377.

10. Robert Frost, "The Secret Sits," in *A Witness Tree* (New York: Henry Holt, 1942).

CHAPTER FIVE

1. Buber's interpretation of Hasidism was a subject of controversy between him and Gershom Scholem. See Gershom Scholem, "Martin Buber's Interpretation of Hasidism," in *The Messianic Idea in Judaism* (New York: Schocken, 1995), p. 243ff; Karl Grotzinger, "The Buber-Scholem Controversy about the Hasidic Tale and Hasidism—Is There a Solution?" in *Gershom Scholem's Major Trends in Jewish Mysticism*, pp. 327–36.

2. Jeffrey Kripal, *Esalen: America and the Religion of No Religion* (Chicago: University of Chicago Press, 2008), describes this history in fascinating detail.

3. Arthur Green's pseudonymous essay on this subject—"Psychedelics and Kabbalah," written under the name Itzik Lodzer—is contained in the anthology *The New Jews*, edited by James A. Sleeper and Alan L. Mintz (New York: Vintage Books, 1971), pp. 176–92.

4. Ramakrishna, *The Gospel of Sri Ramakrishna*, p. 32.

5. Ibid., p. 133.

6. Moses Cordovero, *Or Ne'erav*, part 2, chap. 2 (Jerusalem: Kol Yehuda, 1965), pp. 18–19. Translation mine.

7. Vivekananda, *Living at the Source*, p. 105. In the original source, see vol. 1., p. 325.

8. See Daniel Pinchbeck and Ken Jordan, eds., *Toward 2012: Perspectives on the Next Age* (New York: Tarcher/Penguin, 2008).

9. Robert Levine, *There Is No Messiah and You're It: The Stunning Transformation of Judaism's Most Provocative Idea* (Woodstock, Vt.: Jewish Lights, 2002).

10. David Friedman, "A Cure for Messianic Madness," www.kosmic-kabbalah.com/pages/teachings_kabbalah_art_a_cure.htm.

11. Joel 2:28.

12. Epistle of the Baal Shem Tov, translation mine. See also David Sears, *The Path of the Baal Shem Tov* (Lanham, Md.: Jason Aronson, 1996).

13. Rabbi Menachem M. Schneerson, *On the Essence of Chassidus*, pp. 41–43. Translation mine.

14. It is also an essential Hasidic teaching: the "effusion of new light, of the aspect of the interiority of keter and higher—effusion of the innermost of *Atik*, that is Ein Sof, that is ineffable." Ibid., p. 26. Translation mine.

15. Ramana Maharshi, *Talks with Ramana Maharshi*, p. 256.

16. See Ken Wilber, *Integral Spirituality*, pp. 58–70; and Ken Wilber, *A Theory of Everything* (Boston: Shambhala, 2000), pp. 5–8. Of course, the content of these stages varies greatly from culture to culture; the theoretical underpinning of the models is that the overall structure does not. See Lawrence Kohlberg, *Essays on Moral Development: The Psychology of Moral Development* (New York: Harper & Row, 1981), pp. 250–52; Don Edward Beck and Christopher C. Cowan, *Spiral Dynamics: Mastering Values, Leadership, and Change* (Cambridge, U.K.: Blackwell, 1996).

17. See generally Jean Piaget, *The Essential Piaget*, edited by Howard E. Gruber and J. Jacques Voneche Gruber (New York: Basic Books 1977); and also Piaget's *The Moral Judgment of the Child* (Whitefish, Mont.: Kessinger, 2008).

18. Robert Kegan, *The Evolving Self: Problem and Process in Human Development* (Cambridge, Mass.: Harvard University Press, 1982).

19. Susanne Cook-Greuter, "Maps for Living: Ego-Development Stages from Symbiosis to Conscious Universal Embeddedness," *Adult Development*, vol. 2: *Models and Methods in the Study of Adolescent and Adult Thought*, eds. Michael L. Commons et al. (Milton Park, U.K.: Praeger, 1990).

20. James Fowler, *Stages of Faith: The Psychology of Human Development and the Quest for Meaning* (San Francisco: Harper & Row, 1981).

21. Lawrence Kohlberg, Charles Levine, and Alexandra Hewer, *Moral Stages: A Current Formulation and Response to Critics* (New York: Karger, 1983). But see Carol Gilligan, "In a Different Voice: Women's Conception of Self and Morality," *Harvard Education Review* 47, no. 4 (1977), critiquing Kohlberg's model as androcentric.

22. Beck and Cowan, *Spiral Dynamics*.

23. Abraham Joshua Heschel, *Man Is Not Alone: A Philosophy of Religion* (New York: Noonday Press, 1951), p. 11.

CHAPTER SIX

1. Vivekananda, *Living at the Source*, p. 36 (in original, see 6:133).

2. Quoted in Philip Kapleau, *Three Pillars of Zen: Teaching, Practice, and Enlightenment* (New York: Anchor, 1989), p. 205.

3. Zohar I:241a. The Aramaic is *yistaklun*, which might also be rendered "looks closely."

4. R. Aharon, *Shaarei HaAvodah* 7a–b. In Kabbalistic language, R. Aharon says that *hochmah* and *binah* are insufficient for true knowledge; *da'at* must also involve the lower *sefirot* of emotion and physicality.

5. Schäfer and Dan, eds., *Gershom Scholem's Major Trends in Jewish Mysticism*, p. 347.

6. See, for example, Jan Kersschot, *This Is It*, pp. 8–14, 43–47, 90–91; Ramesh Balsekar, *Consciousness Speaks*, pp. 148–56, 192–95.

7. Wei Wu Wei, *Ask the Awakened: The Negative Way* (Boulder, Colo.: Sentient, 2002), p. 23.

8. The original story is available in *The Essential Rebbe Nachman*, trans. Avraham Greenbaum (Jerusalem: Azamra, 2006). See Aaron, *The Secret Life of God*, p. 150. Aaron suggests that monotheism itself is

just such a ruse; if one doesn't profess it, one seems to be insane, so one professes it as make-believe.

9. R. Aharon, *Shaarei Ha Avodah* 13a.

10. Ibid., 1b.

11. Ibid., 12a.

12. Ibid., 71a–b.

13. Ibid., 4a.

14. Ibid., 7a, 12a.

15. R. Schneur Zalman of Liadi, "Boney Yerushalayim," in Elior, *The Paradoxical Ascent to God*, p. 29.

16. DovBer Pinson, *Toward the Infinite: The Way of Kabbalistic Meditation* (Lanham, Md.: Rowman & Littlefield, 2005), pp. 25–26.

17. Ibid.

18. Ibid.

19. Tanya, 14 (*Likkutei Amarim*, chap. 3).

20. Solomon Maimon, "On a Secret Society, and Therefore a Long Chapter," in *Essential Papers on Hasidism*, ed. Gershon Hundert (New York: New York University Press, 1991), p. 16.

21. Rabbi Shmuel Schneersohn, *Mi Chamocha*, pp. 27, 31. Translation here is mine.

22. Thich Nhat Hanh, *Peace Is Every Step: The Path of Mindfulness in Everyday Life*, ed. Arnold Kotler (New York: Bantam, 1991), pp. 95–96.

23. Ajahn Sumedho, *The Way It Is* (Hertfordshire, U.K.:, Amaravati, 1991), p. 132.

24. Ramana Maharshi, *Talks with Ramana Maharshi*, p. 21.

25. Quoted in Wei Wu Wei, *Ask the Awakened*, p. 15.

26. See Lama Surya Das, *Awakening the Buddha Within* (New York: Broadway Books, 1998), pp. 319–20.

27. See Chokyi Nyima Rinpoche, "Meditation," in *The Dzogchen Primer: An Anthology of Writings by Masters of the Great Perfection*, ed. Martha Binder Schmidt (Boston: Shambhala, 2002), pp. 50–54.

28. Lama Surya Das, *Awakening the Buddha Within*, p. 319.

29. DovBer Pinson, *Toward the Infinite*, p. 91.

30. John of the Cross, *Ascent of Mount Carmel*, I:13.

31. Alan Watts, *The Book: On the Taboo against Knowing Who You Are* (New York: Vintage, 1989), pp. 22–23.

32. *Tiferet HaYehudi*, 176 no. 93. The Hebrew for "rule" is *klal*, which might also mean "general principle," as in there are no general principles for the service of God, only specific paths. See Michael Rosen, *The Quest for Authenticity: The Thought of Reb Simhah Bunim* (Jerusalem: Urim, 2008).

33. Wilber, *Eye to Eye*, p. 33.

34. Green, *Seek My Face*, p. 23.

CHAPTER SEVEN

1. *Imrei Tzaddikim* 18c, trans. Kaplan, *Meditation and Kabbalah*, p. 302.

2. Green, *Seek My Face*, p. xxiii.

3. *Likkutim Yekarim* 2b, 20a.

4. R. Dov Ber of Mezrich, *Maggid Dvarav L'Yaakov* 110.

5. *Shemu'ah Tovah* 79b–80a, quoted in Arthur Green and Barry W. Holtz, eds. and trans., *Your Word Is Fire*, p. 57.

6. R. Aharon, *Shaarei HaAvodah* 2a, 9a.

7. See Jacobs, *Seeker of Unity*, pp. 12–13, 115–18; Naftali Loewenthal, *Communicating the Infinite: The Emergence of the Habad School* (Chicago: University Chicago Press, 1990). R. Aharon's blistering attack on R. Dov Ber's *Tract on Ecstasy* may be found in *Shaarei HaAvodah* 6a–7b.

8. *Tzavaat HaRivash* 68.

9. See *Maggid Dvarav L'Yaakov* 162.

10. R. Yakov Yosef of Polonnoye, *Toldot Yakov Yosef*, Bereshit 8c, in *The Light Beyond*, p. 44.

11. Meister Eckhart, "Always Kissing," *Love Poems from God*, p. 100.

12. Psalms 31:23.

13. Psalms 119:20.

14. BT Sanhedrin 106b.

15. *Likkutim Yekarim* 116a, *Uniter of Heaven and Earth*, p. 90.

16. *Tzavaat HaRivash* 93.

17. St. Francis of Assisi, rendered by Daniel Ladinsky as "He Asked for Charity," in *Love Poems from God*, p. 33.

18. Deuteronomy 16:20; Isaiah 1:16.

19. Exodus 22:22; Deuteronomy 24:20–22; Proverbs 14:31; Proverbs 19:17.

20. BT Shabbat 31a; Leviticus 19:18.

21. Richard Smoley, *Inner Christianity: A Guide to the Esoteric Tradition* (Boston: Shambhala, 2002), pp. 180–83.

22. John 8:32.

CHAPTER EIGHT

1. Sfat Emet, *Otzar Ma'amarim u'Michtavim,* 75f, in Arthur Green, *Ehyeh*, pp. 22–23. Brackets in original.

2. See, for example, *Tzavaat HaRivash* 5–6 ("Attach your thought to Above. Do not eat or drink excessively, but only to the extent of maintaining your health. Never look intently at mundane matters, nor pay any attention to them, so that you may be separated from the physical.").

3. *Likkutim Yekarim* 54, trans. Arthur Green, "Hasidism: Discovery and Retreat," in *The Other Side of God: A Polarity in World Religions*, ed. Peter Berger (Garden City, N.Y.: Anchor, 1981), pp. 117–18.

4. Proverbs 3:6.

5. See Krassen, *Uniter of Heaven and Earth*, pp. 48–49.

6. *Keter Shem Tov* 102.

7. See R. Aharon, *Shaarei HaYichud v'HaEmunah* 216a–b; Elior, *The Paradoxical Ascent to God*, p. 146.

8. Nehemiah 9:6.

9. Zohar III:225a.

10. R. Solomon of Lutsk, *Dibrat Shelomo,* Shemini, 2:25–26, quoted in Seth Brody, "Open to Me the Gates of Righteousness: The Pursuit of Holiness and Non-Duality in Early Hasidic Teaching," *Jewish Quarterly Review* 89, nos. 1–2 (July–October 1998), 14–15.

11. Spinoza, *Ethics*, part 5, p. 14.

12. Quoted in Loy, *Nonduality*, p. 238.

13. Vivekananda, *Living at the Source*, p. 121. In the original source, see vol. 5, p. 270.

14. See R. Aharon, *Shaarei HaAvodah* 45a–b; Elior, *The Paradoxical Ascent to God*, p. 132.

15. R. Schneur Zalman of Liadi, Maamarei Admor Hazaken 26, in Elior, *Paradoxical Ascent*, p. 29. Italics in original.

16. R. Menachem M. Schneerson, *On the Essence of Chassidus*, p. 28.

17. R. Nachman of Bratzlav, *Likkutei Moharan* 64:2.

18. R. Dov Ber of Mezrich, *Maggid Dvarav L'Yaakov* no. 97.

19. Elizabeth Gilbert, *Eat, Pray, Love* (New York: Penguin, 2007), p. 188.

20. Ibid., p. 191. The guru quoted is Swami Muktananda.

21. Aaron, *The Secret Life of God*, p. 173.

22. Rami Shapiro, *Open Secrets*, p. 114.

23. R. Aharon, *Sha'arei HaAvodah* 42b.

24. R. Dov Ber of Mezrich, *Maggid D'varav L'Yaakov* 240.

25. R. Ze'ev Wolf of Zhitomir, *Or Hameir*, Pekudei 85, in Rachel Elior, *The Mystical Origins of Hasidism* (Portland, Ore.: Littman Library of Jewish Civilization, 2006), p. 76.

26. Baba Kuhi of Shiraz, trans. R. A. Nicholson, in F. C. Happold, *Mysticism: A Study and an Anthology* (New York: Penguin, 1991), p. 251.

27. Loy, *Nonduality*, p. 212.

28. R. Aharon, *Shaarei HaAvodah* 14a.

29. Elior, *Paradoxical Ascent*, p. 26.

30. Chuang Tzu, trans. Francis H. Cook, *Hua-Yen Buddhism* (State College: Pennsylvania State University Press, 1977), p. 27.

31. See Loy, *Nonduality*, pp. 248–60; Kevin Hart, *The Trespass of the Sign: Deconstruction, Theology, and Philosophy* (Cambridge, U.K.: Cambridge University Press, 1989), pp. 71–104; Jacques Derrida, "How to Avoid Speaking: Denials," in *Derrida and Negative Theology*, eds. Harold Coward and Toby Foshay (Albany: State University of New York Press, 1992), pp. 88–95.

32. Nicholas of Cusa, quoted in Happold, *Mysticism*, p. 46.

33. DovBer Pinson, *Toward the Infinite*, p. 124.

34. Elior, *Paradoxical Ascent*, p. 67.

35. R. Aharon, *Avodat HaLevy* I, 1, in Elior, *Paradoxical Ascent*, p. 125.

36. R. Aharon, *Shaarei HaYichud v'HaEmunah* 157b.

CHAPTER NINE

1. Michael Lerner, *Jewish Renewal*, p. 408.

2. Rivka Shatz Uffenheimer, *Hasidism as Mysticism: Quietistic Elements in Eighteenth-Century Hasidic Thought*, trans. Jonathan Chipman (Princeton, N.J.: Princeton University Press, 1993).

3. See Martin Buber, *The Origin and Meaning of Hasidism* (New York: Harper & Row, 1966), p. 174; Jerome Gellman, "Hasidic Mysticism as an Activism," *Religious Studies* 42 (2006): 343.

4. Ramesh Balsekar, *Consciousness Speaks*, p. 48.

5. There are those who disagree. The neo-Vedantist writer Jan Kersschot has said that "as soon as it is clear that Beingness is reflected everywhere, there is no point in trying to bring peace and bliss into our lives, or to try and work towards a better world." Kersschot, *This Is It*, p. 67. I would reply that there is "no point" absolutely but that there remains a "point" from the relative perspective.

6. Ramesh Balsekar, quoted at Clearsight, "Wisdom Quotes from Enlightened Teachers," http://peterspearls.com.au/spiritual-quotes .htm.

7. Available at www.youtube.com/watch?v=A9XbcyaJlTo.

8. Tanya, 164 (*Shaar HaYichud*, chap. 7).

9. Timothy Conway, "On Neo-Advaitin Ramesh Balsekar," available at www.enlightened-spirituality.org/ramesh_balsekar.html.

10. Ibid.

11. Ibid. Padmasambhava, the half-mythical founder of Tibetan Buddhism, put it this way: "Do not interrupt conditioned roots of virtue even though you realize appearances to be mind." Padmasambhava, "Taking Refuge," in *The Dzogchen Primer*, p. 151.

12. There may be exceptions. R. Mordechai Lainer of Ishbitz suggested that there are some circumstances in which one may disobey a law, as in the Biblical tales of Judah. And it is possible that the seclusion of R. Menachem Mendl of Kotzk (the Kotzker Rebbe) was an act of quietism. However, these are the exceptions more than the rule.

13. See generally, Robert Kane, *The Oxford Handbook of Free Will* (Oxford: Oxford University Press, 2001).

14. Spinoza, *Ethics and Selected Letters*, part 3, p. 2S.

15. Daniel Dennett calls this the "Cartesian theater" view. Dennett, *Consciousness Explained*, pp. 109–15. On the scientific consensus regarding Cartesian dualism generally, see Dennett, *Consciousness Explained*, pp. 33–39.

16. Ibid., pp. 219, 253–54.

17. Famously, Descartes himself suggested that there is a nexus between the material and the non-material in the pineal gland of the brain. Given what we now know about the pineal gland and its role in consciousness, that Descartes chose it is quite remarkable, even prescient. But even electricity and the various energies of the brain are still material.

18. Ken Wilber's *Quantum Questions* (rev. ed., Boston: Shambhala, 2001) is a terrific anthology of the twentieth-century masters of quantum theory all lining up to say that, while this hypothesis is remarkable, mystical, and amazing, it has nothing whatsoever to do with "thoughts creating reality" or free will.

19. Dennett, *Freedom Evolves*, p. 185.

20. Ibid., pp. 169, 304–5.

21. Ibid., p. 136.

22. Mishna Avot 3:19 (*hakol tzafui, v'reshut n'tunah*).

23. Quoted in Theodore Stcherbatsky, *Buddhist Logic Part One (1930)* (Whitefish, Mont.: Kessinger, 2004), p. 133.

24. See Loy, *Nonduality*, pp. 96–112.

25. Rami Shapiro, *Open Secrets*, p. 104.

CHAPTER TEN

1. Quoted in Joseph Goldstein, *The Experience of Insight* (Santa Cruz, Calif.: Unity Press, 1976), p. 32.

2. Vivekananda, *Living at the Source*, p. 5. In the original source, see vol. 1, p. 501.

GLOSSARY

Aharon Halevy Horowitz of Staroselye (1766–1828): Foremost disciple of Rabbi Schneur Zalman of Liadi, founder of Chabad Hasidism. Wrote works of systematic nondual Jewish theology and practice.

Apophatic: The "negative way" in theology; like *bittul ha-yesh*, divesting oneself of all concepts and images of ultimate reality, all states of mind and all ideas, to arrive at a true knowledge of God as *ayin*, Emptiness.

Aretz: Lit. "land"; more generally, the finite and relative.

Avodah: Lit. "work"; service of God; spiritual practice.

Ayin: Nothingness.

Baal Shem Tov (1698–1760): Rabbi Israel ben Eliezer, the founder of the Hasidic movement.

Bittul ha-Yesh: Lit. "Annihilation of what is"; practice of seeing the emptiness or nonexistence of all things, especially the self.

Buber, Martin (1878–1965): Philosopher and scholar of Hasidism who emphasized dialogical encounter with the "Eternal You."

Carlebach, Shlomo (1925–1984): Charismatic Jewish musician and teacher who began in Chabad-Lubavitch but, with Zalman Schachter-Shalomi, pioneered a spiritual Judaism that crossed denominational lines and emphasized ecstatic, devotional practice.

Cataphatic: The "positive way" in theology; like *hakarat hatov*, recognizing the interdependence and miraculous nature of manifestation to arrive at a true understanding of God as *yesh*, Being.

Chabad: Nondualistically and philosophically oriented sect of Hasidism, founded at the end of the eighteenth century. The sect moved to the town of Lubavitch—thus the term "Lubavitcher" Hasidism.

Cordovero, Moses (1522–1570): Early systematizer of Kabbalah.

Devekut: "Cleaving" to the Ein Sof; being in the Presence of God.

Dov Ber of Lubavitch (1773–1827): Son of and successor to Rabbi Schneur

Zalman of Liadi, and the second Chabad rebbe. Wrote many works on nondual theology and practice.

Dov Ber of Mezrich/the Maggid of Mezrich (1704–1772): The second leader of Hasidism, after the Baal Shem Tov.

Ein Od Milvado: There is nothing else besides God.

Ein Sof: The Infinite; the All.

Guide to the Perplexed: Philosophical masterpiece by Maimonides which argues that all anthropomorphic language in the Bible is mere analogy, and that God is One without differentiation or attributes.

Hasidism: Mystical revivalist movement started in the eighteenth century, emphasizing devotion, ecstasy, and *devekut* as ideals, and Ein Sof as theology.

Heschel, Abraham Joshua (1907–1972): Neo-Hasidic philosopher, theologian, activist, and rabbi largely responsible for the dissemination of Hasidic philosophy in liberal American Judaism.

Kabbalah: Jewish esoteric and mystical tradition which first flourished in the medieval period, emphasizing the structure of Godhead, depth and balance of interpretations and energies, and, in some forms, practical and prophetic applications.

Kadosh baruch hu: The Holy One, Blessed be He; the primary masculine aspect of the Godhead.

Kal v'chomer: A fortiori; how much more so.

de Leon, Moshe (1250–1305): Redactor and likely co-composer of the Zohar, as well as many Kabbalistic works under his own name.

Levinas, Emmanuel (1906–1995): Twentieth century Jewish post-nondualistic philosopher who argued that our experience of undifferentiated Being is interrupted by the presence of the Other, to whom we have ethical responsibility.

Lubavitcher Rebbe: Generally refers to Rabbi Menachem Mendel Schneerson, the seventh and last Chabad Lubavitch rebbe, who widely disseminated Chabad teachings and who some believed to be the messiah.

Luria, Isaac (1534–1572): Often called the ARI (Hebrew for "lion"), Kabbalistic innovator and genius who promulgated new theories of creation, cosmic rupture, and repair.

Maimonides, Moses (1135–1204): Medieval Aristotelian Jewish philosopher, doctor, and legalist who systematized Jewish law and synthesized classical Greek philosophy with Jewish theology and tradition.

Mitzvah/Mitzvot: Commandment; ritual, or ethical act prescribed by Jewish law.

Mochin d'gadlut: Expanded mind.

Mochin d'katnut: Contracted mind.

Nefesh, Ruach, Neshamah, Chayah, Yechidah: The five levels of soul in later Kabbalistic and Hasidic teaching. Correspond roughly to the body, heart, mind, and spirit, with *yechidah* being the union with God that pervades all levels.

Nirvana: In Buddhism, the state of an awakened mind which is free of suffering and rebirth. Also sometimes refers to the unconditioned, nondual reality.

Nisargadatta (1897–1981): Nondual Indian sage who emphasized the view that all is consciousness only.

Plotinus (204–270): Philosopher and metaphysician, founder of Neoplatonism, which held that reality consists of emanations from the One.

Ram Dass (b. 1931): Contemporary nondual Western teacher. Born Richard Alpert, originally a researcher into psychedelics, later one of the leaders of the 1960s and 1970s wave of spirituality.

Ramakrishna (1836–1886): Charismatic, devotional Vedanta sage, teacher of Vivekananda and synthesizer of philosophical and devotional religious practices.

Ramana Maharshi (1879–1950): Enlightened nondual sage who advocated self-inquiry to dissolve the sense of self and other and recognize that all is consciousness.

Ratso v'Shov: Lit., "running and returning." Phrase from Ezekiel 1:14 which has come to stand for any number of oscillations in spiritual life—for example, between expanded and contracted mind, being and nothingness.

Rosenzweig, Franz (1886–1929): Major twentieth-century Jewish existentialist philosopher whose work focused on understanding creation, revelation, and redemption in human terms.

Samsara: In Buddhism, the endless cycle of death and rebirth, in which suffering takes place.

Schneur Zalman of Liadi (1745–1813): Founder of Chabad Hasidism, sometimes called the "Alter Rebbe" (old rebbe) or Baal Ha'Tanya (master/owner/author of the Tanya). Student of Rabbi Dov Ber of Mezrich, successor to the Baal Shem Tov. Brilliant synthesizer of Kabbalistic and philosophical thought into a nondual system of Judaism.

Sefirot: The ten emanations of the Ein Sof; the One as it appears to the Many. Cordovero analogizes the *sefirot* (sing., *sefirah*) to panes of stained glass through which light shines and appears to take on colors.

Shamayim: Lit. "sky," or "heaven"; more generally, the infinite and absolute.

Shechinah: The main feminine aspect of the Godhead; the revealed Divine Presence.

Shema: Lit., "listen." The one-line statement of Jewish faith: "Hear, O Israel, the Lord our God, the Lord is One." Understood in a panentheistic way by many Hasidim.

Sovev u'Memaleh: Lit., "surround and fill." The panentheistic doctrine that Ein Sof surrounds and fills the world.

Spinoza, Baruch (1632–1677): Monistic Enlightenment Jewish philosopher who argued that all the world is of one substance, and that substance is God. Banned as a heretic for questioning the divine authorship of the Bible.

Tanya: Masterpiece of Chabad Hasidism, part of which ("The Gate of Unity and Faith," or *Shaar HaYichud v'HaEmunah*) describes a nondual Jewish philosophy in detail, influenced by Kabbalah and Maimonidean thought.

Tikkun olam: Lit. "repairing the world"; Lurianic Kabbalistic doctrine that through ritual action (*mitzvot*), human beings restore the primordial unity shattered in the process of creation. In recent years, *tikkun olam* has come to mean social justice work which repairs brokenness in the world.

Tzimtzum: Lit. "contraction"; Lurianic Kabbalistic cosmological doctrine that the Ein Sof "contracted into itself" to make space for the universe.

Vedanta: Philosophical strand of Hinduism which emphasizes nonduality. Became popular in the West in the late nineteenth and early twentieth centuries largely through the efforts of Swami Vivekananda and the Vedanta Society he created. Vedanta also influenced the American transcendentalists Ralph Waldo Emerson and Henry David Thoreau.

Vivekananda (1863–1902): Remarkably prolific and articulate Vedanta sage who brought the ideas of Vedanta and nonduality to the West, which eventually helped spark the 1960s spiritual revolution and the New Age movement.

Yesh: Lit. "something"; the apparently existing world; the sense of self and substance.

Zohar: Lit. "radiance"; masterpiece of the Kabbalah which first appeared in the late thirteenth century. A combination of myth, cosmology, biblical exegesis, narrative, and symbol, the Zohar largely consists of conversations among Talmudic rabbis as they interpret the hidden meanings of Torah and the relationship between God and world.

BIBLIOGRAPHY

CONTEMPORARY SOURCES

Aaron, David. *The Secret Life of God: Discovering the Divine within You.* Boston: Shambhala Publicatios, 2005.

Abelson, Joshua. *The Immanence of God in Rabbinical Literature.* New York: Hermon Press, 1969.

Adyashanti. *My Secret Is Silence: Poetry and Sayings of Adyashanti.* Los Gatos, Calif.: Open Gate, 2003.

Balsekar, Ramesh. *Consciousness Speaks.* Edited by Wayne Liquorman. Redondo Beach, Calif.: Advaita Press, 1992.

Beck, Don Edward, and Christopher C. Cowan. *Spiral Dynamics: Mastering Values, Leadership, and Change.* Cambridge, Mass.: Blackwell 1996.

Blackmore, Susan. "Waking from the Meme Dream." In *The Psychology of Awakening: Buddhism, Science, and Our Day-to-Day Lives,* edited by Gay Watson, Stephen Batchelor, and Guy Claxton. London: Rider, 2000.

Boorstein, Sylvia. *That's Funny You Don't Look Buddhist: On Being a Faithful Jew and a Passionate Buddhist.* New York: HarperOne, 1998.

Brody, Seth. "Open to Me the Gates of Righteousness: The Pursuit of Holiness and Non-Duality in Early Hasidic Teaching." *Jewish Quarterly Review* 89 (1998): 3–44.

Broughton, James. *Special Deliveries: New and Selected Poems.* Seattle: Broken Moon Press, 1990.

Buber, Martin. *The Origin and Meaning of Hasidism.* Edited and translated by Maurice Friedman. New York: Horizon Press, 1966.

Buxbaum, Yitzhak. *The Light and Fire of the Baal Shem Tov.* New York: Continuum, 2006.

———. *An Open Heart: The Mystical Path of Loving People.* Flushing, N.Y.: Jewish Spirit, 1997.

Churchland, Patricia, and Terrence Sejnowski. *The Computational Brain.* Cambridge, Mass.: MIT Press, 1992.

Cook-Greuter, Susanne. "Maps for Living: Ego-Development Stages from Symbiosis to Conscious Universal Embeddedness." In *Adult Development*. Vol. 2: *Models and Methods in the Study of Adolescent and Adult Thought*. Edited by Michael L. Commons, et al. London: Praeger, 1990.

Cooper, David. "The Godding Process." Parabola. http://parabola.org/content/view/137/.

———. *God Is a Verb: Kabbalah and the Practice of Mystical Judaism*. New York: Riverhead, 1998.

———. *Three Gates to Meditation Practice: A Personal Journey into Sufism, Buddhism, and Judaism*. Woodstock, Vt.: Skylight Paths Publishing, 2000.

———. *A Heart of Stillness: A Complete Guide to Learning the Art of Meditation*. Woodstock, Vt.: Skylight Paths Publishing, 1999.

Crook, John H. *The Evolution of Human Consciousness*. Oxford: Clarendon Press, 1980.

cummings, e. e. "i thank You God for this most amazing." In *100 Selected Poems*. New York: Grove Press, 1959.

Dawkins, Richard. *The Selfish Gene*. Oxford: Oxford University Press, 1976.

Dennett, Daniel. *Consciousness Explained*. London: Little, Brown, 1991.

———. *Freedom Evolves*. New York: Penguin, 2004.

Derrida, Jacques. "How to Avoid Speaking: Denials." In *Derrida and Negative Theology*. Edited by Harold Coward and Toby Foshay. Albany: State University of New York Press, 1992.

Deutsch, Eliot. *Advaita Vedanta: A Philosophical Reconstruction*. Honolulu: University of Hawaii Press, 1969.

Drob, Sanford. "The New Kabbalah." www.newkabbalah.com.

Elior, Rachel. *The Mystical Origins of Hasidism*. Portland, Ore.: Littman Library of Jewish Civilization, 2006.

———. *The Paradoxical Ascent to God: The Kabbalistic Theosophy of Habad Hasidism*. Translated by Jeffrey Green. Albany: State University of New York Press, 1992.

Emerson, Ralph Waldo. "Brahma" and "Nature." In *Selected Writings of Ralph Waldo Emerson*. New York: Signet Classics, 1965.

Festinger, Leon, Henry Riecken, and Stanley Schachter. *When Proph-*

ecy Fails: A Social and Psychological Study of a Modern Group That Predicted the Destruction of the World. New York: Harper, 1964.

Forman, Robert. *The Problem of Pure Consciousness: Mysticism and Philosophy.* New York: Oxford University Press, 1997.

Fowler, James. *Stages of Faith: The Psychology of Human Development and the Quest for Meaning.* San Francisco: Harper & Row, 1981.

Friedman, David. "A Cure for Messianic Madness." www.kosmickabbalah.com/pages/teachings_kabbalah_art_a_cure.htm.

Friedman, Maurice. *Martin Buber's Life and Work: The Early Years 1878–1923.* New York: E. P. Dutton, 1981.

Frost, Robert. "The Secret Sits." In *A Witness Tree.* New York: Henry Holt, 1942.

Gaard, Greta, ed. *Ecofeminism: Women, Animals, Nature.* Philadelphia: Temple University Press, 1993.

Gellman, Jerome. "Hasidic Mysticism as an Activism." *Religious Studies* 42 (2006): 343–49.

Gilbert, Elizabeth. *Eat, Pray, Love: One Woman's Search for Everything Across Italy, India, and Indonesia.* New York: Penguin, 2007.

Gilligan, Carol. "In a Different Voice: Women's Conception of Self and Morality." *Harvard Education Review* 47, no. 4 (1977): 481–517.

Goldstein, Joseph. *Insight Meditation: The Practice of Freedom.* Boston: Shambhala Publications, 1993.

Green, Arthur, and Barry Holtz, trans. and eds. *Your Word Is Fire: Hasidic Masters on Contemplative Prayer.* Woodstock, Vt.: Jewish Lights, 1993.

Green, Arthur, trans. "Hasidism: Discovery and Retreat." In *The Other Side of God: A Polarity in World Religions,* edited by Peter Berger. Garden City, N.Y.: Anchor, 1981.

Green, Arthur. *Ehyeh: A Kabbalah for Tomorrow.* Woodstock, Vt.: Jewish Lights, 2004.

———. *Seek My Face, Speak My Name: A Contemporary Jewish Theology.* Lanham, Md.: Jason Aronson, 1994.

Happold, F. C. *Mysticism: A Study and an Anthology.* New York: Penguin, 1991.

Hart, Kevin. *The Trespass of the Sign: Deconstruction, Theology, and Philosophy.* Cambridge, U.K.: Cambridge University Press, 1989.

Heschel, Abraham Joshua. *The Ineffable Name of God: Man: Poems*. New York: Continuum, 2005.

———. *Man Is Not Alone: A Philosophy of Religion*. New York: Noonday Press, 1951.

Huxley, Aldous. *The Perennial Philosophy*. New York: Harper, 1944.

Idel, Moshe. *Absorbing Perfections: Kabbalah and Interpretation*. New Haven, Conn.: Yale University Press, 2002.

———. *Hasidism: Between Ecstasy and Magic*. Albany, N.Y.: State University of New York Press, 1995.

Isherwood, Christopher, and Swami Prabhavananda. *How to Know God: The Yoga Aphorisms of Patanjali*. Hollywood, Calif.: Vedanta Press, 2007.

Jackson, Carl. *Vedanta for the West*. Bloomington, Ind.: Indiana University Press, 1994.

Jacobs, Louis. *Seeker of Unity: The Life and Works of Aaron of Starosselje*. London: Vallentine Mitchell, 2006.

———. *Hasidic Prayer*. Oxford: Littman Library, 1993.

James, William. *The Varieties of Religious Experience*. Cambridge, Mass.: Harvard University Press, 1985.

Kamenetz, Rodger. *The Jew in the Lotus: A Poet's Rediscovery of Jewish Identity in Buddhist India*. San Francisco: Harper San Francisco, 1994.

Kane, Robert. *The Oxford Handbook of Free Will*. Oxford: Oxford University Press, 2001.

Kapleau, Philip. *The Three Pillars of Zen: Teaching, Practice, and Enlightenment*. New York: Anchor, 1989.

Kegan, Robert. *The Evolving Self: Problem and Process in Human Development*. Cambridge, Mass.: Harvard University Press, 1982.

Kerouac, Jack. *On the Road*. New York: Penguin Classics, 2002.

Kersschot, Jan. *This Is It: The Nature of Oneness*. London: Watkins, 2006.

Keyes, Charles F. "Buddhist Economics and Buddhist Fundamentalism." In *Fundamentalisms and the State*, edited by Martin E. Marty and R. Scott Appleby. Chicago: University of Chicago Press, 1993.

Klein, Jean. *Be Who You Are*. Translated by Mary Mann. Salisbury, U.K.: Non-Duality Press, 2006.

Kohlberg, Lawrence, Charles Levine, and Alexandra Hewer. *Moral Stages: A Current Formulation and Response to Critics*. New York: Karger, 1983.

Kohlberg, Lawrence. *Essays on Moral Development: The Psychology of Moral Development*. New York: Harper & Row, 1981.

Kornfield, Jack. *Meditation for Beginners*. Boulder, Col.: Sounds True, 1998.

———. *A Path with Heart: A Guide through the Perils and Promises of Spiritual Life*. New York: Bantam, 1993.

Krassen, Miles. *The True and the Real: Neo-Hasidic Reflections on the Nature of Reality*. 2006. www.rainofblessings.org.

———. *Uniter of Heaven and Earth: Rabbi Meshullam Feibush Heller of Zbarazh and the Rise of Hasidism in Eastern Galicia*. Albany: State University of New York Press, 1999.

Kripal, Jeffrey. *Esalen: America and the Religion of No Religion*. Chicago: University of Chicago Press, 2008.

Lerner, Michael. *Jewish Renewal: A Path to Healing and Transformation*. New York: Harper Perennial, 1995.

Levine, Robert. *There Is No Messiah And You're It: The Stunning Transformation of Judaism's Most Provocative Idea*. Woodstock, Vt.: Jewish Lights, 2002.

Loewenthal, Naftali. *Communicating the Infinite: The Emergence of the Habad School*. Chicago: University of Chicago Press, 1990.

Loy, David. *Nonduality: A Study in Comparative Philosophy*. New Haven, Conn.: Yale University Press, 1988.

Matt, Daniel. *God and the Big Bang: Discovering Harmony between Science and Spirituality*. Woodstock, Vt.: Jewish Lights, 1998.

Merzel, Dennis Genpo. *Big Mind, Big Heart: Finding Your Way*. McLean, Va.: Big Mind, 2007.

Michaelson, Jay. "The Buddha from Brooklyn." *Forward*, November 26, 2004.

———. *God in Your Body: Kabbalah, Mindfulness, and Embodied Spiritual Practice*. Woodstock, Vt.: Jewish Lights, 2006.

Nisargadatta. *I Am That: Talks with Sri Nisargadatta Maharaj*. Translated by Maurice Frydman. Durham, N.C.: Acorn Press, 1973.

Nishitani, Keiji. *Religion and Nothingness*. Berkeley: University of California Press, 1983.

Otto, Rudolph. *Mysticism East and West: A Comparative Analysis of the Nature of Mysticism.* New Haven, Conn.: Meridian, 1958.

Piaget, Jean. *The Essential Piaget.* Edited by Howard E. Gruber and J. Jacques Voneche Gruber. New York: Basic Books, 1977.

———. *The Moral Judgment of the Child.* Whitefish, Mont.: Kessinger, 2008.

Pinson, DovBer. *Meditation and Judaism: Exploring the Jewish Meditative Paths.* Lanham, Md.: Rowman & Littlefield, 2004.

———. *Toward the Infinite: The Way of Kabbalistic Meditation.* Lanham, Md: Rowman & Littlefield, 2005.

Plant, Judith, ed. *Healing the Wounds: The Power of Ecological Feminism.* Gabriola Island, B.C.: New Society, 1989.

Prager, Marcia. *Path of Blessings: Experiencing the Energy and Abundance of the Divine.* Woodstock, Vt.: Jewish Lights, 2003.

Ramana Maharshi. *Talks with Ramana Maharshi: On Realizing Abiding Peace and Happiness.* Carlsbad, Calif.: Inner Directions, 2000.

Rosen, Michael. *The Quest for Authenticity: The Thought of Reb Simhah Bunim.* Jerusalem: Urim, 2008.

Sack, Bracha. "Rabbi Moshe Cordovero's Doctrine of Tzimtzum." *Tarbiz* 58 (1989): 207–37.

Schachter-Shalomi, Zalman. *Credo of a Modern Kabbalist.* Victoria, B.C.: Trafford, 2006.

———. *Jewish with Feeling: A Guide to Meaningful Jewish Practice.* New York: Riverhead Books, 2005.

———. *Paradigm Shift: From the Jewish Renewal Teachings of Reb Zalman Schachter-Shalomi.* Edited by Ellen Singer. Lanham, Md.: Jason Aronson, 2000.

———. "A Triumphalist Table of In/Compatibility of Other Religions with Judaism." *Zeek* at Jewcy.com, February 2008. www.zeek .net/802zalman/.

———. *Wrapped in a Holy Flame: Teachings and Tales of the Hasidic Masters.* San Francisco: Jossey-Bass, 2003.

Schneerson, Menachem M. *On the Essence of Chassidus.* New York: Kehot, 1986.

———. *Torat Menahem: Hitwwa'aduyyot 5743.* Vol. 2. New York: Lahak Hanochos, 1993.

Scholem, Gershom. "Martin Buber's Interpretation of Hasidism." In his

The Messianic Idea in Judaism and Other Essays on Jewish Spirituality. New York: Schocken, 1995.

———. *Kabbalah.* New York: Plume, 1978.

———. *Origins of the Kabbalah.* Translated by Allan Arkush. Princeton, N.J.: Princeton University Press, 1987.

———. *Major Trends in Jewish Mysticism.* New York: Schocken, 1974.

Sears, David. *The Path of the Baal Shem Tov.* Lanham, Md.: Jason Aronson, 1996.

Shapiro, Rami. *Open Secrets: The Letters of Reb Yerachmiel ben Yisrael.* Rhinebeck, N.Y.: Monkfish, 2004.

Shatz Uffenheimer, Rivka. *Hasidism as Mysticism: Quietistic Elements in Eighteenth-Century Hasidic Thought.* Translated by Jonathan Chipman. Princeton, N.J.: Princeton University Press, 1993.

Smoley, Richard. *Inner Christianity: A Guide to the Esoteric Tradition.* Boston: Shambhala Publications, 2002.

Stcherbatsky, Theodore. *Buddhist Logic: Part 1.* 1930. Reprint. Whitefish, Mont.: Kessinger, 2004.

Surya Das, Lama. *Awakening the Buddha Within.* New York: Broadway Books, 1998.

Thich Nhat Hahn. *Peace Is Every Step: The Path of Mindfulness in Everyday Life.* Edited by Arnold Kotler. New York: Bantam, 1991.

Tolle, Eckhart. *The Power of Now: A Guide to Spiritual Enlightenment.* Novato, Calif.: New World Library, 2004.

Torwesten, Hans. *Vedanta: Heart of Hinduism.* Jackson, Tenn.: Grove Press, 1994.

Trungpa, Chögyam. *Cutting through Spiritual Materialism.* Boston: Shambhala Publications, 2008.

———. *The Myth of Freedom and the Way of Meditation.* Edited by John Baker and Marvin Casper. Boston: Shambhala Publications, 2002.

Walsh, Roger. *Essential Spirituality: Exercises from the World's Religions to Cultivate Kindness, Love, Joy, Peace, Vision, Wisdom, and Generosity.* New York: John Wiley & Sons, 1999.

Warren, Karen. *Ecofeminist Philosophy.* Lanham, Md.: Rowman & Littlefield, 2000.

Waskow, Arthur. *Godwrestling.* New York: Schocken, 1987.

Watts, Alan. *The Book: On the Taboo against Knowing Who You Are*. New York: Vintage, 1989.

Wei Wu Wei. *Ask the Awakened: The Negative Way*. Boulder, Colo.: Sentient, 2002.

Wilber, Ken. *Eye to Eye: The Quest for the New Paradigm*. Boston: Shambhala Publications, 2001.

———. *Integral Spirituality: A Startling New Role for Religion in the Modern and Postmodern World*. Boston: Shambhala Publications, 2006.

———. *No Boundary: Eastern and Western Approaches to Personal Growth*. Boston: Shambhala Publications, 2001.

———. *Quantum Questions*. Rev. ed. Boston: Shambhala Publications, 2001.

———. *A Theory of Everything*. Boston: Shambhala Publications, 2000.

Wolfson, Elliot. "Eneiric Imagination and Mystical Annihilation in Habad Hasidism." *ARC: The Journal of the Faculty of Religious Studies* 35 (2007): 131–57.

CLASSICAL JEWISH SOURCES (IN ENGLISH)

R. Azriel of Gerona. "The Explanation of the Ten Sefirot." In *The Early Kabbalah*. Edited by Joseph Dan. Translated by Ronald C. Kiener. New York: Paulist Press, 1986.

Baal Shem Tov, R. Israel. *Tzava'at haRivash: The Testament of the Baal Shem Tov*, trans. by Jacob Immanuel Schochet. New York: Kehot, 1998.

Bahya Ibn Pakuda. *The Book of Direction to the Duties of the Heart*. Translated by Menahem Mansoor. Oxford, U.K.: Littman Library of Jewish Civilization, 2000.

Green, Arthur, and Barry Holtz, trans. and eds. *Your Word Is Fire: Hasidic Masters on Contemplative Prayer*. Woodstock, Vt.: Jewish Lights, 1993.

Greenbaum, Avraham, trans. and ed. *The Essential Rebbe Nachman*. Jerusalem: Azamra, 2006.

Kaplan, Aryeh, trans. *The Light Beyond: Adventures in Hassidic Thought*. New York: Moznaim, 1981.

Lamm, Norman. *Religious Thought of Hasidism: Text and Commentary*. Jersey City, N.J.: Ktav, 1999.

Maimon, Solomon. "On a Secret Society, and Therefore a Long Chapter." In *Essential Papers on Hasidism,* edited by Gershon Hundert. New York: New York University Press, 1991.

Matt, Daniel C. *The Essential Kabbalah: Heart of Jewish Mysticism.* New York: HarperOne, 1996.

R. Menachem Nahum of Chernobyl. *The Light of the Eyes.* Translated by Arthur Green. Mahwah, N.J.: Paulist Press, 1982.

R. Nachman of Bratzlav. *Rabbi Nachman's Wisdom.* Translated by Aryeh Kaplan. New York: Breslov Research Institute, 1984.

Schneersohn, Rabbi Shmuel. *Mi Chamocha.* 1869. Reprinted, with English translation by Rabbi Yosef Marcus, as *True Existence: A Chasidic Discourse from Chabad-Lubavitch.* New York: Kehot, 2002.

R. Schneerson, Menachem M. *On the Essence of Chassidus.* New York: Kehot, 1986.

CLASSICAL NON-JEWISH SOURCES

Analayo. *Satipatthana: The Direct Path to Realization.* Birmingham, Ala.: Windhorse, 2004.

Buber, Martin, comp., and Paul Mendes-Flohr, ed. *Ecstatic Confessions: The Heart of Mysticism.* Translated by Esther Cameron. Syracuse, N.Y.: Syracuse University Press, 1996.

Candrakirti. *Lucid Exposition of the Middle Way.* Translated by Mervyn Sprung. Boulder, Colo.: Prajna Press, 1979.

Chuang Tzu. *Hua-Yen Buddhism.* Translated by Francis H. Cook. State College: Pennsylvania State University Press, 1977.

Cloud of Unknowing. New York: Penguin, 1978.

Conze, Edward, trans. *Buddhist Wisdom: The Diamond Sutra and the Heart Sutra.* New York: Vintage, 2003.

Deutsch, Eliot, and Rohit Dalvi, eds. *The Essential Vedanta: A New Sourcebook for the Advaita Vedanta.* Bloomington, Ind.: World Wisdom, 2004.

Hafiz. *The Gift: Poems by the Great Sufi Master.* Translated by Daniel Ladinsky. New York: Arkana, 1999.

Katz, Jerry. *One: Essential Writings on Nonduality.* Boulder, Colo.: Sentient, 2007.

Ladinsky, Daniel. *Love Poems from God.* New York: Penguin, 2002.

Meister Eckhart. *Meister Eckhart's Sermons.* Sermon IV: "True Hearing" on Ecclesiasticus 14:30. Translated by Claud Field. Grand Rapids, Mich.: Christian Classics, 1909.

Nisargadatta. *I Am That: Talks with Sri Nisargadatta Maharaj.* Translated by Maurice Frydman. Durham, N.C.: Acorn Press, 1973.

Padmasambhava. "Taking Refuge." In *The Dzogchen Primer: An Anthology of Writings by Masters of the Great Perfection,* edited by Martha Binder Schmidt. Boston: Shambhala Publications, 2002.

Pascal, Blaise. *Pensées.* Translated by A. J. Krailsheimer. Rev. ed. New York: Penguin, 1995.

Plotinus. *The Enneads.* Translated by Stephen Mackenna. New York: Penguin, 1991.

Prabhavananda, Swami, and Christopher Isherwood, trans. *Shankara's Crest-Jewel of Discrimination (Viveka-Chudamani): Timeless Teachings on Nonduality.* Los Angeles, Calif.: Vedanta, 1970.

Ramakrishna. *The Gospel of Sri Ramakrishna.* Recorded by Mahendranath Gupta. Translated by Swami Nikhilananda. New York: Ramakrishna-Vivekananda Center, 1942.

Ramana Maharshi. *Talks with Ramana Maharshi: On Realizing Abiding Peace and Happiness.* Carlsbad, Calif.: Inner Directions, 2000.

Saint Augustine of Hippo, Sermon 88, 5.

Schleiermacher, Friedrich. *On Religion: Speeches to Its Cultured Despisers.* 1893. Reprint. Whitefish, Mont.: Kessinger, 2008.

Schmidt, Martha Binder, ed. *The Dzogchen Primer: An Anthology of Writings by Masters of the Great Perfection.* Boston: Shambhala Publications, 2002.

Spinoza, Baruch. *Ethics and Selected Letters.* Edited by Samuel Shirley. Indianapolis, Ind.: Hackett, 1982.

Vivekananda. *Living at the Source: Yoga Teachings of Vivekananda.* Boston: Shambhala Publications, 2001.

TABLE OF BIBLICAL AND
TRADITIONAL RELIGIOUS SOURCES

The following traditional religious sources are referenced in this book. Page numbers are to the standard print editions, where available.

HEBREW BIBLICAL SOURCES

Genesis 1:2, 28:12, 28:16
Exodus 3:14, 6:3, 22:22, 25:8, 32:8, 57:7
Leviticus 19:18
Numbers 5:3, 12:8, 14:21
Deuteronomy 4:35, 4:39, 6:4–5, 10:12–13, 16:20, 24:20–22, 30:11, 30:14
Isaiah 1:16, 6:3, 8:17, 21:11, 45:5, 63:10–11
Ezekiel 1:14
Joel 2:28
Malachi 3:6
Daniel 12:3
Proverbs 3:6, 14:31, 19:17, 25:2
Psalms 16:8, 31:23, 51:11, 65:2, 84:12, 103:19, 119:20, 139:7–12
Nehemiah 9:6
I Chronicles 28:9

RABBINIC SOURCES

Mishna Avot 3:15, 3:19
BT Berachot 64a
BT Shabbat 31a
BT Sotah 5a
BT Baba Batra 25a
BT Sanhedrin 39a, 103a, 106b
Yerushalmi Taanit 1:1

Genesis Rabba 9:7, 68:9
Exodus Rabba 2:5
Deuteronomy Rabba 7:8
Lamentations Rabba 25
Song of Songs Rabba 2
Pesikta d'Rav Kahana 1:4

KABBALISTIC AND HASIDIC SOURCES

Zohar I:18b, I:241a, II:1b-2a, II:85b, III:225a

R. Samuel Kalonymous, *Shir HaYichud*

R. Moses Cordovero, *Or Neerav*, part 2, chap. 2; *Perek Helek* 206b; *Elimah Rabbati* 24d–25a

R. Hayyim Vital, *Etz Hayyim* 1:1b–1d, 8:1

R. Isaiah Halevy Horowitz, *Shenei Luchot HaBrit*, Shavuot 189b

R. Israel Baal Shem Tov, *Tzavaat HaRivash* nos. 5–6, 68, 76, 93

R. Israel Baal Shem Tov (attr.), *Keter Shem Tov* 2b, 51b, 02; *Sefer Baal Shem Tov,* Bereshit 15, Vaetchanan 13

R. Yaakov Yosef of Polonnoye, *Toldot Yakov Yosef*, Bereshit 8c, Yitro 54b; *Ben Porat Yosef*, 50b

R. Dov Ber of Mezrich, *Likkutei Amarim*, 26b; *Maggid Dvarav L'Yaakov*, nos. 92, 110, 162, 240; *Shemu'ah Tovah* 79b–80a; *Torat HaMagid* II, p. 162

R. Dov Ber of Mezrich (attr.), *Or Ha'Emet* 2b

R. Levi Yitzhak of Berdichev, *Kedushat Levi*, Mishpatim, 190

R. Schneur Zalman of Liadi, *Likkutei Amarim* (Tanya), 14, 54, 154, 155, 156, 159, 161, 164; *Likkutei Torah,* 20c; *Maamarei Admor Hazaken*, 26; *Iggrot Baal haTanya u'Bnei Doro*, 97–98

R. Aharon of Staroselye, *Shaarei HaYichud v'HaEmunah*, 2b–3b, 20b, 157b, 216a–b; *Shaarei HaAvodah*, 1a, 1b, 2a, 4a, 5a, 6a–7b, 9a, 10b, 12a, 13a, 14a, 42b, 45a–b, 71a–b; *Avodat HaLevy*, I, 1

R. Menachem Mendel Schneersohn (Tzemach Tzedek), *Torah Or*, Ki Tisa, 172

R. Dov Ber Schneersohn, *Torat Hayyim*, Bereshit, 243c–d

R. Shmuel Schneersohn, *Mi Chamocha*

R. Menachem Nahum of Chernobyl, *Meor Einayim*, Noah; Vayetze; *Hanhagot Yesharot*

R. Nachman of Bratzlav, *Likkutei Moharan* 33:2, 64:2
R. Zeev Wolf of Zhitomir, *Or Hameir*, Pekudei, 85
R. Solomon of Lutsk, *Dibrat Shelomo*, Shemini, 2:25–26
R. Aryeh Leib Alter (Sfat Emet), *Otzar Ma'amarim u'Michtavim*, 75f
R. Yaakov Yitzhak of Prysucha, *Tiferet HaYehudi*, 176 no. 93
Imrei Tzaddikim, 18c
Likkutim Yekarim 2b, 14d, 20a, 115b–116a, 117b
Or Ha Emet 2b

NON-JEWISH SOURCES

Aitareya Upanishad 3.3, Rig Veda
Mandukya Upanishad 1.2, Atharva Veda
Chandogya Upanishad 6.8.7, Sama Veda
Brhadaranyaka Upanishad 1.4.10, Yahur Veda
Diamond Sutra
Heart Sutra
Nagarjuna, *Mulamadhyamikakarika*, 25: 19–20
John 8:32
St. Augustine of Hippo, Sermon 88, 5
John of the Cross, *Ascent of Mount Carmel*, I:13
Plotinus, *Enneads* 5.1.7, 5.2.1, 6.9.4, 6.5.6

INDEX

material world, 108–12
  as dream, 79, 112
  spiritual materialism, 167
Matt, Daniel, 6
matter, 217–18
meditation, 152–66
  and nondual Judaism, 86
  contemplation, 152–55
  insight, 158–63
  relation between Jewish and Buddhist, 133
Meher Baba, 79
Meir ibn Gabbai, Rabbi, 44
Meister Eckhart, 78, 94, 194
memaleh kol almin, 40, 55–56, 83
Menachem Nahum of Chernobyl, Rabbi, 71, 99
Meor Einayim (R. Menachem Nahum of Chernobyl), 71
Merton, Thomas, 78
Merzel, Dennis Genpo (Genpo Roshi), 26, 36, 163, 165
messiah, Jewish belief in, 138–41
messianic age
  and evolving consciousness, 139–46
  Hasidic view of, 139–41
  and nonduality, 142–46
Mi Chamocha (R. Shmuel Schneersohn), 21, 69
Midrash, 44, 55, 227n5
Miller, Henry, 110–11
mitzvot, 13, 92, 192
m'lo chol ha'aretz kvodo, 51, 52–53, 65
monotheism, 53, 62, 99–100
Moore, Thomas, 123
Moshe de Leon, Rabbi, 58, 59
morality. *See* ethics
Muktananda, 79
multiplicity, 102, 109
mystical experience
  Hasidic views of, 32
  importance of, 31
  limitations of, 33–34
  and nonduality, 30–31
  and ordinary experience, 42
  problems with, 32–33
mysticism
  and atheism, 30

  and community, 129
  relation to religion, 2

Nachman of Bratzlav, Rabbi, 72–74, 150, 195
nature, 22, 39–40, 68, 94, 113, 121, 192, 214
  and sense of self, 145, 212
  in the Tanya, 68
necessity (of events), 99–101
nefesh, 30, 38–40
negative theology, 180, 202
neo-Hasidism, 74–76, 130–31
Neoplatonism, 28, 130
neshamah, 30
New Age, 86–89
Nicholas of Cusa, 202
nirvana, 70, 85, 101, 102, 103, 109–10
Nisargadatta, 12, 79, 81, 94, 205
non-distracted non-meditation, 164–66
nonduality
  and beliefs, 39
  "benefits" of, 3–4, 36, 126
  definition of, 1–2, 17–19, 57
  as delusion, 220
  depiction of, by Jewish sources, 2–3, 18, 27
  historical development of, 129–35, 140–41
  knowing of, 12–14, 17–18, 30–33, 78–79
  as philosophical position, 28–30, 173
  and religious myth, 6, 44–45, 60, 92, 93–108
  stages of realization of, 7–12
non-self, 19–26

On the Essence of Chassidus (the Lubavitcher Rebbe), 140
oneness, as distinct from nondualism, 11
Otto, Rudolph, 121

Pali Canon, 82–83
panentheism, 53–54, 58
  difference between pantheism and, 55, 75
  in works of Baal Shem Tov, 63
pantheism, 6, 59, 74–75
  difference between panentheism and, 55, 75
PaRDeS (method for interpreting Torah), 45
Pardes Rimonim (Moses Cordovero), 62